Views from My Boathouse

Musings of a City-Raised, Small Town Journalist

Gail Galotta

Illustrations by Nancy Sundstrom Wolfe

Copyright © 2018 by Gail Galotta

Cover photograph and illustrations by Nancy Sundstrom Wolfe

In memory of my father,
Wallace R. Sundstrom

Acknowledgements

My family's encouragement throughout the years has helped to bring this book to fruition. I was fortunate to have parents who showed interest in my writing from the time I was a child and gave me a typewriter to aide in this creative endeavor. My mother continues to inspire me with her enthusiastic support. I also want to thank my brother, John Sundstrom, and his wife, Nancy, for whom my writing was an appreciated Christmas gift each year; my brother-in-law, Jim Wolfe, who offered advice on this book's concept; and my brother-in-law, Martin Straka, who remained a faithful reader of my newspaper columns. I am especially grateful for my sister Nancy's support and her wonderful illustrations that adorn these pages. I owe years of gratitude to my sister, Carol, my most ardent fan and cheerleader. Finally, I thank the two special men in my life: my son, Grant, for his witty reviews of my writing over breakfast that always concluded with "Good job, Mom;" and my husband, Richard, who has sustained me with his sage advice and loving support and who good-naturedly allowed me to exploit his foibles in such a public expression.

Preface

As a young girl my favorite places to write were in my bedroom from which I viewed our backyard, and at the end of a dock from which I dangled my feet. These early creations in pencil, which I still possess, remind me of the locations that inspired them: my home in Chicago and the lake cottage in Michigan. They are still at the heart of everything I write.

After a lifetime of "windy city" winters, it might be expected that I would turn my head toward warmer regions, but, instead, I looked north. When a piece of lake property became available, I also pointed my husband in that direction. "It's on the water!" I said enthusiastically.

And so we bought fifteen acres of woods on a lake in the Upper Peninsula of Michigan. In the dead of winter. Sight unseen.

Sort of. I was certainly familiar with that chain of lakes, having spent part of my childhood summers there at my grandparents' cottage. My father was born in a nearby town, a location our entire family returned to over the years that included excursions to the lake. So, perhaps, it isn't surprising that a city girl who grew up next to one of the Great Lakes ended up near a small town on another *great* lake.

Not that our new home did not present its challenges. We are city people, and life in the U.P. is very different from life in Chicago. But when it was time to retire from our teaching careers, we decided it was also time to move north and start a new life. And that has been...a journey.

Some of that journey is expressed in this book. The rest is, well, a little of this and that: personal experiences, childhood memories, family tales, and my "boathouse philosophy." Yes, there really is a boathouse.

Sort of. With the exception of existing boathouses, these structures are no longer allowed on the water. However, we were permitted to build a garage a short distance from the shore. Our construction also included an octagon-shaped room perched atop its flat roof from which an expansive view of the lake and woods might be observed. Designed by my husband (a project that I hoped would fuel his enthusiasm for this move), the room opened to the roof, where ample deck space provided for entertaining and relaxing.

But it was the tower itself that caught one's eye from the lake, its seven windows glinting like a beacon at the lake's end. And it was in this second-story retreat that I found my muse. Here, surrounded by the same views that had influenced my childhood fantasies, I now wrote fiction in the form of short stories and plays as well as articles for a local newspaper.

My weekly column carried a general purpose to entertain, and toward that goal I offered humor and sentimentality—and a bit of story-telling—in five-hundred words or less (usually). I had accumulated a faithful readership as a columnist, and I enjoyed that journalistic relationship. Many of my essays—on which the following versions are based—are now extended to a broader audience outside this hamlet in the Northwoods.

These musings are the *views from my boathouse*. I may appear to have my head in the clouds much of the time—but my feet are never far from the water.

Contents

Chapter 1

U.P. Tails and Wood Tick Trails

Our War with the Pine Needles

Sure, we saw the pine trees when we moved here. They looked beautiful against the summer sky and provided a picturesque background for our new home. "And," we exclaimed with glee, "no leaves to rake!" Two months later September arrived. The autumn winds unleashed the slings and *arrows* of nature's outrageous fortune, turning our struggling yard into a haystack and transforming our house into a giant porcupine. Pine needles are ingeniously designed by nature to resist the blades of lawn mowers, escape the tines of garden rakes, and defy the grasp of bare hands. That didn't stop my husband from trying. He spent hours picking up needles from among the landscaping stones and sidewalk cracks, the process of which wore away his fingerprints. "Great," I told him. "Now you can lead a life of crime without being traced."

But while he was concentrating on the ground, I looked up to find our quaint Craftsman-style home adorned with an antiquated thatched roof. The needles had literally gone too far. This was war! Richard began a series of attack plans that were executed in a progression of frenzied, futile maneuvers. It didn't take long to realize that our ladders weren't high enough to reach the eaves. Our windows only afforded a teasing poke with a broom from awkward angles that also fell short. In a moment of wild imagination, the leaf-blower was considered, but it also proved a *distant* threat.

Just as Richard's determination had reached obsession, my son arrived for the weekend. It wasn't long before Grant was scheming alongside his father with theories of acrobatic feats performed with extension poles affixed to various household objects. Finally, he emerged from the basement and announced, "I've got it!" The secret weapon was a red, plastic dinosaur with menacing claws. The childhood toy that had once stalked Lego cities and wreaked havoc on tiny Matchbox cars was now the Godzilla of gutters, tethered to the end of a nylon rope. (The other end of the rope was held by two knuckleheads.)

But after several tosses from a shaky ladder, it was apparent that the "plasticsaurus rex" could do little more than bounce off the firmly-matted bed of needles. That is, until it bounced behind the chimney—and stayed there. While Grant and Richard took turns yanking the rope from various angles, I muttered to myself over a sink of dishes. However, the repeated thuds on the roof from another object sent me outside.

"What are you doing with that football?" I queried. But it was apparent that their plan was to dislodge the dinosaur from the chimney by knocking it loose with a football. Both athletes demonstrated their throwing abilities from assorted yard lines, but all efforts failed to achieve the desired goal. I feared they would simply damage the shingles. Finally, the Hail Mary was delivered, and the dinosaur's tail wobbled enough to free the rope and secure a happy landing. However, victory was short-lived: the *football* now occupied the evasive spot behind the chimney.

By now an assembly of neighbors had gathered to watch as another football was sought for the final touchdown. After a series of launches with the new weapon, the original ball was finally set free, fell to the ground, and was quickly retrieved. The crowd cheered. Still, despite the field goal, the pine needles held steady in their position of victory. I decided that enough was enough. Stomping across the yard in that manner that most women reserve for only the most serious of reprimands, I finally called foul and took the footballs away from both teams. Next I unfettered the dinosaur so that it could return to its extinction in the toy box.

Autumn came and went with no more discussion of the silent monster that slept above us. It wasn't long before the bitter winds of winter roared over the house, followed by layers of snow that accumulated on the roof. Even when it melted, sliding in large clumps down the dripping eaves, not a single pine needle relinquished its impervious hold on the shingles.

Then in May a sudden storm passed over with ominous dark clouds. But instead of yielding the expected rain, the clouds released a shower of hail that pounded our roof for several minutes. Suddenly, in a wave of surrender, a shadow passed the window before crashing to the ground. It was the matted heap of pine needles, ironically defeated by nature itself.

That summer eased blissfully along, green and soft and quiet. Puffs of smoke from the charcoal grill sent harmless signals to the cloudless sky. Birds skimmed over the verdant yards and twittered from their camouflage among the lush trees. Rains misted the lawns, and sunlight mottled the leaves with a gentle breeze. The truce had lulled us into contentment.

Then September returned.

Even a Dog Can Have Fishing Fever

It was a sweltering July when we moved here. After hours of unloading boxes, we headed for the cooling lake water. Bella paced on the shore and walked out just far enough to convey her concern for our safety. At just a year old, she had never ventured farther than it took to wet her paws.

Those paws were big. After all, her Labrador and standard poodle background was genetically skilled in water retrieval. But Bella had never been put to task, and now her beloved family was drifting toward unknown danger. Another instinct kicked in, and she bravely moved her long legs through the water until they disappeared beneath her. A final shout of encouragement from the swimmers, and she was earth-bound no more. Bella could swim.

As much delight as she found in swimming, the lake soon held a stronger incentive for her. She stared into the shallow water along the shore, occasionally jerking her head and slapping at the surface. We tried to get her attention, but a serious distraction was keeping her spellbound. She had discovered fish.

I understand fishing. I like fishing. I have a brother-in-law who lives for fishing. But, unlike Bella, he will come home at night without being dragged by the collar. (Well, I better check with my sister about that.) The problem was that Bella didn't know how to *stop* fishing.

After breakfast she bolted for the lake. Her routine was the same: a scan for minnows along the shoreline, a plunge in the direction of moving shadows, and a pursuit that went on for hours. Her swimming pattern repeated itself along the stony bottom, through the reeds, around the boat, under the pier, and back to the shore. Within weeks the sun had bleached her black hair to a color our groomer described as "a bad dye job." After a month the other fishermen knew her by name. By the end of the summer she had lost nine pounds.

We increased her food and insisted on a mid-day nap. At the sound of the whistle, I could spot her head lifting from the water and watched as she begrudgingly shook off and dragged herself home.

But it wasn't long before she was whimpering at the window. Rainy days were like a Greek tragedy. In winter she dreamed of fishing. In early spring, she pawed at the ice in hopeful anticipation. Finally, that tail was moving like a rudder among the teasing minnows.

Let me answer the question that everyone asks. No. At least we've never seen her catch one. But like every good fisherman will tell you: It's the ones that got away.

June Is Busting out All Over

Longer days are here again. With more hours to enjoy outdoor activities, it's nice to finally relax at the end of the extended day. A cool drink, a soft breeze, and...what's all that noise? Oh, yeah. It's June, the noisiest month of the year.

I don't mean the daytime noises of lawn tools, watercrafts, or children playing. They provide a traditional background for summer that usually disappears with the setting sun. I'm talking about that other world of sounds that creeps up with the evening shadows and intensifies as darkness closes in. There is no escape from this barrage of sound. It is nature's creatures of the night. Every night. And they won't shut up.

Now don't get me wrong. I love nature, and I'm a very tolerant person. Woodpeckers can knock on my dead trees all day; geese can honk at my dog for hours; and cows can complain till...the other cows come home. But the creatures that haunt the night are downright annoying.

Take, for example, the lovely whippoorwill. Its distinctive pronunciation of its own name is, no doubt, an important element for mating and is charming to hear...the first few times. But we could set our clocks by the first chirp at 11p.m. that begins hours of relentless repetition. No wonder the deer head for the roads at night. And just how many partners is that bird calling?

In fact, the night is filled with romance...if you are a frog or a cricket. No one else has a chance with all that distracting noise. With a croak here and a chirp there, the average human can barely finish a sentence. The hills are alive—with a cacophony that makes your ears ring.

Even the smallest sounds can be a source of torture at night. Regardless of where it's been hiding all day, as soon as you begin to drift towards sleep, the elusive mosquito buzzes over your head. You swat the air, bury your face in the pillow, and hope it will go away, but it never does. Oh, you may land a few good slaps to your own face, convinced you've smashed the insect, but it predictably returns a few minutes later just as you are slipping into unconsciousness and hums into your ear. The pattern repeats itself until you fall asleep from exhaustion. The following morning there is blood on your face and pillow. You assume that you have killed it. But that night the monster returns, buzzing that tiny chainsaw in your ear. All night. To quote Dracula: "Listen to them. The children of the night. What music they make." He must have been tone deaf.

One Rainy Tuesday Has Two Versions

This is a tale of two Tuesdays. It was the best of times; it was the worst of times. Actually, it was only *one* Tuesday, but there are two entirely different versions of that rainy day: one male, one female—of course.

The rain was not going to affect my plans for a day trip with my sister and friends. We had arranged to take a pottery class and do a wine tasting tour. However, my husband and brother were scheduled to dig post holes in the yard. Since our ground is more rock than dirt, they reserved a bobcat with a power auger for the job. "You'll have that done before lunch," I cheerily remarked to my husband as I bounced out the door. Then the typhoon began.

Under normal conditions a steep hill can be a challenge for heavy machinery. But in the rain the bobcat became the mechanical bull of a cowboy's nightmares. My brother eased the beast along with caution but could not predict its movements on that slippery slope. He lurched forward and then, inevitably, slid backwards and sideways. My husband watched in horror as the beast reared up and threatened to throw John under its tracks.

...Meanwhile, I noticed a steady rain through the window of the pottery studio where we ladies remained warm and dry as we leaned over our craft projects. "I'm going to paint flowers on my ceramic tile," my sister announced. I told her that would be pretty. I dabbed my brush into the blue paint for my landscape. Classical music played in the studio's background. I sighed with satisfaction and decided to add some trees to the landscape of my water scene.

...Back at home the pounding rain turned the grassy slope into underwater seaweed. Although the auger hammered through tree roots and cracked stones like eggs, John felt vulnerable at that slippery angle. Richard attacked the less accessible holes with a manual post hole digger. Eventually, both men resorted to shovels. They slammed the tools into the ground as their clothes grew heavier with the pelting rain.

..."I find this a little dry," I related to the group as I set my wine glass on the counter. After exhibiting our crafting skills at the art studio, we journeyed down the road to a country winery that resembled a quaint barn, but that only added to its rustic charm. The sampling of local brews had piqued our interest. "Let's try that cherry wine next!"

...Sweat, rain, and mud now also covered my brother-in-law and nephew, who must have heard Richard's and John's groans of desperation from across the lake and joined in their efforts. When my sister and I returned, all four of them were on their knees, burrowing into the earth like animals pursued by demons. I recognized my husband's voice beyond a pyramid of rocks, but something in his tone told me that I had better not inquire how his day had gone.

As I quickly retreated to the house, I decided that it probably wasn't the best time to tell him how mine had gone, either.

Intruder Is No Match for Superheroes

It was after midnight when the sound of muffled thuds awakened me. I jolted to consciousness when I realized that my husband and son were struggling with something, and judging from the sound of things, they seemed to be losing.

The sounds grew louder as they moved upstairs. Since Bella was not barking, I was fairly certain that there wasn't an intruder in the house. Finally, I got out of bed to see what antics they were into at that hour. When I opened the door to ask, Grant met me with a concerned warning, "Get back and close the door, Mom! It's a bat!"

Just the word *bat* would have been sufficient. From my side of the door I could hear the scuffle move down the hall to the guest bedroom. At last I heard my husband say, "Got him!" I opened my bedroom door as my son carried a weighted bag down the stairs. My husband's sweating face announced, "It was a big one."

They explained that while watching a movie they were surprised by a dark shadow that swooped over their heads. The rest of the story sounded like a plot set in Gotham City. Using their special weapons—a broom and pillows—my superheroes pursued the forces of evil throughout the house and to an early death. Batman and Robin had been victorious.

They returned to the scene of the crime long enough to replace the furniture and remake the bed. "Good job!" I told them, but my mind was already focused on how the bat got in and how many of his friends were with him.

I have long been acquainted with the fluttering creatures that arrive after sunset on summer evenings, especially at my grandparents' cottage at the lake where on occasion a bat would enter through the chimney. The following scenario then involved a lot of shouting while my grandmother angrily chased it toward an open door with a broom.

In the 1960s vampire movies gained popularity, and I watched in horror as the dreaded vermin transformed themselves into second-rate actors who nonetheless gave an adolescent audience the chills. (It never occurred to me that the female characters were dressed rather provocatively for a cold night in an unheated castle— but that's show biz.) A crucifix was only a temporary defense as the victims eventually succumbed to the charms of the undead. Perhaps it was the cape. Regardless, I wondered why no one bothered to shake a broom in their direction.

I am not taking any chances. In case my superheroes are asleep the next time something winged and unexpected flies across the ceiling, I will have a broom *and* a crucifix next to the bed.

Harvest Bounty May Not All Be Welcome

The harvest moon is shining down on depleted gardens, but there are still plenty of surplus vegetables to share. Maybe too many.

My father used to say, "You don't want to sit on your porch too long or someone will give you a zucchini."

It's not that I don't like zucchini, but I can only eat so much of it myself. Yes, I've put them in breads and cakes. That doesn't fool my husband. He can find any trace of vegetable in any recipe, despite my efforts to camouflage them. He has the sensory skills of a narcotics-sniffing bloodhound. I've known him to detect a fleck of broccoli hidden under a layer of cheese sauce, and extract the chocolate from the fiber in an Ex-Lax.

Besides, some vegetables grow to science-fiction proportions. I've seen zucchini that requires two people to hold up each end. (I believe that certain tribes of Indians hollowed them out to make canoes.) It seems that the less desirable a food is, the more abundant it is. After nursing my tomatoes along all summer, I only had enough for two salads. Strawberries grow like pearls in oysters. But those fall squash go from seed to pulling down a fence in two days.

Deer cabbage is a good example of this. Hunters carry off tire-sized cabbage by the truckload to use as deer bait. There is a myth that the deer eat so much of it that they develop severe cramps and make for easier targets. There is another belief, just as credible, that when the men run out of chili at their camps, they resort to eating the cabbage themselves, thus providing a natural fuel for keeping warm on those cold November nights in the woods.

Despite their daunting size, cabbages have a mystical appeal. A friend of ours was recently lured by an appealing sign that advertised these leafy heads. By the next morning the trance had worn off, but he still had to deal with a car trunk filled with cabbage. He began by giving some to the couple who live next door to us. A day later I arrived home to find a cabbage the size of a bushel basket on *my* kitchen counter. My husband shrugged and said it was a gift from our neighbors. Aha! The green monsters were infiltrating house by house! Was there no stopping them!?

"You could make stuffed cabbage," my husband suggested.

"You hate cabbage," I retorted. (I could have sworn that the cabbage moved.)

"I know, but I'll eat the stuffing part."

After a few days the wilting leaves of the cabbage hung over the kitchen drawers and threatened to take root. My mother stopped by and remarked innocently, "Is that a cabbage?"

"Yes," I said sweetly. "It's for you."

Setting a Trap Requires Skill and a Hot Dog

With the whole morning ahead of me to get down and dirty with some outside projects, I headed to the yard. But not only did my best laid plans go awry, something was also afoot—four "foots" to be exact. At first I dismissed a slight rustling in the bushes as a stray bird, but when I passed by again, I was stopped in my tracks by a pair of much larger eyes.

It was a raccoon. Not that I expected it to understand English, but *shoo* is universal for "Get out of here!" He simply moved closer to the front door. So I flagged down my husband by standing on my toes and frantically waving my arms—a universal gesture for *Help*! He gave me that "this-better-be-good" look because he had to get off of the lawn mower—which really irritates me because I turn the vacuum cleaner on and off a dozen times for his inquiries about where his glasses are, whether the mail came, or when lunch will be ready. So I think that any request to get rid of a potentially rabid rodent is certainly off-switch worthy.

Only last week I had called upon my husband's fearless pest-removal skills to rid my garden of a pine snake. Except this one was entangled in nylon mesh intended to protect plants. I refused Richard's request that I hold the shovel from which the snake dangled while he cut away the excess mesh. But I did get him the scissors. I also encouraged him on—from a safe distance, of course.

As it turned out, his raccoon-herding technique was no better than mine, except that he added a threatening gesture with the shovel that apparently is *not* universal. The raccoon just stared at us. It was obviously sick. Richard suggested that our neighbor could probably shoot it. My mind immediately conjured up the gallant scene from the film *To Kill a Mockingbird* in which Gregory Peck shoots a rabid dog, but I dismissed this option when I considered that our neighbor's aim might already be hampered by his morning beers. Besides, I didn't want blood on my patio. Instead, I called a professional and waited from inside the house, keeping an eye on our unwelcomed friend through the kitchen window.

I found out that professional nuisance control requires a cage—and some poking and chasing. The wily raccoon managed to run into the next yard, where I lost sight of both expert and culprit. When the man returned empty-handed, he suggested putting food out to lure the creature into the trap (which also describes how I get Richard to where I want him). But just as I started cutting a hot dog into bite-sized pieces, the man returned with news of his completed mission and intension to turn the critter loose to frolic in some faraway meadow. Sure.

By then it was lunch time. Richard would be hungry, and I suddenly thought of a new method for enlisting his help with a few things I needed him to do. That hot dog wouldn't go to waste, after all.

Neighbors Are Voice of Experience

In every place that we have lived, we have been fortunate to have nice neighbors. As another bonus, we have always lived next door to older and wiser homeowners. This is especially valuable when you are unfamiliar with the area, inexperienced with owning a house, or just plain naïve. In other words, we've learned a lot from our neighbors over the years.

We should be pretty knowledgeable by now, but our present environment made us feel more like old dogs just trying to learn new tricks. Until now. We just acquired new neighbors. They are also transported city people, and they are not acquainted with the particulars of Michigan's Upper Peninsula. Much to our surprise and amusement, we are assuming the role of the older and wiser couple next door.

The basis of our advice has nothing to do with common sense: It's simply relating what we know now that we didn't know then. Looking back, that's a pretty long list. I recall working on our house prior to moving in. Our former neighbor popped in while we were painting and invited us to come over later for a drink. The visit was a welcomed break, but on the return home we became disoriented in the dark and had trouble locating our own house. We stumbled confusedly through the brush and trees that separated our properties.

It hadn't occurred to us that there were no street lights. From then on we carried flashlights with us.

That wasn't the only difference from life in suburbia. We were told that our well could go dry in the present drought, an omen that restricted our use of the hose and consequently turned our yard into a desert. A further annoyance was that cable service was not available, and the only way to get TV reception was via a satellite dish that looked like aliens landed in the front yard.

We also learned that winters here can be life-threatening for humans, but wood ticks can survive an ice age. During the most active tick season—which is basically the entire summer here—we are mindful that the parasites often enter into the house with us. Watching television is periodically interrupted by one of us making a mad dash from the couch to remove one that has decided to settle onto our stomachs or backs for the night. Before we go to bed, we perform the nightly "tick check" on each other—a routine that is generally considered foreplay in Michigan's U.P.

Some things we learned the hard way. For example, have your snow blower ready in October. (And don't store it away until May.) You can put feed out for the birds all winter, but come March, it is bear bait. We also discovered that the local deer are related to Santa's sled team because they can fly over any fence shorter than the Great Wall of China. And if septic tanks are not pumped out every few years, the consequences will be a reminder that you will never forget.

We've passed along some of our acquired wisdom to our new neighbors, like staking out their driveway so they can find it after the first snow, and checking themselves for ticks as soon as the snow melts. It's the least we homesteaders can do for newcomers.

Clever Mice Need a Better Mousetrap

A wooden plaque hung on the wall of my grandmother's kitchen. It pictured a terrified woman standing on a chair. Beneath her, staring up from the floor, was a mouse. Although the caption was in Swedish, no translation was needed. "Eek!" is a universal expression.

Mice are the uninvited guests that have a habit of moving into our home when we do. Our last house was in a suburb that encroached upon farmland. We took up residence in November; the field mice had occupied the basement since October. Assuming squatters' rights, they were in the kitchen when I came down to make breakfast, and they played hide-and-seek with each other under the furniture at night. One of them even held the door open for my husband when he left for work each morning.

Northern rodents are equally bold. While the pine snakes were tossed out by workers during construction, the mice hid in corners, fattening themselves on crumbs from the crew's lunches. The little creatures cheered when our belongings arrived: our boxes provided perfect rent-free homes for their newly acquired neighborhood.

Not that we were going to stand for this. My husband is somewhat of an expert at mouse extermination. In Chicago it is considered a form of hunting, and it is always open season. We've tried the poison pellets, but there is always the possibility that the victim will crawl under an appliance to die. Those sticky mouse motels might stop them in their tracks, but then you not only have to deal with a live mouse, but one that's now really ticked-off, too. Our weapon of choice is the simple mousetrap. Amateurs use cheese; we prefer peanut butter. (Chocolate also works, but my husband is prone to eating the bait.)

However, we have been less than diligent this winter. As a consequence, at least one vermin infiltrated our basement. I reported the unmistakable smell of its corpse to my husband. He, as usual, couldn't smell anything. Nonetheless, his bloodhound wife tracked the culprit's whereabouts to the storage area. As we removed each box of holiday decorations, I imagined the mouse crawling through my Christmas village and frolicking with the bunnies in my Easter collection. I still wasn't satisfied when the last carton revealed nothing. There was only one place left; unfortunately, it was between two walls. I held the flashlight beam on a small, gray lump while my husband probed the distance with a long pole attached to duct tape. I closed my eyes and held my breath as he withdrew the makeshift trap and announced the horrible consequence: "It's only lint!" This was immediately followed by, "Can I have lunch now?"

The defeat left no recourse. Although the foul odor would eventually dissipate, the mouse would remain in the recesses of the wall. There was nothing I could do but set my revenge—and another trap—for the next intruder. They always return to the scene of the crime.

Harsh Winter Is Nothing New

Anyone who lives in this area is used to U.P. winters. There are variations in the severity each year, of course, but you can expect a reasonable amount of cold and snow at this time. I know that the recent cold spell was a little extreme and hung in there a lot longer than usual, but we just bundled up and dealt with it. That's what we do.

That wasn't so easy for my aunt and uncle who were visiting us for two weeks over the holidays. After moving to Florida in 1966, their blood kind of thinned out. (Too much sun and citrus, I guess.) The one winter trip they made to Chicago years ago was a mild and snowless one so they haven't seen what a real winter is for decades—until they came up here.

They arrived with an assortment of cold weather garb, but there's a big difference between below freezing temperatures and *freezing* temperatures. My aunt naively donned earmuffs, which did little more than protect her earrings while the hair on her head stood up like icicles. And her corduroy jacket may as well have been cardboard for the insulation it offered in sub-zero conditions. She shivered over her coffee each morning when I announced, "Look! It's up to sixteen degrees," and then added softly, "below zero."

My uncle, on the other hand, was eager to embrace the cold. He loaded his mittens with hand warmers and accompanied me on walks through the woods. It was a little challenging for him to manipulate his camera and narrate the journey at the same time. He paused to record close-ups of the snow as if he were on the film crew of *Doctor Zhivago*. I encouraged him to keep moving lest we turn into ice sculptures ourselves. But he stopped when something else appeared in his lens.

"Oh, look! There's Grant digging for gold!" Actually, my son was trying out a metal detector, despite the frozen terrain.

(Chicago weather honed his survival skills; the tenacity he got from me.) No gold, but he did come up with a bottle cap and a shell casing. Around here hunting and drinking go together like, well, snowmobiling and drinking, ice fishing and drinking, and watching, celebrating or cursing the Green Bay Packers and drinking. So I am not surprised.

We returned home just before dark, about the same time that people in Florida are having brunch. But this is the U.P. so I gave my uncle a beer. After his second one, the feeling in his fingers and toes returned. It doesn't take long to learn the local survival skills.

My aunt wasn't as easily persuaded. Sure, she had a great time spending the holidays with all of us, and she appreciated how beautiful everything looked outside with the snow—just like a Christmas card, which is about as close to winter as she wants to get.

"Next time we'll visit in the warm weather," she said when they left.

Right now I can't remember when that is.

Power Outage Tests Survival Skills

A heavy snow, a flickering of the lights, and the house was suddenly filled with that conspicuous silence that only a power outage can achieve. Well, at least I had finished the breakfast dishes and a load of laundry. I would just catch up on some small tasks. Little did I realize how many of these required plugging-in.

The weight of this wet snow had compromised the overhead lines that are so vulnerable in this area. With the phones out, Richard used his cell phone to call the electric company. But by habit he plugged it in to charge it afterwards. "Dad..." my son began, and then they both laughed at the futility of this gesture. But when I later cautioned Grant about playing games on his phone and wearing down the battery, he said smugly, "I can charge it in my car."

Yeah, about that car...the garage opener is electric, too. We could bypass it, but that didn't work out too well the last time. Well, at least the snow blower fit through the service door. There's nothing like working up a sweat while clearing a foot of snow from the driveway, only to catch a chill when you come into an unheated house afterwards. "I could go for a cup of hot chocolate," my husband said with such yearning that I nearly attempted to heat some up with a candle—well, as near as a moment of idiocy gets to a reality.

Grant's work on the drive prompted another urge, and I reminded him that the toilets were limited to one flush. "You can go up the hill like Bella and do your business in the snow." (Not too many years ago he would have enjoyed this little adventure.)

As the afternoon wore on, I contemplated the necessity of electricity for indoor activities. Without sufficient light I couldn't work on projects in my craft room or basement. Writing on my laptop would only last as long as the battery. Without power, I couldn't sit and listen to music. Even reading became challenging as the gray afternoon drifted into early darkness. It was getting colder, and we couldn't exactly warm ourselves by an electric fireplace. And what about cooking? I had planned to heat up leftovers from Christmas dinner. Were we destined to eat cold mashed potatoes in the dark? Would we have to forage for branches under the snow and make a fire on the patio to keep warm? How long would it be before we were reduced to shaking bird feeders for sunflower seeds and gnawing on balls of suet?

Suddenly, the lights popped on! We were saved! Then, from the other room a voice called, "Can you make us some sandwiches?" *That* I can do!

Outside Creatures Should Have Boundaries

Well, I can't go into the basement anymore. I don't mean that I am not physically able to go down there. I guess you could call it a psychological problem. More accurately, it's a situation of boundaries. Why can't outside creatures stay outside?

Believe me, when I run into one of them in the great outdoors, I step the other way. Sometimes I even run the other way. I never want to surprise anything that might be lurking behind trees, in culverts, under mounds of leaves or hanging from a branch. "Walk loudly and carry a big stick" is my motto. So what gives them the right to squish their furry, slimy, or slinky bodies through the tiniest crack to enter my abode? A little respect, please!

While I'm on the subject, it wouldn't hurt for them to make a little noise so they don't startle a person. A light scratching, a flip of a tail…any warning would be appreciated. This would have helped recently when I encountered an uninvited visitor in the basement. I had just finished my routine on the treadmill and walked over to turn off the radio. Something small and dark wriggled along the floor. Immediately, I recognized the little intruder as a snake.

My scream aroused two responses. First, the snake curled against the wall in fear. The second was from my husband who groaned down the stairs, "Now, what?" I wasted no time in bounding up the steps and demanding that he capture the scoundrel immediately. I handed him the dust pan—I don't know, it just seemed like the appropriate tool for the job—and pushed him toward the basement door. After all, it could have slinked off and found a hiding place under the tool bench or freezer.

Even after my husband captured the snake ("This little thing?") and put it outside, my mind was racing with scenarios. "How did he get in? What if he has family here? There could be more of them! And what if he comes back?"

This certainly wasn't the first time we've been visited by home invaders. Over the years our residences have been infiltrated by bees, ants, mice, birds and even bats. I came home from work one day to find wall pictures on the floor and the curtains ripped. I thought we had been robbed. It turned out that our special guest was a squirrel. After enlisting the help of our neighbor's dog, I stood on a chair and shook a rug until the frenzied chase ended with the squirrel exiting through the door.

I guess I can't stay out of the basement forever. After all, it is my house. Will someone please tell that to all creatures great and small?

Onset of Winter Halts Projects

By now all the birds have built their shelters and are burrowing into them before the snow flies. That's the way I feel when winter arrives. It's not that I don't love many aspects of winter, especially skating and skiing, but my outdoor projects must come to a halt. Even with that knowledge, I always seem to be scrambling to get just a few days in before the cold hits. Each November I am flying around like Auntie Em in *The Wizard of Oz*, reluctantly entering the cellar before the storm hits. But I'm not ready to take cover in that cellar, yet. I still have a few things to do outside.

I begin my doomsday lament in September. My husband is just entering the house with a bounty of tomatoes when I bombard him with omens. "Get the green tomatoes in here now! It's going to freeze tonight. You better get our rowboat put away before the animals take refuge under them! We have to pound some stakes into the ground to mark the driveway for the snowplow. And what about the Christmas lights? We have to put the decorations in the yard *now*, or we'll be using a sledge hammer to secure Santa and his reindeer to the lawn!"

This year I added another project to my list. My epiphany came to me while I was walking in our woods with Bella. We have enough woods that the trees make it park-like, especially for the children in my family. It's a great place for a scavenger hunt and scary adventures. The idea came to me to put up small wooden signs that marked the location of the little creek and big pine and circle of cedar trees. I could put them on posts along a path.

That meant digging holes for the posts, which meant clearing brush and trees for a path, which meant a lot of work, which meant I had "a lot of 'splainin' to do" to my husband. Instead, I minimized my project as "a little digging" and waited until Richard was occupied with his own work near the lake before I entered the woods with my tools. Then the sky darkened and the rain began. By the second post even Bella had deserted me, and I could hear Richard calling my name. I was now soaking wet, covered in mud and muttering into the post holes.

But I continued because time was running out, and I would soon have to take shelter from the storm—from the oncoming cold and threat of snow. I had to finish today: tomorrow was winter. That's a long time to regret unfinished business. Besides, winter's the time to develop new projects for spring. As long as the weather cooperates, my schemes will come true.

Hunting Season Is Ladies' Paradise

Lots of people have to-do lists tacked to their refrigerators. But in November the abundance of notes can scarcely be secured by mere door magnets. The activity list is only matched by the contents of bulging purses that include coupons, gift ideas, and credit cards. The men are gone. The women are unleashed. It's hunting season.

As a newcomer to this area, I was unaware of the nuances of deer season. My knowledge was largely based on a vague memory of my grandfather and great uncles retreating to their camp around Thanksgiving. The women didn't seem to mind. In fact, my grandmother gaily attended to her baking and errands with an enthusiasm that bordered on joy. But I didn't understand the real interest that women had in hunting season until I moved here.

The signs were unmistakable, but I misunderstood them. For example, the newspaper featured ads and articles directed to "hunting widows." At first my reaction was one of sympathy. How nice of the community to think of these lonely women at this time of the year. Upon later contemplation, I was also perplexed. Why were there so many functions for hunting widows? Could there be that many unfortunate women whose husband's befell the same fate? I pondered the scenario of hunters mistaking their brothers-in-law for deer. The idea of promoting shopping sprees for their widows seemed a little insensitive, but, then again, there's nothing like a bargain to lift the spirit.

Eventually, I learned that these "widows" consisted of any woman whose husband goes off into the woods to shoot deer every November—which is basically every woman except me. I also found out that hunting season offers a lot more to women than bus trips to shopping malls. During those two weeks they indulge in activities their husbands generally dislike: seeing "chick flicks," shopping for clothes, going out for drinks with the girls, and redecorating the house. They bond with their girlfriends, go off their diets, and dispose of their husband's old clothes. But these things don't happen by chance. It takes a clever woman to make hunting season a holiday for *her*.

She has to know, for example, that's it's not only safe for humans to eat deer apples, but when baked into desserts and sent to the camps, the men tend to stay there even longer. Hence, church bake sales serve a dual purpose of community service by raising money for those less fortunate *and* encouraging ample restoration for harried housewives.

Likewise, "deer cabbage" is not restricted to baiting purposes, unless one considers the benefits of luring a man with the versatile vegetable. I've heard that the aroma of cabbage soup will so arouse a man that he can be persuaded to put the Christmas lights up in October. And promising to cook a recipe for any venison dish is a U.P. aphrodisiac (not recommended for men with high blood pressure).

A woman just has to remember to reserve some charm for his return. That way he won't notice the new furniture or his missing wardrobe until at least Christmas.

Letter to a U.P. Snowbird

Dear Snowbird,

So, you're leaving us again! After all we shared through the summer and fall, you are still going. No wonder you had that smug expression on your face when the temperature first dipped below zero in November. You already had your bags packed for a warmer place.

I have heard about the charms of Florida, Arizona, Texas, and other states that are *not* Michigan. Although I am not fond of places that have an average temperature higher than my body temperature, I can appreciate that some people like it. Some claim that you don't even feel the heat because the air is so dry. I think that is the same description that Hell uses in its brochure.

If you plan to play golf all winter, you better become the expert that all of your friends will expect you to be. After all, you can't exactly get by with that old excuse that you're just rusty from months of not playing. That's our excuse, and we've earned it.

"Yoopers" (as residents in the U.P. affectionately refer to themselves) take pride in restoring a baby-like softness to their skin over the winter. The only area that is allowed to glow from a chance exposure to sunlight is the back of the neck. This can happen in two ways: shoveling snow and leaning over a hole in the lake while ice fishing. If you show up with more of your body tanned than that, people will assume you're from out of state.

Personally, I think that sunshine is overrated. There's nothing like forty-six consecutive days of cold and snow to build character. In fact, Yoopers have so much character that they have to temper it with drinking a lot of beer just so they can appear humble.

Oh, I've heard about the warmer habitats that have beautiful plants and wildlife that can be enjoyed all year. But the locals here like to give the animals a break. After being chased with guns all fall, the wildlife deserves to curl up in the woods while hunters mind their own business all winter.

I also know that many of you can pick fresh citrus from your backyard trees. That sounds nice, but leaning over the produce section in a store seems a lot safer than risking an encounter with scorpions and snakes while crossing the yard. As for the availability of all the freshly-caught seafood in places like Florida, that's all well and good, too. But we like our fish ready-frozen, direct from the hole in the ice and transported by snowmobile. Besides, it will take until spring to get through all that venison in the freezer that everyone was giving away before they took off for their tropical getaways. Someone's got to eat it.

You're still going? Okay, but don't say you weren't warned. By the way, close the door on your way out. It's cold out there!

Chapter 2

Alley Cats, Pirates and Mermaids

City Has Small Town Neighborhoods

If you've never lived in a large city, you may not fully understand the significance of its neighborhoods. In many ways a city neighborhood can be as intimate as a small town. At least this was the way it was in Chicago when I grew up.

Our neighborhood was a composite of ethnic groups, many of whom still held to the traditions of their previous homelands. The older houses, like the ones on our block, were often occupied by families who had relatives living on the same street. Most men held blue collar jobs, especially at the steel mills and factories on the perimeter of South Chicago where I lived.

When the prairies were prepared for the post-war housing boom, I played in the freshly-poured foundations and watched the construction of homes that would soon be occupied by our new neighbors. Eventually, the inhabitants of these brick bungalows became friends with whom we shared our lives for many years. Although our backgrounds and nationalities may have differed, living in the same neighborhood gave us a commonality that my generation, in particular, identified with more than an individual's nationality. The Polish kids on our block made their first communions; the ones in the new houses on Euclid celebrated Hanukah; and most of the rest of us attended the Lutheran Church. But we all played together in backyards, basements and alleys. I wasn't so much the descendant of Swedish-Irish immigrants as I was simply one of the girls on Jeffery Boulevard who went to Joseph Warren Elementary School.

Most families only owned one car, but many relied on buses or walking to reach their daily destinations. However, there were few reasons to leave the neighborhood. Everything we needed was there. The corner grocery, the hardware store, the cleaners—they were all just down the street. Everyone relied on local businesses, which thrived quite well with this arrangement.

For many years my world was contained in a small circle that rarely extended beyond my neighborhood. I went to school across the street. The schoolyard was merely an extension of my yard. We often sat on our front steps on summer evenings and watched the teenaged boys play baseball. Church was one block down on the corner. I was there several times a week for Sunday school, choir practice, youth league, and even Girl Scouts.

Of course, such a tight environment also meant that everyone knew everyone else—and their personal business. People conversed over fences, lines of laundry, and open car hoods. Every neighborhood had its oddball, but, overall, we looked out for each other. If my mother called me from the back door, several neighbors echoed the message as I headed home.

Many years and many moves later, I still think of my little world in that neighborhood as home.

Prairies Held Mystery and Adventure

There was an excitement to spring when I was a child because playtime outside was extended by several hours. The warmer weather also meant that our activities were expanded to the more distant parts of our city neighborhood. For us that meant the prairies, open areas of undeveloped land which had not yet been affected by the post-war building boom.

Access to the prairies was via the alleys which bordered our house on two sides. Though a source of perpetual dust or mud for the cars, they provided magical avenues to adventure for us. We were alley cats, hiding behind trash cans, running over black cinders (some of which I still bear in a scar on my knee) and foraging for small treasures among the rusted bottle caps.

But these crude pathways led to one prairie that extended for an entire city block and, though bordered by civilization, provided a jungle-like setting for our play. Adults never entered the confines of this wilderness, but we alley cats knew its secrets. Our legs were soon enveloped in weeds that smelled like onions and wild sunflowers that towered over our heads. The low areas often flooded and attracted snakes. But where the prairie rose into hills of clay, chunks of fool's gold sparkled in the sun. In other words, it was a kid's paradise.

Imagination was a key element of our play, and the prairie afforded extravagant fantasies. Within this natural setting were also items left by humans, such as tobacco tins, a single glove, a comic book, even construction materials, most of which we stepped over and ignored as part of the prairie's eclectic ambiance. But there was one curiosity that proved resourceful: A discarded section of cement provided the perfect deck of a submarine, and its protruding pipe—rusted and bent as it was—served as the periscope. As captain, I surveyed the horizon and gave orders to my small crew, who scrambled through the waves of surrounding brush.

The prairies exuded mystery. One day, while scaling one of the mounds of clay, I found the shriveled remains of an animal paw. The discovery was hailed as a great wonder by the gang, and I carried it proudly in my pocket all day. Simple chases through the prairie weeds were transformed into acts of heroism as I bestowed invisible protection with the petrified talisman. Even my mother's insistence that the claw be tossed away before we contracted rabies did not diminish its allure.

A rat's foot was not the only item that posed a threat in the prairie. Many were hidden from view as we ran with our games. On one occasion my unfortunate leap landed on a wooden board with an exposed nail. Of course it broke through my tennis shoe and entered the center of my foot. I hopped home—board still attached to my foot—hoping that I wouldn't get in too much trouble. Upon my mother's urging I sat on our back porch steps, leg extended, while a neighbor yanked on the board. A crowd had gathered in the alley, and I proudly proclaimed that it didn't hurt a bit. Despite my protests, I still ended up at the doctor's office for a tetanus shot, which was probably a wise decision considering all the other rusty encounters I had incurred over the years.

But a little old nail wasn't going to deter an alley cat with nine lives, and I was back in the prairie within a couple days. Who knows what adventures I could find there next?

Schoolyard Dares Are Hard to Resist

Remember how difficult it was to turn down a dare when you were a kid? It often began when someone on the playground boasted about an impressive feat he had accomplished, like dangling from the top of the fire escape by his feet. Or it may have started with a hypothetical situation conjured up on a boring summer afternoon, like "I'll bet you're too afraid to go into that abandoned house alone?"

Of course, such a suggestion frightened me. But there is a tone that all kids recognize when someone is questioning their bravery. It is the same inflection that is used to admonish someone too young to be included in the activities of the older kids. In other words, "You can't play with us."

Girls were not excluded from this kind of challenge in my neighborhood. In fact, we girls had an image to maintain. No boy was going to outrun, outsmart, or outdo anything we did. I may have been all pigtails, party dress and patent leather shoes on Sunday, but on Saturday I ran through the alleys in worn-out Keds and scabby knees. When lines were drawn in the gravel of a schoolyard, the challenge rivaled any cowboy showdown at high noon. We nine-year-olds were unarmed, of course, but our reputations required ammunition. Flinch when a dead snake was thrown at you, and you would suffer an endless taunting at the hands of reptile-totin' bullies.

My most memorable challenge came on a Saturday afternoon while a group of us sat on the fire escape steps that were constructed in the narrow courtyard between the main school building and a one-story annex. From this second-story landing on the fire escape, we could look down at the annex roof and the lower ground level of the main building's basement. In fact, if one was careful, he could jump from that fire escape perch and reach the annex roof. But, if he wasn't careful, he could fall twenty-some feet onto the cement outside the boiler room.

And, of course, that was the challenge. More accurately, it was the mandate. My best friend, who was known for her fearless antics, expelled a defying laugh and took the first leap. She landed—barely—onto the tarred surface of the annex roof, rolled a short distance, then stood up with a triumphant smile that invited the next challenger. The group froze. Suddenly, I heard my voice answer, "I'll do it!" That was it: I was already ensnarled in the net that fate had cast.

I tried not to look at the ominous cement two stories below. Then I leapt, hitting the tarred roof solidly on my feet with a jolt that shook my body, as well as my senses. I immediately regretted the risk I had taken, which could have just as well turned out to be disastrous, if not deadly. But it taught me a strong lesson: There is a difference between being brave and being *foolish*.

Neighborhood Had Characters

The people in our South Side neighborhood were typical of those found in most Chicago neighborhoods: an eclectic mix of ages, ethnicity, occupations, and personalities. Even as kids we knew which houses to approach when trick-or-treating, and which houses were most likely to be guarded by real witches and ghouls. We stayed clear of certain characters the way we avoided angry dogs. But that didn't mean we eliminated all encounters.

The old man next door always seemed a frightening figure because he wore a gruff expression and didn't talk to us. That didn't stop us from stealing cherries from the trees in his yard, but it gave us hesitation when our balls went over the fence. His wife seemed to rule the roost, and her henpecked husband sought peace and quiet in an unusual way. One day we noticed boards nailed like steps on the roof of his two-story house. My father said that they looked suspiciously like those from a wooden construction horse that was coincidentally missing from a street project on the corner. Thereafter, when Mr. McDonald wanted to get away from his wife, he climbed onto the roof to hide, pulling the ladder up so that she wouldn't find him.

There seemed to be a lot of disgruntled men in the neighborhood, even my best friend's father. We weren't allowed to play at her house when her father was home because he "didn't like noise." I suspected that he just didn't like kids. He spent a lot of time in his garage polishing his fancy, white Lincoln Continental. I don't know why. He never drove it anywhere.

There were the "stay-inside" people that you rarely saw and wondered what secrets were behind their drawn curtains. Entire families eluded us for years, stirring up speculation of separations, divorce or worse ("Do you think he killed his wife and buried her body in the yard?").

And there were the "outside" neighbors who never went inside. They were always on their front steps or hanging over their backyard fence, just kind of waiting for you to come by so they could engage you in conversation. One of these men didn't even bother to get fully dressed. He just stood by his gate in his undershirt, always with a can of beer in his hand, which I imagine was the only sustenance he could get under those circumstances.

There was Annie the Goat Lady, so-named because she raised goats in her yard next to the railroad tracks. There was also Crazy Margaret, who used to stand at the bus stop, waving her arms and ranting to strangers—and then to herself after they left. And there were the eccentric members of one family who were all supposedly geniuses. None-the-less, the mother was a large woman who wore her husband's t-shirts and no bra, and their daughter was prone to hysteria and once bit my friend in the leg. I assumed that intelligence wasn't such a smart thing, after all.

But the most colorful character was probably Rose, the card lady. Rose was, as my mother explained, "slow-witted." Yet she was a well-known figure all over the South Side, selling cards door-to-door with intimidating veracity. Once, while my mother was having coffee at a neighbor's, the two women spotted Rose coming up the walk with her bag of greeting cards. They tried to hide under the table, but there was no escaping Rose, who persisted at the kitchen window above them. Nor did it do any good to refuse or tell her to come another time. "When?" she would ask. "Oh, six months," you'd say. Then, without even writing it down, six months to the day she would be pounding on your door with her monomaniacal edict, "You buy cards!" Everyone did—eventually.

Most neighborhoods have some character—we had a whole cast of them!

Weeds and Wildflowers Make Great Scents

The edge of the yard was overgrown with weeds that included wildflowers and dense ferns. Prepared with boots and gloves, I whacked at the tall grass with my sickle. Bent over in my purpose, my head was soon devoid of any thoughts. Then a familiar smell entered my nostrils, and my mind searched for the memory it triggered. Ah! Prairie perfume.

I am not merely referring to a fragrant field. I mean, quite literally, a perfume made from prairie plants. More specifically, the wildflowers found in the prairies—and the alleys—of my Chicago neighborhood when I was a kid. Who would make such a perfume? My sister and I did. And we sold it.

True, we knew very little about the fragrance business. The dime store sold tiny bottles of cologne with exotic names like Blue Waltz. And our grandmother gave us each a bottle of Orange Blossom, the exotic essence of Florida. Somehow, we thought our ingenuity could compete with these fragrances. After all, wasn't cologne just flower-scented water?

Our naivety launched our first entrepreneur endeavor. It was summer, and the prairies were filled with floral opportunities. As pretty as some of them looked, weeds didn't have much, if any, smell. We decided to add a more pungent flower to the recipe: marigolds. They were abundant in yards, and no one would miss just a few from a garden. Pulling our wagon through the alley, we discreetly snatched an assortment of colorful blooms that included our neighbor's prized roses. We assumed she'd be happy to contribute to our cause.

Manufacturing took place in our basement. The ingredients were simple: petals and water. These were added to empty pickle and jelly jars. What we lacked in quality was made up in quantity. When the concoctions turned a murky yellow a day or two later, we figured our perfume was potent enough to attract customers. We used Mom's colander to strain out the flowers and resealed the jars. Using our best crayon techniques, we crafted labels bearing flowers and alluring names. Once loaded into the wagon, the jars of urine-colored cologne clanked over the sidewalk as we called out, "Perfume for sale!"

Remarkably, we managed to sell a few bottles, mostly to neighbors who may have felt some sympathy for our efforts (and had not yet discovered the snipped chrysanthemums in their yards).

Our basement retained that peppery smell for days. Funny how a whiff of freshly cut weeds and wildflowers will bring that sentimental scent back so many years later.

Papergirls Find News That's Fit to Print

We were not discouraged when our fragrance business folded after its first week. Apparently, homemade perfume was not a hot item in our neighborhood. I came up with another scheme to make money, something a lot easier than hauling jars of flower water in a wagon.

The idea came to me one afternoon when the newspaper arrived. A newspaper! But there were already several papers in Chicago. Besides, I knew less about front page news than I did about making perfume. But I had watched enough *Superman* episodes to know that a good paper relied on good reporters. If Lois Lane could find a story, so could this twelve-year-old.

My sister agreed that a neighborhood newspaper was a better idea than peddling perfume, but what would we write about? Using the "you-go-that-a-way" strategy I had observed in television Westerns, we split up and took to the sidewalks. Armed with pad and pencil, we were ready to pounce on any lead. When we finally convened in the editor's office (our basement), it was generally noted that our neighborhood was the epitome of peace and quiet.

I did have one story that could serve for our headline. Some street repairs were being done at the corner of our block and 92nd Street. After a suitable but unproductive time for brainstorming, we decided to check the real newspaper for inspiration. The pages inside proved to be more promising. After all, not every item had to be breaking news. We took particular notice of "Dear Abby" and the want ads.

The creative process turned out to be less trouble than the printing process. Pounding out copies on the old typewriter was frustrating when I had to start over every time I made a mistake. Eventually, I resorted to making several copies by using multiple sheets of carbon paper. Ironically, there was more ink on my face and hands than on the pages.

Our newspaper consisted of one double-sided sheet of paper. The lead story, entitled "Danger for Children," gave a stern, albeit brief, warning about heavy equipment and potholes. We listed items for sale, including a friend's go-cart and my father's car parts. Our tribute to the comics was the inclusion of corny jokes. Carol solicited readers who might have a problem that she could solve in her advice column, "Dear Carol." Her only other article was a lament about the ordeal of writing and typing thirteen copies for distribution. It ended with the clincher, "I wonder if it was worth it!!"

But at ten cents a copy, we sold enough to earn a trip to the corner store. Carol's journalistic question lingered in our thoughts as we sucked on popsicles. Yup. It was worth it.

Fear of Strangers

Most young children have a natural fear of strangers, and that is probably a good thing. You should never trust someone you don't know, and there are enough sad outcomes in the news to remind us how true this is. My first experience with this lesson came at an early age.

My sister and I were six and eight, respectively, when we and a neighbor boy entered a construction site down the street. The area had previously been a prairie and was a favorite place for make-believe adventures as pirates or explorers. When the prairies were bulldozed for houses, we still ventured there, if only to investigate the foundations that were our catacombs.

On this particular Sunday our destination was a freshly-poured basement over which the studs for walls had been newly erected. Our goal was to gather the metal slugs cut from the electrical outlets. These silver "coins" were our pirate money, and we picked through the sawdust as intently as if it were a treasure of gold. Satisfied with our booty, we turned toward home. But our steps were apprehended by a man who now stood blocking our way.

I remember the man's appearance distinctly, as the image would return to haunt my dreams for years thereafter. He was very tall and wore a white suit, which even on this warm Sunday seemed oddly out of sync with the crude surroundings of the prairie. His hair was black and slicked down so that it glimmered in the summer sun. But it was his smile that most betrayed him, calm and insincere, even as he implored us with his subterfuge.

"A workman lost his ring. Could you help look for it?" He gestured toward the shell of a house from which we had just emerged. Our faces must have registered some confusion for he continued to explain. "He lost it in the basement. If you find it, I'll give you a reward."

Bobby moved forward, and Carol leaned in questioningly. Perhaps sensing my caution, the man stepped closer and added with emphasis, "I will give you ten dollars if you go down there and find the ring." Though I knew his dark eyes hid something sinister, he was an adult, and I felt helpless. When Bobby moved toward him, acquiescing to the stranger's request, I froze in panic. Carol took a hesitant step in his direction. I knew that we shouldn't follow, but

my heart was thumping inside my chest, and I was unable to speak.
Just then a voice bellowed down the street. It was Bobby's mother
calling him home. As if released from a spell, we ran.

Carol and I were breathless when we reached our back door.
We dove under the kitchen table and clung to each other in fear. Our
childish babbling must have sounded like more make-believe to my
mother, who soon returned to her household tasks. We remained
under that table for a long time. And so our ordeal remained a secret
between the two of us.

But we had seen evil, and we would never forget the man in
the white suit.

Highlights of a Saturday Halloween

Forget a lunar eclipse. Forget Haley's Comet. There is only
one rare phenomenon that matters in the prime years of childhood. It
is the holy grail of trick-or-treaters: the Saturday Halloween.

The greatest Halloween memory of my youth was on a
Saturday in 1959. We anticipated the holiday for weeks. No rushing
to get into costumes after school. No speeding down the sidewalks to
reach every house before dinner. No hurrying home for curfew with a
disappointing booty in our bags. No school that day—or the next.

My sister and I were in our costumes and ready when my best
friend arrived that morning. We made a giggling trio along the
sidewalks, kicking brown leaves in anticipation of the day's journey.
We began with our closest neighbors, who greeted us with
compliments and homemade treats. These were simpler, safer times.
Our city neighborhood was as familiar to us as our backyards, and we
were trusted to traverse its streets and alleys as we did every day on
foot or on bicycles or roller skates.

By afternoon the neighborhood was bustling with tramps and
princesses, witches and robots. Holding masks and drooping
hemlines, they stomped up porch steps and formed a line. Someone
pushed the doorbell. Another peered through a window. "Here they
come!" The door opened with a phantom hand that reached out to
their opened bags. Then, with a "thank you" tossed into the air, the
masqueraders took flight for new pursuits.

The day was ours, and the excitement spurred our feet to skip down paths of Candyland. For the mere token of a pirate's patch or fairy's wand, all sweet things were ours. We only paused to check our sacks, inhaling scents of chocolate bars, licorice sticks, and popcorn balls. Such enchantment!

We scurried from house to house, up one side of a block, crossed at the corner, and then moved down the other side. The pattern eventually led to streets whose names were less familiar. Our bags sagged with the weight of candy, coins and apples. The sun dipped behind the rooftops, and the last echoes of "trick or treat" floated across the lawns. Pumpkins glowed in dark windows. Bare branches, like witches' arms, shook warnings in the cold wind, and we scattered like leaves along the sidewalks.

Somewhere a goblin squealed and disappeared in the shadows. No doubt there would be cackling over backyard bonfires while the day's treasure was sorted and counted. The bounty would last well through November; the memory of its acquisition would last much longer.

Decades later this Saturday Halloween is still remembered as my sweetest.

It Happened on Main Street

Chicago is where I grew up, but I always considered Norway, Michigan my other hometown. My father, who was born and raised there, often returned with us to visit his parents. The block my grandparents lived on was next to Main Street, and the sounds and sights of the downtown's businesses were part of our experience, especially in the summer.

The downtown shops provided just about anything that you needed—and even more that you might desire. Main Street was the shopping hub for Norway and the surrounding area, and it supported a variety of businesses that included several grocery stores and three bakeries. I would awaken in the morning to the smell of freshly baked bread and the sound of delivery trucks unloading at the back entrances. Voices from the shops' back doors, as well as from apartments above, echoed down the alley.

Every building on Main Street offered something of interest. A trip to the dime store, for example, was a treat even if we didn't make a purchase. If we strolled across the street, our generous great uncle, who frequented the hotel bar, usually came out with candy bars or potato chips for us. Proprietors knew all of my relatives; in fact, they knew all of their customers.

There was a formality to Main Street that was upheld by town residents then. My grandmother, especially, respected the unwritten dress code. Hat and gloves would not be out of the question, but certainly one did not patronize shops in a housedress. When her grown daughter embarked on an errand downtown, Grandma was adamant. "You can't walk down Main Street in *that!*" she said of my aunt's casual outfit.

Main Street bustled with pedestrians who stopped to exchange greetings, news, and gossip. "Guess who I saw on Main Street today?" was a question that preceded the appearance of a grocery bag through the door at home. One of my great aunts developed a nervous condition that became agitated in grocery stores. As soon as she got into the checkout line, she was struck with an irrepressible call of nature. Invariably, she'd abandon her groceries and run home. Too embarrassed to return herself, someone in the family had to collect her items later.

One of my best Main Street memories occurred on the cusp of my teen years. Grandma announced that there was a street dance to be held downtown, right around the corner from us. My initial dread and self-consciousness eventually dissipated once the music of the local band began. I'll never forget how we girls laughed and danced that day. And it happened on Main Street.

Pasty Picnics

My grandmother believed in serving a hot dinner in the middle of the day, even in the summer. The meal coincided with the warmest part of the afternoon and seemed excessive given the temperatures. However, when dinner was ready, we were expected to be, as well.

Grandma was not a stern woman. On the contrary, she loved to laugh and have fun. As a young woman she had left her family in

Sweden for the opportunities that America promised. By the time she settled in Michigan, she had learned the benefits of hard work. But the girl in her never ceased to enjoy all that life could offer. I believe it was this spirit that captured my grandfather's heart.

My grandmother shared this joy with my father and his two sisters. In spite of what they lacked during the Depression, they thrived on what they had. As many women did then, my grandmother could make soups and stews out of bones and scraps. As she did for her children, Grandma delighted in preparing food for her visiting grandchildren. Her hot oven competed with the outside temperatures. We stopped our play when she called us for dinner and sat in the sweltering dining room over plates of hot *flaskpannkaka* or steaming *potatiskorv* and *rotmos*.

Sometimes, when my grandfather went to his camp, my grandmother planned a picnic lunch that we would bring out and share with him. All morning the kitchen was bustling with preparations. Crust was rolled out to accommodate the filling of potatoes, meat, and onions. While the pasties baked, Grandma and her sister, Augusta, loaded a basket with pickles, fruit, cake, and cookies. The pasties were then wrapped in waxed paper and covered with newspaper to keep them hot.

The camp was a log cabin that my grandfather built in the woods along the Sturgeon River. Though the distance was only about 20 miles from town, it seemed a long car ride to the little girls sitting in the backseat beside a basket that emanated with enticing aromas. In anticipation of our arrival, Grandpa had moved a table and chairs outside onto the grass and placed bottles of locally-made Odill's soda in a metal pan of cold water that he pumped from the well. The women spread a tablecloth onto the table and arranged the contents of the basket.

My sister and I played along the river until the call for dinner was heard. Wildflowers, placed in a glass, completed the traditional picnic table that Grandma remembered as a child in Sweden. She didn't talk about it, but there was something in her face that reflected the memory of those earlier days. "Ya, it is good," she said surveying the table. "We eat now."

I will always remember fondly those pasty picnics at the camp.

Summer Mermaids

My mother's parents purchased a cottage at Hamilton Lakes in the 1940s, just a few years before she and my father met as teenagers there at the beach. My father lived only minutes away in town. After they married and settled in Chicago, they still returned to these settings to visit family. Consequently, for years my sister and I benefitted from the proximity of these two places, as well as the love and attention of so many relatives. Summers in Michigan were the highlight of my childhood, but the lake retreat, in particular, held a special enchantment for us.

The cottage was perched on a hill and nestled among pines and birch. Inside, the small rooms contained cozy nooks for conversations or reading. But during the day it was impossible to ignore the brilliant lake that opened at the bottom of the stone steps my grandfather made. It seemed that I spent more time in the water than I did on land. My bathing suit never completely dried because I wore it most of the day. We weren't allowed to wear wet suits inside so at lunch time we either ate outside or changed in the garage and then carried our dripping suits to a clothesline that was strung between two pines near the outhouse. The rope always sagged with wet towels and suits, and they were usually tugged off again for use while still damp. Even pulling the cold fabric over my suntanned skin never discouraged another escapade to the shore.

We spent hours each day at the resort beach nearby. The cabin renters, many from Chicago, sat in Adirondack chairs that cast shadows along the shore, measuring the afternoon like sundials. But we children were the true keepers of time, reflecting the light from squinted eyes and glistening arms until our bodies were mere silhouettes against a coral sky.

My sister and I pretended that we were mermaids and wriggled through the water with our ankles locked in make-believe fins. We assumed names like Water Lilly and Seaweed and imagined pursuits by fishermen with menacing nets. I opened my eyes under the water and watched the minnows disappear beneath the diving raft's metal drums. My legs felt the currents of cold springs while my outstretched arms floated in the sun-warmed upper layer. With my nose just above the surface, I inhaled the lake's unique, ineffable scent.

We stayed in the water until our lips were blue with cold and the sun dipped behind a purple horizon. We shivered up the stone steps of our hill and dripped a path to the garage. After peeling away our wet suits, we scurried to the clothesline and draped them among the evening's shadows. Of course, they would still be damp the next morning. It didn't matter. We would don our magical fins and return to the water once again as the two summer mermaids of the lake.

Vacation Bliss Ends

Nothing broke the carefree mood of my childhood summers more than those back-to-school sales. Advertisements for school supplies and clothing invaded the newspapers and store windows with the same alarm one might associate with emergency provisions before an impending storm. There I was, innocently scanning the comic books at the lake store or strolling down Main Street, when the dreaded word *school* entered my idyllic world of summer bliss.

But it was still August! With the shadow of school looming ahead, we eked out every precious drop of summer. We donned bathing suits after breakfast and stayed in the water until our skin turned the color of a bluegill's belly. The log fires held off the night's chill as we lingered with one more ghost story and a second bag of Campfire marshmallows.

But the Labor Day countdown loomed like an execution date that even the upcoming county fair could not obliterate. Although there would be no time for shopping at home before the Chicago schools opened on Tuesday, our mother was also reluctant to leave the cheery confines of the cottage. But on a cloudy afternoon she would drive us to Iron Mountain for new shoes and underwear, stopping on the way back for cones of our favorite flavor of ice cream, blue moon. Finally, Mom conceded that we better head to the dime store for our supplies. So we begrudgingly scanned the aisles for notebook paper and Crayola boxes while ignoring the displays of comic books and beach toys. On Monday we grabbed our soggy suits from the clothesline and squeezed into the back of the station wagon for the long drive back to the city.

In the 1950s the car ride from the lake cottage in Michigan to our house on the South Side of Chicago took us over eight hours. We watched as the lakes and woods and little towns receded behind us and the darkening line of pines disappeared from our vision above the suitcases. We traversed Milwaukee via local streets in those years, and the choking pace accelerated our car sickness. We reached the outskirts of Chicago in darkness, but the baked streets sent exhausting heat through the open car windows. Our house was reached just as one of us was on the verge of throwing up.

We stumbled into the house and proceeded upstairs with the luggage, slowing with each step of mounting heat. I unpacked my new underwear and placed it next to my school supplies. My damp bathing suit was a limp reminder of another world I had left only that morning. Waves of anxiety and unrelenting heat kept me awake for hours. Morning came too soon.

And so, another school year began. Our classrooms were decorated with construction paper leaves and promises of cool, crisp days. I leaned my elbows on the sticky, lacquered desk and daydreamed of breezes—not of autumn, but those of returning summer at the lake.

Summer Heat Triggers Memory

When the hottest days of the season linger in the heavy air, one in particular will flicker before me until my slow breaths draw the memory close, and it all comes to back to me.

Having just turned thirteen, the summer's possibilities peeked like sunbeams behind the hung laundry, exposing more of the sky with every clothespin I dreamily removed. Many times my backyard reveries were interrupted by the friendly voice of Mr. Stein, spewing his cheerful banter before moving on down the alley. He lived in the building behind us, sharing the second floor apartment with his two sisters. All three siblings were middle-aged and unmarried.

"A pretty girl like you," he would say as I blushed, "must have a boyfriend already!"

His genial teasing would also be directed at my best friend, who accepted it with the same casual disregard that she had for everything else. Susie lived downstairs from Mr. Stein. She knew that he was seeing a woman that his sisters disliked, an opinion the women stressed many times to Susie's mother over slices of coffee cake as they stirred cream and disapproval into their cups. But the drama had little effect on Susie, who enjoyed the freedom bestowed upon a last child who was generally ignored, allowing her to disappear for hours without interference—which was her plan when she entered the garage for her bike on that fateful day.

I found out what interrupted those plans at supper that evening when my mother was beckoned by a knock on the back door. I sat at the kitchen table, deciphering the whispers that engaged my mother and a neighbor on our porch.

"Yes, he was depressed after his girlfriend left him."

"He carried a rope in his pocket for days, but, of course, no one took that seriously..." Our tiny kitchen felt suffocating as I struggled to grasp the details of Mr. Stein's death. The horrific image hovered in the oppressive August air like the distorted heat waves over the asphalt streets.

When Susie entered the garage that afternoon, she must have paused only a moment to flick on the light before discovering the gruesome scene. Mr. Stein hung from the ceiling. His stocky body dangled from a section of clothesline which had been tossed over a rafter and wound about his neck. An overturned step ladder beneath him confirmed the self-inflicted act in which he had choked to death. Susie had seen the bulging eyes and protruding tongue that resulted from a struggle that probably took several minutes. She fled through the yard and up her stairs.

Her father had already discovered the body and notified the police—something he had neglected to tell his daughter.

I didn't see Susie again until school started. By then the incident had faded from neighborhood gossip. Even my friend had retreated into her demeanor of casual disregard, and any emotional traces incurred were undetectable in her pale blue eyes. We never discussed what had happened.

But, when the heat of August becomes oppressive, I think of how that other summer ended—and my journey to adulthood began.

Some Glamour May Be Unrealistic

One of my favorite summer activities when I was young was reading comic books. A dime was never better spent than on the latest shenanigans of Little Lulu or Richie Rich. But my very favorite characters were Archie and his friends, especially in the September issue.

That was the back-to-school issue, which featured the perpetually beautiful teens, Betty and Veronica, in clothes that any fashion-conscious girl would drool over. They posed in plaid, pleated skirts with coordinating sweater sets while holding books—just to let you know that they were studious as well as stunning. Their clothes reflected their exciting social life: elegant suits for travel, eye-catching casual wear for football games, and gorgeous gowns for all those school dances they attended. According to Betty and Veronica, high school was a fashion show.

Meanwhile, I was in grade school, and my new school clothes were as practical and predictable as the eight-count box of crayons and two Ticonderoga pencils we added to the previous year's supply box. I may have wanted trendy, pointed flats like Betty or Veronica, but a pair of gray oxfords would be more sensible. And if I dreamed about a rainbow of sweaters to coordinate with different outfits, the one with the Scottie dogs that my grandmother knit for me would just have to suffice, whether over my corduroy jumper, plaid dress, or snow pants.

But glamour was as close as my Barbie doll case. Inside, the ultimate model of sophistication and fashion posed on tiny black mules. Most of my doll's clothes were meticulously made by my talented grandmother, but the Barbie catalogue contained visions that fulfilled a girl's fashion fantasies: "Solo in the Spotlight" was a black, mermaid-style dress for singing in a nightclub, and "Garden Party" suggested green lawns and rose-colored cocktails. "Orange Blossom," the smart, bridesmaid ensemble, could even inspire Ken to propose, and the airline stewardess uniform, complete with travel bag and winged pin, represented the most glamorous profession any woman could imagine.

By the time I entered high school, the images that Betty, Veronica, and Barbie represented seemed a little unrealistic. My fall wardrobe consisted of a few sensible skirts that could be worn with simple blouses from J.C. Penny. I went to football games in jeans like all the other girls, and my party dresses were far from "solo in the spotlight."

But I learned to appreciate the little splashes of glamour, like my first pair of high heels and a pretty new shade of lipstick. After all, school was more than attracting another *Jughead*, and my aspirations were higher than serving lunch in the clouds. I was going to college. And *that* seemed glamorous enough to me!

Money Saved Is the Stuff of Dreams

My experience with earning and saving money began when I was eleven years old. And, although it is no Dickens' tale of drudgery in the workhouse, I was a diligent saver and made every penny count. That's a good thing since my early salaries were best described in cents.

Getting paid fifty cents an hour to take care of neighborhood children certainly beat lugging pop bottles in my wagon to the corner gas station for a return deposit of two cents each. My reputation as a reliable and responsible sitter earned me consistent Saturday night jobs, most of which were for the young families on the next block. They all had two children and lived in recently-constructed, identical, brick bungalows with new furniture encased in clear plastic. My responsibilities were certainly not challenging, but there was rarely anything to eat as a snack except tasteless matzo crackers (which made my grandparents' hardtack seem like coffee cake in comparison). Each couple went out from exactly 7 p.m. to midnight. That meant I earned exactly $2.50. On the rare occasion that they were fifteen minutes late, I received an extra dime.

But even a dime was a significant profit for an adolescent girl in the 1960s. I enjoyed counting those dollars and planning how I might spend them. When my savings reached a sufficient amount, a trip to Evergreen Shopping Plaza was planned. Located just outside of Chicago, it was the suburban area's first mall, and it was a mecca of shopping splendor under one roof. The excursion required extra money for bus fares and, because it was a much-anticipated highlight of the day, lunch at Woolworth's restaurant. For only ninety-nine cents, a meal consisting of a hamburger, small drink, and fries could be enjoyed from a swiveling perch at the counter.

My meager income taught me to be a wise shopper. Although our mother bought us new outfits for school each fall, supplementing my wardrobe was a personal luxury. I might admire a pretty dress and even try it on in a shop's dressing room, but my sensible inner voice told me that a more practical skirt and two blouses might be purchased for the same amount. I learned that a cardigan sweater was a better investment than a trendy top and that clothes for school were more important than special-occasion fashions. But whatever I purchased, transporting it home on the bus and laying it out on the bed to admire later were rituals that filled me with delight.

But my small income from babysitting money was not all spent on clothes for myself. My father had taught me the value of saving, and I always kept a reserve of funds for purchasing birthday and Christmas gifts for my family. I look back now with wonder at how I did this throughout high school while earning so little. But I guess the lessons it taught me were worth much more.

Songs of Summer

The seasonal sounds of grass-cutting, boat motors, and humming insects had not yet heralded summer to my idle ears. Then a Beach Boys' tune came on the radio, and my sleeping mind suddenly awakened at the first line, "Wouldn't it be nice...?" Ah...it's summer again!

Or, more accurately, "Wouldn't it be nice to have *that* summer again?" *That* summer of days at the beach, songs on the radio, and boys on the phone. *That* summer when I was young and pretty and full of dreams. Even now it opens in my mind like a blossom that cannot wilt, forever nurtured with an endless string of sunny days and dewy nights.

I have often wondered how much of that girl I have taken with me through the years, and how much of her I have left behind. Perhaps the best I can do is to recall the girl I used to be, the one that looked out at the beginning of one special summer and believed that the magic would never end. I suppose that the past is usually remembered as a simpler time, but that summer was as enriching an experience as it was an uncomplicated time in my life.

Still somewhat shy, I possessed a carefree attitude that ultimately led to confidence. I liked talking to boys, and my heart jumped with excitement when the phone rang. My girlfriends and I watched them parade up and down the beach. Although we pretended that our sole purpose was to get sun, we were secretly flattered when boys chose to pick us up and toss us into the waves. Every blanket on the beach had a transistor radio tuned into WLS. *Good vibrations.*

It was the summer of long hair streaked with Summer Blonde, short sundresses in *mod* prints, and two-piece bathing suits with bright daisies or polka dots. It was the summer of neighborhood garage bands (that all played "Louie, Louie"), bicycle rides along the lakefront, and drives to Rainbow Beach or Carl's hot dog stand.

I had begun playing the guitar that spring, just long enough to have callouses on my fingertips and sufficiently enough to accompany my friends and myself in singing. We would gather in my yard, and I would strum the chords while our voices echoed the words of some familiar tune. I even found the courage to sing at a coffeehouse—once. And I composed my own songs, translating my poems into little melodies that floated through my bedroom window on summer afternoons and landed, like my daydreams, onto the soft green below.

At night I wrote, filling a diary with frivolous details and secret hopes, unaware of the woman who would eventually translate those dreams in unforeseen ways. Oh, to be that girl again that summer: young and pretty and full of dreams! *Wouldn't it be nice?*

Beatles Left a Lasting Impression

When the *Grammies* featured a performance by Paul McCartney and Ringo Starr, I was struck by the fact that these musicians first came to America's attention over half a century ago. Of course, that television appearance wasn't exactly a Beatles' reunion, but it did stir up memories for those of us who grew up with their music playing in the background.

I remember their appearance on the Ed Sullivan Show in 1964. Their hair was longer than that of any boy I knew. Their attire of close-cropped jackets, slim pants, and boots put a fun and sexy twist on the traditional black suit. The four had humor and charm, and when they smiled—nearly laughed—into the television cameras, every American girl fell in love.

I was too young to have been affected by the Elvis phenomenon. The only music I really listened to in my early years was that which my parents tuned into on the radio, and they didn't listen to rock and roll. So when the Beatles performed on the very show that entered our living room every Sunday night...well, it was a far cry from Topo Gigio, the Italian mouse puppet! The next day our teacher gave each of us a topic for an impromptu speech, and mine was to be a personal impression of the Beatles. I was tongue-tied and could only offer a few words in self-consciousness, but it was the introduction to my preferences for our generation's popular music.

How could I—still a young girl—know that the Beatles' songs would accompany me through high school and into college? How could I know then that their voices would make me smile and their melodies make me dance? That my girlfriends and I would lie on the floor and listen to the album *Rubber Soul* over and over? That a few years later I would play "Blackbird" on the guitar? And a few years after that I'd select my favorite songs from the *White Album*, embracing the lyrics with a passion that ignited my own poetry?

In a way the Beatles' songs were my own. Even the simpler tunes and sillier songs had significance. Someday, I hoped, someone would say to me, "I want to hold your hand" or even, "Do you want to know a secret?" As I grew older (and wiser), other songs resonated in significant ways and kept me company as if the Beatles were growing up and changing with me.

My generation took the Beatles' breakup and the subsequent deaths of John Lennon and George Harrison as personal losses. Although their music still haunts the air and continues to be translated by other artists, it is the Beatles themselves we mourn and those times that make us "long for yesterday."

In tribute I recall these words from my favorite Beatles' song: "Though I know I'll never lose affection for people and things that went before, / I know I'll always stop and think about them, / In my life I love you more."

Childhood Companions Create Neverland

In the carefree days of my youth, I spent part of every summer at my grandparents' cottage. And for several of those golden years, my sister and I were accompanied in our adventures by two boys, exactly the same age as ourselves, who were the annual houseguests of the neighbor in the next cottage.

The brothers' stark differences from one another may be attributed to the fact that they were adopted and not biological brothers. Dick was freckled, funny, and fearless, leading us on excursions with a wooden sword or water reed whip. Bill was slender, sensitive, and scholarly, hesitating before following and often stopping to offer cautionary advice that floated like a receding echo behind our enthusiastic chants. But he always acquiesced, and so we were always four—as natural to the lake as the four winds that swept its surface from all directions. We all rose at once in the morning with the sound of the first screen door and faded at night with the last of the fireflies. But in between was a world we created for each other: skydiving from white clouds, rescuing mermaids among seaweed, and capturing spirits from campfire flames.

The boys stayed in their host's boathouse, which also served as our clubhouse and afforded the perfect pirate lookout. Since we weren't allowed to take the rowboats out ourselves, we built our own boat, of sorts, a raft fashioned from discarded logs and scrap lumber, and upon which we took turns navigating the waters of our pretend ocean while the others kicked alongside. Eventually, my mother put an end to raft travel, saying that it was too dangerous because motor boats couldn't see us. We scoffed. Couldn't see pirates and mermaids?!

But we could. We heard the beat of Indian war drums pounded out on oatmeal boxes and witnessed the arrival of aliens attired in cardboard space suits. Emboldened by our camaraderie, we placed pennies on the railroad tracks and waited until the caboose rattled into the distance before recovering the copper Lincolns that had been flattened to smooth, oblong disks. Such were the heated adventures that culminated in a cooling, afternoon swim. Not until the sun lit the lake's surface with a pink glow did we surrender to the land, only to meet again later under the lavender clouds that turned to smoke above our campfire. Our voices, animated with stories, drifted above the flames and up to the stars. For several moments our upturned faces were four moons reflected in that silver light. At last we moved in our own constellation, a rotating pattern of the game "starlight, moonlight" under the shadowed pines. When the darkness ended our play, we shot like comets across the yard, our farewells echoing in the still, still night.

"Goodnight."

"See you tomorrow."

"Goodnight."

The adults drifted on the periphery of our world, occasionally calling us, as from a distant planet, to come in for dinner. Some afternoons the boys' mother read to us, positioned in a Windsor chair near the brick hearth. Dick's body succumbed to impatient twitches, already plotting our next adventure for later that evening. But Bill absorbed every word, sharing her appreciation for a writer's skill and style. Though so different from one another, they were both the lost boys of *Peter Pan*, orphans in our world of make-believe each summer, one in top hat, the other laughing at his flight around the moon.

And so we flew for several years. We expected to be together every summer. My sister and I would climb out of the station wagon and ask, "Have the boys gotten here yet?" Then, in the time it took to pull on our bathing suits, we would join them at the shore, unaware of how our steps into the water measured our winter's growth. For us, summer erased the distance of time.

Then, one summer, the boys didn't come. We continued our games alone—by day, unpursued mermaids at the beach; at night, playing Sorry and Parcheesi in the den. Unseen campfires sent smoky reminders through the pines, and distant laughter taunted us.

We eventually learned the reason for their absence: The boys' father had passed away quite suddenly. Although he had been a vague figure to us, it was the father's connection to the neighbor that had precipitated the family's visits. Our hearts ached with the possibility that with him gone, the boys might not return. And when they didn't come that summer—or the next—we knew that our Neverland would never be the same.

A few years later on a hot summer afternoon, our grandfather drove us from town, where we were staying, to the lake. After a brief swim at the old beach, he walked us back to the cottage to say our farewells to our other grandparents.

Suddenly, we spotted a boy's figure coming toward us on the road. Our adolescent self-consciousness vanished when we recognized Dick—alone—on his way to the beach. We exchanged greetings and polite inquiries. He was taller and markedly older. But he smiled broadly, still revealing a faint scattering of freckles under his summer blue eyes. Could we go to the beach, he wanted to know. Our hearts thumped with eagerness, but Grandpa reminded us that we had to go back to town where Grandma was waiting with dinner. We would surely see him again. Dick nodded, but there was something in his face that made my heart ache—perhaps it was a lack of faith in promises. Even as the distance grew between our passing figures on the road, I could sense his acceptance that our paths would continue in opposite directions, that we'd never meet again. We were on our way to town when he must have entered the water alone, bracing himself against the cold water, with a grimace that resembled the bold smile.

We never saw the boys again. But when summer returns, I wonder if they, as I, can still see our four figures running through the pines and birch or silhouetted on the surface of a brilliant lake. If only in the memories of mermaids and lost boys, we may still hear those voices calling under the stars.

"Goodnight!"

"See you tomorrow!"

"Goodnight!"

Chapter 3

Can You Make Me a Sandwich?

Old Shirt Finally Gets the Boot

My husband has a hard time accepting the finality of "rag land," the final resting place for clothes that have expired. Sentimental fool that he is, his fondness for certain items is not diminished by mere rips or stains. In fact, he seems to take pride in relating their stories: "These holes in the sleeves are from the embers of a fire I built with my nephews."

Some of his favorite shirts have borne their stains so long that they are named for the foods that damaged them. For example, I might tell him, "It's cool out. You'll need a jacket with that short-sleeved lasagna." But it gets to a point when the go-to favorite just isn't going to *go* anywhere anymore. In another words, it becomes a rag.

Years ago my husband was coerced into giving up a favorite sweatshirt. My children chimed in that it was ugly even *before* the stains adorned its image of a giant cowboy boot. Finally, Richard relinquished it to the rag pile. For a while it was utilized for polishing his car, but, eventually, he used it to mop up oil on the garage floor, a terminal stage for any rag.

However, *somehow*, that disgusting, oil-soaked rag found its way into the laundry. Holding it by the sleeve—as one might hold a dead mouse by the tail—I quickly returned the disgusting sweatshirt back to the garage, where it was eventually forgotten.

Then, several months later, my husband entered the kitchen en route to his Saturday morning errands. On his chest was a blurred figure surrounded by what looked like bullet holes. It was the cowboy boot sweatshirt, resurrected (again, *somehow*) from the bowels of the garage rag pile. I screamed. The children dropped their spoons into their cereal bowls. The mere idea that their friends might recognize their father in such an atrocity sent them into a wail of protest.

"What's wrong with this shirt? It's clean!" (Aha! He put it in the wash on purpose!)

After Richard removed the shirt, I sneaked it back into the garage, where its future use added enough grease to destroy any hope of salvation—or so I thought. A few months later I was washing a load of old towels for cleaning windows when I caught a glimpse of a cowboy boot. (Will the diabolical thing never die?!) I choked the water out of it and buried it in the garbage.

Apparently, that's where my husband thinks I hide his Christmas gifts because it wasn't long before he was snooping through one of the trash bags. "Hey! Look what I found!"

I finally gave up. And, yes, the sweatshirt found its way to our new home—no worse for *wear*, I might add. I just hope that my son chooses a bride with a sense of humor. I wouldn't be surprised if my husband wears it to the wedding.

Marriage Requires a Division of Labor

As soon as I entered the bathroom, I noticed the empty roll of toilet paper. Of course, I grabbed another one from the vanity drawer and installed it. Now, there are only two of us living here so I just had to ask the obvious question of my husband, who responded, "Oh, yeah. I would have replaced it, but I didn't know where you kept them." If there is any mystery left in our marriage, it certainly is not where I keep the toilet paper.

Nor do I hide the vacuum cleaner, laundry soap or ingredients to make a sandwich. According to my husband, I have more skill with these things, especially the art of putting meat and cheese between two slices of bread. Actually, Richard has vacuumed the rug, washed clothes, and even made himself a sandwich, but he is right: I am better at these things.

But in fairness to my husband, there are things that he does that I refuse to do. For example, I have never mowed the lawn. However, I always offer him a cold drink when he comes in, and I say things like, "Oh, you look exhausted. Take a five-minute break." I also do not use the snow blower, but I am happy to make him hot chocolate when he comes in—that is, after his fingers thaw out enough to hold the cup. Nor have I ever washed the car, not even in a car wash (a claustrophobic's nightmare), but I do turn the garden hose on for him—usually.

There are jobs that we do together out of necessity. For example, if we have to give Bella a bath—she loves to roll in something just before we have company—it requires both of us. I do the scrubbing while he pours the water over her and promises a treat if she holds still. Of course, there is the annual putting up of the outdoor Christmas lights, an activity which requires balance on a shaky ladder and dexterity in untangling wires, generally culminating in a mutual effort with duct tape. There is also the occasional do-it-yourself project that takes one person to read the directions out loud while the other person ignores her and assembles it backwards.

Like most couples, a comfortable arrangement has evolved over the years: He washes the windows and kills spiders; I cook the meals and clean up dog vomit. There aren't any rules, just an understanding—and maybe a little extra on each of our parts once in a while. When I am not home, he will record my favorite shows. In appreciation, I will make him a sandwich. When it comes to a division of labor in a marriage, all efforts are a labor of love.

Dance Steps Don't Always Lead to Romance

I can blame it on Cinderella. Her story was literally a rags-to-riches tale, all because she went to a ball. According to the Disney version, Cinderella skipped the buffet and mingling and went right to the event's main focus: dancing— proving once again that "dance equals romance."

While no one ever forced me to sweep cinders out of a fireplace, I looked forward to going to dances. Visions of ballroom dresses danced in my head long before I ever stepped onto a real dance floor. I had plenty of inspiration from television, especially Loretta Young, who opened each of her shows with a few twirls to show off her gown. But I knew dancing required more than a party dress. One did have to know the steps. A gentle sway while gazing into someone's eyes only happens in the movies. My experience was a robotic box step with a perspiring teenaged boy, usually executed while gazing at the exit sign across the gym.

Besides, by the time I was old enough to attend dances, most of the actual movements across the floor were expressed individually. Most of us bounced like marionettes held at safe distances from one another lest our strings become entangled. There were always a few slow songs, and, depending upon who asked you to dance, it was either an exciting suggestion that someone liked you (which you and your girlfriends would analyze later) or an agonizing experience of close body contact with someone who picked his nose during math class.

Through the years I have pursued experiences that would, at least, give me some satisfaction of expressive movement. I took a Latin dance class in college. According to the instructor, "You don't want to be a wallflower when they play a rumba." As an adult I tried beginning ballet (a year of learning nothing but foot positions), dance-exercise classes (like the chorus line in a bad musical), and square dancing (no partner or skills required). But I yearned for real dancing—the kind that Fred Astaire and Ginger Rogers exhibited on extravagant movie sets.

Some years ago I convinced my husband to join me for ballroom dancing lessons. Richard truly followed the beat of a different drummer—just not one that went with the dance. I finally resorted to counting the steps out loud, but when we occasionally switched partners, he looked like a pilot trying to pull his plane out of a nosedive. We even practiced at home although it wasn't easy when the dog jumped up on us and hopped along on her hind legs.

Eventually, an occasional song on the radio would inspire us to dance, and I'd feel a little like Cinderella at the ball. But when the music stopped, Richard usually asked, "Now, can you make me a sandwich?" The steps I take into the kitchen are my Prince Charming's favorites.

Lost Spouse Causes Lost Temper

Most people who know me think that I am a fairly calm, rational person, and this is true most of the time. But on the rare occasions when I do lose my temper, I can explain my behavior in a way that every woman understands: Sometimes my husband just drives me nuts.

I'll use one recent example, which falls under the category of "not listening." Oh, he pretended he was listening, but I recognized his not listening expression so I repeated myself as he was going out the door, "It's next to the barber's, across from the bridal shop." Too much information, apparently, for all he got out of that was that someone was going to get a haircut.

That someone was Bella. She was leaping in anticipation of the ride although she always goes berserk the moment the car moves. (We have to use tranquilizers on long trips, and I'm never sure if I should give them to the dog or my husband.) Anyway, on this morning he was taking her to a new dog groomer in town. But a half hour after he left, the groomer called.

"He's not there?!" I responded in panic. Even with the constant distractions from Bella, the trip is no more than fifteen minutes. My mind ran in circles. Maybe the car broke down. After all, it had over 200,000 miles on it. I also remembered that he left his phone at home because it wasn't charged. Certainly if he had an accident, someone would get ahold of me. But what if he was in a ditch somewhere? I imagined the two of them stranded on the side of the road. Bella is a smart dog, but she's no Lassie. I decided to get in my car and look for them.

With every mile I felt relief that he wasn't hurt, but when I finally reached the groomer's and found that he still wasn't there, I began to feel another emotion—*really mad*! My pursuit was now accompanied by wild thoughts. Maybe he was having an affair. Nah. Who wants an older man with an old car and a neurotic dog—I mean, besides me? Then I had a hunch.

As soon as I pulled into the McDonald's parking lot, I spotted the car. There they were, their two heads bent over a bag of hash browns. "So," I hissed through my open window, "you blow off the dog's appointment and go out to breakfast!"

Bella looked surprised and then returned to licking crumbs off the seat. Richard tried to defend himself by explaining that the shop was closed and he was going to go back later. Apparently, he confused the groomer's shop with a beauty salon a block away. His logic: "It had scissors on its sign."

You could hear my tirade bouncing off the golden arches and down the street to where I followed him to the groomer's. At least, this time, I know he heard me.

Storage Keeps Problems Are Out of Sight

The area in question was hidden from view until another project led to its door, literally. If the storage under our basement stairs could speak, it would say, "Look away! I'm hideous!" But it was too late. We came; we saw; we had to conquer.

Unlike storage places in a garage or closet, the recesses under the basement stairs can go unnoticed for years, like castle dungeons where neglected prisoners eventually turned into skeletons. Well, it was time to get rid of our own skeletons and investigate those dusty boxes. Not easy with everything that was piled up behind the door under the stairs. At first I tried to pull items out by reaching through the open studs of the back wall, but it was no use as the boxes would not fit through those narrow openings. Finally, I told my husband we would have to disassemble the stack of tightly wedged containers that blocked the door. And so, the fun began.

The first obstacle was a rocking horse. His head bobbed over a tower of heavy cartons that anchored his legs to the floor. One by one, Richard removed the boxes and placed them around the basement. I began opening their lids, revealing contents of mostly useless and forgotten items. "Do we have to keep these?" I moaned. It was a question I would repeat throughout the entire dirty process. Meanwhile, he evaluated each item with fascination. "Hey! Remember this keychain?" (I could scarcely remember the car for which the attached key was intended!) "Look at this pile of letters from my cousin!" I looked: They were from 1959. Maybe it was because none of these things were mine, but I just couldn't understand my husband's attachment to what I viewed as junk. I guess he's just sentimental.

So is my son. The rocking horse—and child's rocking chair, toy trucks, and baseball books—are special items that we are storing for him. Once these were dragged into the light, I ventured into the crawlspace. I had to crouch way down in order to reach the smallest recess, dragging the vacuum cleaner hose with me. I tugged hard on a cardboard box filled with old VHS tapes, under which was a pile of rodent poison a mouse had apparently stockpiled. It was at this point that I heard the sound of a cue stick hitting balls across our pool table. "Sure I can't help you in there?" my husband called. He didn't hear me gritting my teeth.

While I sucked up the granules of mouse poison with the vacuum, I contemplated a wild impulse to throw out all the boxes that held Richard's phonograph records, teaching materials, and other assorted, useless paraphernalia.

But it was too late. Just as I crawled out and attempted an upright position, he walked over and said with enthusiasm, "Now I'll help you put them back!"

The Flu Bug Is a Real Pest

I hadn't had the stomach flu for many years, but the signs were impossible to ignore. As I dashed to the bathroom, my husband's caretaker mode kicked in: He put the TV on pause so the program he was watching wouldn't be disrupted by the sound of my retching.

I collapsed next to the toilet and wondered if I would blackout before I threw up. My husband waited down the hall, the same distant position he assumed when I gave birth to our two children. That was fine with me. If I was going to die on the bathroom floor, I didn't want the last words I hear to be, "So, are you done yet?"

In fairness, he did help me into bed after arranging the blankets at an interesting sideways angle, anchored by the dog on one side. I was too sick to care. In case I suffered a repeat performance, he left a bell on the nightstand. The tiny ornament was a souvenir from a recent wedding. However, its single tinkle was feeble at best when I reached for it during the night.

Where was that ginger ale he promised me? I finally dragged myself out of bed and leaned against the doorway as I shook the gold bauble, but the faint jingling was hopelessly lost under the blaring sound of the television. As parched as I was, I knew I couldn't make it down those stairs. With some effort, I called out to him, but it was soon apparent that he was asleep.

The idea of a bell at the bedside was a good idea and one that I used several years ago when Richard was sick. Actually, it was a small cowbell, but every time it clanged, I felt like I was being summoned to the tower of Notre Dame by Quasimodo, except that I was the one developing a hunchback from carrying trays of food and drinks up the stairs every fifteen minutes. Not that he needed to ring anything. His sickbed moaning could be heard by the neighbors, let alone the members of his household. By the third day of his illness, the bedroom looked like a diner. If I heard him say "feed a cold" one more time, I was going to spread Vicks on his toast and tell him it was apple jelly.

In contrast, the bell I was using now was little more than a jingle bell whose purpose was better suited to adorn the hat of a Christmas elf. Oh, well. By morning I was feeling better and could even be sympathetic to Richard's complaint that he had an uncomfortable time sleeping in the chair. He made toast and ceremoniously delivered it to me on a plate. "See how evenly the jelly is spread?" I complimented his culinary skills and told him that I hoped he didn't get sick.

Boy, do I hope he doesn't get sick.

Marriage Thrives on the Little Things

It's the little things about the other person that make you fall in love. After you're married, it's the little things about each other that drive you crazy. If you're married long enough, it's the little things that keep the two of you from *going* crazy.

My husband's knowledge of language and films were attractive attributes when we were dating. And we still enjoy discussing books and movies. However, early in our marriage I used those very interests as weapons of revenge. On one occasion my temper got the best of me, and I tore pages out of his favorite dictionary and tossed them out our apartment window. (I later picked them up in the parking lot and taped them back into the book.) Another incident that occurred years later was sparked by his habit of flipping through the channels during commercials. I was trying to watch a movie, and the distraction put me over the edge. Hiding the remote was too simplistic. After he went to bed, I removed the batteries and threw them away.

I have to admit that I have a few quirks that have plagued my husband, as well. He may respect my interests, but he also believes I have a compulsion to multi-task. It's true that I can go into the kitchen to make him lunch and get sidetracked reorganizing the kitchen cabinets. But I can also make a sandwich with one hand and take notes for my newspaper column with the other.

Yet there comes a point when you just have to ignore each other's idiosyncrasies and deal with it. I hate pumping my own gas so he isn't surprised when he gets in the car and has to drive to the next town on empty. He hates waiting for me to get ready to go out so I've learned to do my hair in the car and dry my nails by hanging my hands out the window. After all these years we've learned to accept each other's failings and avoid triggering arguments: I know that he can't remember my friends' names, and he knows that I can't stand his friends' political views. For the sake of the other, we have both mastered the polite smile.

That doesn't mean there aren't the occasional moments of nails on the blackboard. I've pondered strangling him if he swatted one more fly over me when I'm trying to sleep. He claims that I make an annoying clicking noise in my sleep that keeps him awake. I don't see how that could be true. He couldn't possibly hear anything over that freight train that whistles through his nose every night. Recently he woke me up with a persistent nudging. "What!" I hissed.

He leaned over with sincere concern. "You stopped making that clicking sound, and I wanted to make sure you were still breathing."

After all these years it's the little things that keep romance alive.

Innocent Questions Can Be Revealing

Who could have predicted that such an innocent question could provoke such an uproar? As several members of my family settled into conversation after dinner, my sister, Nancy, suddenly chirped up with a hypothetical situation: "If you were single and wanted to date someone through a computer service, what age would you like that person to be?"

There was an ulterior motive in this proposal: My sister had previously solicited an answer from her husband, and the response surprised her. His maximum age limit was a decade younger than she was. "So," she had retorted, "you wouldn't even consider dating someone my age?" Obviously, his explanation did not satisfy her. She decided to find out what others would consider an appropriate match for themselves.

Carol and I, who are close in age, both felt strongly that we wouldn't want to date anyone more than ten years younger than ourselves—although we admitted that, in general, women outlive men so a slightly younger husband might be a prudent choice. At least for the woman.

When it was my brother's turn to respond, he judiciously looked at his wife and answered, "Well, I guess she should be my age—like my wife."

My husband—who had heretofore been lost in his own reverie—was then asked the same question. Without hesitation he blurted out, "Age twenty-eight to forty." The room erupted in hoots of laughter.

"What!" I screeched. "You would replace me with someone half your age?!"

He tried to justify his selection as merely a fantasy. "So," I responded sarcastically, "it's just your *secret desire* to replace me with a much younger woman!"

"Of course not," he said sweetly (obviously sensing the hole he had dug for himself). "How could I ever replace you?" If that didn't quite convince me, it certainly quelled the crowd.

Nancy then presented another query, "How old do you *feel*?"

The answers to that question were also revealing as most of us felt considerably younger than we actually are. We shared a common philosophy that without a mirror to reflect our physical image, we often forget our chronological age and simply act our spiritual age.

This discussion led my husband to propose his own question: "What age would you *like* to be?"

Suddenly we were all in a wistful state. Some chose their early adulthood; others returned to their childhood years. Even my son turned back the clock to a blissful age ten. He explained, "Why not? All you have to think about is candy and baseball cards." That fantasy made sense to all of us.

My husband, on the other hand, had a lot more *'splainin'* to do on the way home.

Watching TV Show Is a Remote Chance

I love Sunday nights. Why? Because I have a standing reservation with *Masterpiece Theatre*—and any other British drama that flashes across the screen with period costumes, quaint countryside, and dainty teacups. I don't ask for much: just a few hours of undisturbed fantasy without anyone asking me to make him a sandwich while he switches to another station during the "boring parts."

Boring is a relative term. While I might think that managing an English estate or maintaining proper etiquette among the different classes is fascinating entertainment, there are those for whom excitement is best generated by aliens, zombies, and superheroes. I am respectful of this difference and will wander off to the kitchen or bedroom when I hear a barrage of gunfire (although even *I* know that bullets have no effect on aliens, zombies, and superheroes).

I think that men are attracted to certain shows because they are loud and have shiny objects. Like the knife show, an infomercial that runs continuously and never alters from its winning format: an array of knives displayed on a slowly-moving turntable, described in enthusiastic detail by a man who can hardly believe how beautiful and inexpensive these knives are. His Southern accent and the rotating, shiny blades will stop any man in his tracks.

My husband thinks that I am attracted to certain shows because of the actors' British accents. Actually, that sometimes proves to be an obstacle when some characters are difficult to understand. So that I don't miss one clue in the mystery of who killed the arrogant uncle, or one poetic line of unrequited love between the wealthy baron and the governess, I have my husband adjust the television to include the words at the bottom of the screen. "Oh, she thinks he *loathes* her, not *owes* her!" I exclaim. (By now Richard is sleeping.)

Actually, there is one other program to which I am addicted, and it is not British. Richard records *Dancing with the Stars* for me on Mondays so that I can watch it later commercial-free. I have learned how to fast-forward through the ads by myself, but if Richard is operating the remote, he tends to skip over what he considers "filler." I don't consider dramatic film clips that highlight the dancers' struggles to overcome strained muscles *filler*. Nor do I consider the charming banter of the hosts or advice of the judges to be frivolous. I want to see every moment of the dancers' background stories, struggles with tangos and jives, and shocking eliminations.

So just put that remote down, Mister Quick Draw—or I might decide to skip the *boredom* of making a sandwich.

Communication Suffers Power Outage

When I am out of town without my husband, I usually speak with him daily by phone. Most of our conversations involve what came in the mail or what each of us is having for dinner. Not exactly sparkling conversation, but that's what married people talk about. So I shouldn't be surprised when after several minutes Richard says, "Well, I'm about talked out, aren't you?"

That's his tactful way of telling me that *he* is finished talking. It's a little easier to pick up his subtle hints in person. Like when he stops making eye contact or begins reading something or repeats that robotic "uh huh" response, which indicates that he is no longer listening. If I feel it's important, I get his attention by blocking his view of the television, but usually I don't have anything that important to say.

Let's face it, "I'm making meatloaf for dinner," is not exactly an exciting news flash. Not that I can't make "a mountain out of a meatloaf." I can talk about anything. And he knows that. So it's really my fault that the length of my monologues is not relative to a topic's importance. Who wouldn't tune out someone who spends more time explaining how she gets stains out of clothes than she does explaining how her car got scratched or dented?

I also understand that there is a small window of opportunity when engaging my husband in a story I really do want to relate. If it starts with a great opener like "I just encountered a bear in the yard," I have his full attention. But if my conversation begins with, "I know you don't like cooked vegetables, but I saw this recipe…" I will have lost him at the word *vegetables*.

And I know better than to expect him to listen with any concentration when he is hungry. Actually, feeding him has two benefits: He is in a better disposition to listen, and chewing limits his ability to interrupt me. Some of my best opportunities to tell him something unpleasant have been done while I am serving him dessert (as in "I'm sure this project will not take us more than a couple hours—more chocolate sauce on that, dear?").

Conversely, it doesn't require much concentration on my part to interpret his one-word expressions that can express anything from a political commentary to inquiring about dinner. Oh, there are times when he is very long-winded, like when he is trying to explain something to me about football or baseball. I listen patiently, even though I have no interest in sports and don't care to retain any information about games I'll never watch or play.

"Oh," I try to say with interest, but when my responses turn to "uh huh," he gets the hint. Sometimes our best method of communicating is simply being quiet.

Fast Food Has Lingering Effects

Most people from Chicago are familiar with the hamburger chain, White Castle. Years ago, when they were only fifteen cents each, ads for the square-shaped favorites encouraged people to "buy 'em by the bag." Our digestion was a little better back then, but we still indulge on occasion. After all, adults know their limits. And feeding them to a dog should be one of them.

That's why I am still angry with my husband, son, and brother-in-law, who shared their bag of loaded buns with our dog. Although people love the combination of meat, grease, and onions, there is a reason why these popular burgers are also known as "sliders." They should come with a warning: "Eat responsibly."

Unfortunately, it was too late for that when we left my son's house the following morning. We weren't even out of the driveway when I noticed a strong odor that I suspected came from the dog. Richard insisted it was from the lingering scent of White Castle hamburgers that were transported in the car the night before. Really?

By the time we got onto the toll road, it was pretty clear that I was right. Bella pushed her head between our seats and panted with anxiety. I alerted Richard that we should pull over.

"I'm not going to pull over here for no good reason."

The *good* reason emerged a few seconds later—all over the back seat. We rolled the windows down and flew to the next exit, entering a gas station and emergency mode at the same time. Richard carefully gathered up the old sheet that covered the back seat—or, as it turned out, *almost* covered. I will spare my readers the details, but it was very much like changing a messy diaper in an airplane bathroom.

Meanwhile, I ran to the gas pumps for paper towels, which I dipped into a blue solution that is universally known for its cleaning inadequacies. Richard minded Bella as I made trips back and forth between the pumps and car.

The temperature outside had dipped to sixteen degrees, and the wind nearly drowned out my voice as I shouted across the lot, "This is your fault!"

"How is it *my* fault?" Richard queried. In answer I held up the soiled paper, dunked it into the trash, and hissed, "You fed her those hamburgers!"

It was a long ride home with intervals of opening the windows so we could replenish the air in our lungs. Immediately upon arrival, I gave Bella a bath and scrubbed the interior of the car as if it were radioactive. It's clean and fresh now. However, if Santa brings any stocking stuffers this year, a couple of those car deodorizers would be very much appreciated.

Cabin Fever

When cold weather keeps you indoors for too long, the results can be nerve-wracking. It could be the lack of sunlight or claustrophobia or even the knowledge that winter is far from over. But whatever the cause of cabin fever is, driving each other crazy is one of the symptoms.

It's not an intentional assault on the other person's psyche; it's just a slow and tedious wearing down of one's tolerance. One morning in early December you call each other to the window to watch the pretty snowflakes. Then an afternoon arrives when you are inspired to make a snowman together. That evening (by that I mean 3:30) you watch the sunset while drinking hot chocolate. By January you find the sound of his slurping up the marshmallows in his mug extremely annoying. By mid-winter you have banned hot drinks altogether.

That doesn't stop him from making them for himself. You can tell when you come home and find that the inside of the saucepan has a stubborn ring of hardened chocolate. He couldn't find the marshmallows because "You've hidden them somewhere where I can't find them!" (If you really wanted to hide treats, you'd put them next to the laundry soap or ironing board.)

But for some reason the television remote is male territory. You may want to curl up on a cold night with a warm romantic comedy, but he is visiting another planet via a science-fiction movie in which aliens that have been frozen in ice are plotting an attack on earth. Apparently, even extraterrestrials can get a little testy in frigid temperatures. As the wind howls, you glance with irritation at your spouse and wonder what planet spawned him. Or maybe *you* are the creature from outer space. Soon the mother ship will come and beam you up to a place where it is never winter—like Florida.

Meanwhile, there are earthly duties to perform, and your patience is running thin. The dog has to be walked. She has crossed the room several times in an attempt to get attention. Your husband is feigning sleep. As you put on your coat and boots, a feeble voice calls, "Oh, I could have taken her out." Then he adds, "Get the mail on the way back."

You plod through the deep snow to the street but forego tunneling to the mailbox. After all, you just walked the dog in a blizzard. As far as you're concerned, the mail can stay there all winter. And you let him know that as soon as you get inside and encourage the ice-encrusted dog to leap into his lap, a rude awakening that jumpstarts him to snow-blowing duty.

The sight of him struggling down the driveway thaws your frozen heart a little, and you decide it wouldn't hurt to make him some hot chocolate. And maybe some marshmallows, too. After all, it's a long winter.

Old Boots Cross the Line

This Christmas my son gave his father several pairs of socks that he accompanied with this message: "Now you can get rid of those awful socks you wear!" My husband looked bewildered. "What's wrong with them?" Well, one reason was that you could put your fist through the holes. In truth, all of his socks were just two buttons shy of being hand puppets.

Not that he minded the holes. He probably didn't even notice how they looked—just as he doesn't notice how terrible his boots look—which is why I had to spray-paint them. Let me explain: I didn't paint the entire boot, just the toes. You see, Richard has a favorite pair of rubber moccasins that have served in many combat zones: the jungle (cutting trees and brush), the swamp (dredging the lake), and even an arctic prison (pushing a snow blower). Over the years he has literally worn off the tread so I bought him an identical pair that could be worn out in public. To distinguish the new ones, I painted the tips of his old boots a bright white.

Apparently, they were not bright enough. While the shiny new pair stayed at home, the ragged, "chew toy" originals accompanied their master to town on errands. At first Richard wondered why a store clerk was staring at his feet. When he looked down, he was even more perplexed: Was there snow on his shoes? But there was no snow—only a broad stripe of white spray paint, intended as a version of caution tape that should not be crossed.

Maybe Richard just has something for boots. After all, that "boot shirt," an old sweatshirt with a huge cowboy boot on the front, took years to die. When it became too soiled to be worn, it was thrown into the rag pile and used to clean up oil up in the garage. But, oblivious to the new stains, my husband found it and wore it again—and again—and again. It should have had a cat on the front because that shirt certainly had nine lives.

I am simply trying to make a point about recognizing when something should no longer be making appearances in public. It's like the expiration date on dairy products: you can dance with danger for only so long before someone pushes it one day too far and then throws up curdled milk—which looks very much like what happened on the toes of those old boots.

Meanwhile, the new boots are tucked inside the shoe rack in the laundry room, just waiting for a public appearance. They are next to the like-new snow boots that he doesn't like to wear because they "take too long to zip up." If it came down to a choice between practicality and ease, my husband would be wearing slippers to cut the lawn. I could deter that by gluing dog toys to the toes, but I really don't think he would notice.

A Fish by Any Other Name

I want to make it clear that I love fish—in rivers, in lakes, in aquariums—just not on my plate. But here in the U.P. the Friday night fish fry is a year-round tradition; people will wait for hours in a local bar for a plate of fried cod with a side of coleslaw. So when I order a burger, it is usually accompanied with a sort of apology: "I don't like fish."

Not that people with good intentions haven't tried to convert me. They make very sincere suggestions. "How about a light fish?" (No, *skinny* fish still taste like fish.) "How about shrimp?" (Nope—still seafood.) Soon they grow a little incredulous. "You must like lobster?" (*Must* I?) Finally, "Not even a tuna fish sandwich?" (Not even. But I like bread.)

Presentation doesn't alter the food or disguise it, either. If you hate liver, cooking it with onions just means you are eating an onion-flavored internal organ that still tastes like liver. Likewise, if you don't like crab, blending the crustacean with cream cheese in a dip does not sweeten the deal.

Most people have some type of food that they don't like. Maybe we're born with a certain aversion to a vegetable, or maybe we got sick after eating a particular meat, or perhaps a favorite pet became Sunday's lamb chops. Years ago, during a Sunday dinner of fried chicken, my little sister found out that the piece of crispy meat on her plate was once a live hen running about the barnyard. That bit of information led to more discoveries, like where hamburgers come from and why the Thanksgiving turkey has legs. She never quite got over that. I guess it didn't help that we teased her by imitating the sound of animals during dinner.

My husband, on the other hand, is not a fan of cooked vegetables. (He doesn't jump up and down for the raw ones, either.) Oh, he'll make an exception for green beans or corn, but the sight of broccoli is like a crucifix to a vampire: he thinks that a respectful distance will spare his life. He once read that the reason that some people do not like broccoli is because their taste buds are more sensitive and their discriminating palate identifies it as bitter. This discovery vindicated him in his own mind and even made him feel superior to those of us with unrefined taste buds and crude palates.

However, I fail to recognize any signs of refinement when he has something with scales and a tail sticking out of his mouth.

Still, we respect each other's culinary preferences: He doesn't balk at my broccoli, and I don't cringe at his shrimp. Besides, if we still have room for dessert, we'll often order something chocolate to share. In that, we both show great taste.

Finding Perfect Dress Is Imperfect Quest

When it comes to purchasing clothes, men have it a lot easier: Their pants and shirts are sized by inches. If a woman could purchase items by such precise measurements, she would save herself time trying on a dozen same-sized dresses that vary in fit a dozen ways. Of course, there are other reasons to try before you buy.

And no, it doesn't help to simply hold the dress up and imagine yourself in it—unless your shoulders are shaped like a plastic hanger. Actually, the only thing gleaned by holding up a dress is that it does or doesn't look good on that plastic hanger. The real test is in the dressing room. Many a harsh truth is revealed via florescent lights and a full length mirror—that, and a husband whose opinion you solicit.

Such was the case recently when my husband accompanied me on a shopping trip. I needed a new dress for an upcoming occasion. After making sure he had lunch first, I assured him that I wouldn't be long and he could sit in the "husband's chair" that was placed—mercifully—nearby. I also promised him we could stop for candy afterwards.

Now, I can navigate the racks and sniff out a dress like a hound dog on a rabbit's trail, but the prize is rarely in the first hole. So I gather any garment in my size that catches my eye, even if I have to strip a store mannequin or climb a display to achieve that goal. Often my sister is along to assist me in this endeavor, and if my mother accompanies us, I have a nice balance of comments on the dresses— somewhere between "harlot" and "hospital gown." The result is usually a compromise of a little black dress with a conservative neckline.

But my husband wanted to see me in each dress. He especially liked a red one, but it just didn't fit right. His opinion? "It really accentuates your chest!" Well, the red one was out! I also tried on a black dress that I liked and modeled it expectantly. Richard looked skeptical. "That one is a little tight over your rear, isn't it?" One more strike and the candy store was out!

I went through the rest of them like Goldilocks at the home of the Three Bears: "Too big," "Too small," "Too hot," "Too...hospital gown." Finally, I settled on a sweet number with a classic neckline and full skirt—very Audrey Hepburn—and it fit!

On the drive home I handed Richard samples of the chocolate he had just purchased. After all, he had earned his treats. That reminded me: It was past Bella's dinnertime, and she would be hungry. Bella—my little bundle of dark fur—now there's a girl who is always stylish in classic basic black.

A Saturday Valentine's Day

Valentine's Day is on a Saturday this year, which makes it easier for most people to celebrate. Falling, as it does, on the traditional date night gives even more reason to celebrate in public with a movie and nice dinner. In fact, it seems appropriate that one should honor the occasion by going out—which is why I wish Valentine's Day was *not* on a Saturday.

It's not that I don't celebrate Valentine's Day: My husband and I will certainly have an exchange of sentiments and sweets. But Saturday makes it seem a little more significant, more of a special occasion. And by *special* I mean something more than my typical Valentine's offering of a special breakfast. Actually, it's not that special. It's just one of the rare occasions when in addition to making the usual fare of oatmeal or eggs, I also fry bacon. But having Valentine's Day on a Saturday suggests that we should probably go out and have someone else fry the bacon—or fish or steak. Or we should go somewhere and order lobster, even though I hate seafood. And we should order champagne, even though Richard prefers Pepsi.

That's a lot of holiday pressure for two people who do not regard Saturday as date night—or it hasn't been for the past several years. Weekends don't have the same meaning since neither of us has had to get up early and go to work anymore.

Not only do we have the luxury of going to a movie on a Tuesday night, we have the advantage of avoiding the weekend crowds. It doesn't seem that long ago when Saturday nights had to be planned days in advance so a babysitter could be reserved. Sunday through Thursday nights were never an option because we had to get up early the next morning for work. Now we just get up early in the morning for no particular reason. In other words, we are getting older.

I thought about just having some friends come over for dinner instead. But then I wondered if they might prefer celebrating the Saturday Valentine's Day alone in a more special, romantic setting. After all, they are also mature couples who have been married for years and...wait a minute. They're married: They don't want to be alone!

Our wedding anniversary is in October and has coincided in some years with Sweetest Day, a holiday which created larger crowds in the Chicago restaurants. Of course, back then we were happy to be out on a Saturday night and really didn't mind waiting for a table or, for that matter, waiting in line for a good movie.

But now? Well, date night doesn't even have to be at night. In fact, we might celebrate Valentine's Day on Saturday morning. Yeah. I'll make a special breakfast: I'll fry bacon.

What Is Cherished Most Changes Least

Part of the attraction of traveling is to see new places, but this trip also included a return to a location that we hadn't seen since we honeymooned there. It would be fun, we figured, to drive to the Smoky Mountains and revisit what we remembered of little Gatlinburg, Tennessee.

It didn't take long to discover that what we remembered was completely gone. The shocking transformation began miles before in the previously sleepy towns that now were connected to Dollywood by a string of rhinestone-studded billboards. But when we entered Gatlinburg, the change had made the town unrecognizable. The area was circumvented by an unending traffic jam from which cars might access the Smoky Mountains National Park, although that destination seemed to elude the majority of tourists who instead veered off the main street into public parking lots. For an additional fee, one could board a trolley car and stop at every corner to watch the slow-moving mass of pedestrians waddling from popcorn stands to souvenir shops, presumably in search of local color.

We tried in vain to find the little motel where we had stayed or even recognize the corner on which it had been nestled. Gone also was the privately-owned restaurant that served fresh trout, no doubt replaced by one of the many food chains represented along the strip. The businesses themselves seemed to spill out onto the street, blending into a series of carnival tents; one "barker" even tried to entice us with matching tattoos. Our visit, albeit brief, was ended with a hasty departure away from the carnival lights and back through the corridor of highway that so blaringly advertised its attractions.

A light rain distorted the view from the rear window, and the Smoky Mountains were scarcely discernible against the dark clouds. I thought of the park's beauty that had first impressed us forty years ago, how we had walked under canopies of blazing gold and even rode horses along a mountain trail. That other October now seemed like a dream that had faded with time.

I felt a lump rise in my throat as I realized that the past was impossible to recapture, for we were not the same, either. The inevitable experience that life yields has altered us, for better and for worse. But we have made the journey together, and we have our memories. And it was one memory in particular that nudged my brain the next morning. "Maybe on the way home we could stop at that little town in Indiana. Remember…?"

We had first visited Nashville, Indiana about thirty-five years ago as a getaway that included the beautiful scenery of Brown County State Park. Now, as we drove the distance from the highway, I was encouraged that the natural landscape still dominated the area. We were delighted that the Brown County Inn, which looked exactly the same, had a vacancy. And it was a relief to find that the town's main street had retained its original character: unique shops housed in quaint cottages, many featuring the crafts of local artisans, some of whom have been there for decades. Even the little theatre where we saw a live performance of the play *Harvey* years ago had not changed its rustic appearance.

"Remember," I began my sentences as I recalled moments from our earlier trips: the toy xylophone we purchased here as a gift for our baby daughter, the caricature artist who did my portrait on the street, and the deer our children fed in the park. The entrance to that park was just across the stream that flowed behind the inn, and we continued our reminiscing as we made our way back over fallen leaves of sycamore and maple.

Richard, slowed by his sore knee, urged me ahead so I could take photographs. I paused on the footbridge and looked down the path to where it curved into the woods. It was a short distance, but I felt the sadness of a more significant separation: that of time. Still recovering from my head injury after being thrown from a horse this summer, I felt especially vulnerable, weaker, and, yes, older.

But there was comfort in this surrounding's familiarity. The inn's restaurant still served homemade dishes in the same country ambiance. And the indoor pool was still there. After dinner I swam its length several times, alone with my thoughts and the images of my own children splashing and laughing within the same confines years ago.

When I returned to the room, my husband was stretched out on the bed. "Someone must have thought this plywood storage box was a great idea for a headboard," he laughed. The décor, which was a little worn and dated, would soon be updated by the new owners who planned to renovate the 1974 establishment. Coincidentally, that was the year we were married.

"Yes," I thought to myself, "forty years is a long time." But as I cuddled up next to my husband, I realized that being "a little worn and dated" seems to suit us just fine.

Chapter 4

Expect Turbulence

Expect Turbulence When Flying

I don't care for flying. That's why on this particular trip I was delighted to have the distraction of my own movie screen. After selecting the Oscar-nominated film, *Queen*, I quickly discovered that headphones had been omitted from my seat pouch. My disappointment must have been audible because the man next to me offered me his headphones. "However," he warned, "only one earpiece works."

Undaunted, I plugged in just as the movie began. The characters moved across the tiny screen to the sound of soft clicks. Clicks? I glanced at my neighbor, who was keeping a steady rhythm on his laptop computer. I looked back at actress Helen Mirren, whose vocal interpretation of Elizabeth II was probably perfect, if only I had sound. Hitting the control button was futile as my audio was broken. That explained why I didn't have headphones.

But I had not given up hope of experiencing the movie. I nudged my Good Samaritan. "Excuse me, but I don't have any sound. Do you think that I could plug into your armrest?" Before he could answer, I was leaning over his lap in an effort to stretch the cord to his control panel.

But the computer presented an obstacle, and the only way I could access the sound was if I rested my head on my neighbor's chest. I actually considered this, but the man's startled expression discouraged further pursuit of this awkward and rather intimate position.

Suddenly, I had an idea: The cord would reach my seat if it was placed *behind* the man. I muttered a scattering of directions as I plunged my left arm between his back and the seat while using my right arm to untangle the wire from his laptop. Then, by threading the sound cord under his seatbelt, around his left hip, and circling his waist, I was able to ease another few inches toward my seat. I gave a final tug, and the man lurched forward, thus allowing me just enough cord to don the headphones. So, tilting my head toward his shoulder and pressing the audible plug to my right ear, I was able to compensate for the mute side enough to hear the film.

But something wasn't right: the Queen sounded more like the prime minister. When she spoke without moving her lips, I realized that the soundtrack was from an entirely different film. My eyes focused on the channel buttons under the man's left elbow, but he was absorbed in the business of that giant clam that remained open on his lap. Oh, well. I had missed too much of the film already. Without comment I gave the cord a hard pull. The man jolted as the released plug shot around his waist and snapped back into my waiting hand. I pretended not to notice the irritated look on his face and placed the headphones on his keyboard.

"Changed my mind," I said and resigned myself to a very long flight.

Fireworks Spark Challenges

Who doesn't love a grand display of fireworks? They were always a part of our Fourth of July celebration when we visited our grandparents in Michigan, and that tradition continues in the small town's impressive show. The brilliant lights against the night sky are just as beautiful and exciting as they were when I watched them as a child although it seemed a lot easier to experience firework displays back then.

Maybe I didn't notice the mosquitoes when I was young because I was so absorbed in the drama going on above me. But when I had my own children, part of my responsibility was to swat these pests away from our blanket and lawn chairs. I didn't really need to look up anyway as I could picture each firework from *whistle* to *boom* to *crackle*.

One year the explosives seemed too close, and my niece jumped up with alarm. Someone near us (any crowd averages about one idiot per fifty people) lit a firecracker that sprayed hot fragments across the ground. After that I made up my mind that sitting in a car was a better way to see the real show.

But parking has its own challenges, especially in the coveted spots that offer the best views. Ask my mother. She knows exactly where those places are. Even if you don't ask her, she will tell you. She will tell you many times, even as you are parking in one of the spots she pointed out.

Her commentary runs something like this: "Not here! I can't see around that pickup truck. Pull into that other space." But she changes her mind: "No, this is too close to a tree. Back out and pull in over there." But that spot is still not right: "No, too close to those people who look drunk." This is the narration that sent my (usually) good-tempered sister over the edge one year. After being told to back out of one-too-many "perfect" spots, Carol got out of the car, threw the keys, and shouted "Park it yourself!" That was enough fireworks for one night.

We were back to the blanket the following year. However, we settled for a less crowded area on a hill near the golf course. I covered my ankles in defense of the mosquitoes and soon became all-absorbed in the light show. Suddenly, we heard shouting a short distance away. By the time we realized what was happening, it was too late. We were soaked with the spray from in-ground sprinklers that were coincidentally timed with our entertainment. As the nozzles spun water across the unsuspecting crowd, they jumped up, one group at a time. It reminded me of the "wave" that people do at ballgames, except that this one was accompanied by screams.

My husband had stayed home and was waiting outside when I returned. As I approached—my wet hair dripping onto my mosquito-bitten face—he gave me some news.

"Did you know that you can see the fireworks from *here*?"

Yeah, but what fun is that?

Houseplant Succumbs to Death by Neglect

When all is said and done, I think I gave it an exceptional run. After all, I had the thing for six years and two months. That's about a third of the time it takes to raise a child, for heaven's sake. And before you judge me for my actions, be mindful that I did not ask for this responsibility. It was thrust upon me in the guise of a hostess gift.

"Here," our houseguest said as she placed a large pot in my arms. "It's a—(something I can't remember)—plant. It's almost impossible to kill." I looked at the tall stalks with vibrant leaves and thought to myself, "But it is *possible*."

This wasn't my first experience with indoor plants. I've seen the best of them go down with everything from root rot to forget-me-not. I've transformed English ivy into English tea leaves and turned potted geraniums into crematoriums. So, unless this green monster was made of plastic, it was doomed to the same fate.

We started out on polite terms. I placed the pot in the front hall, which afforded sufficient light, and watered it with some regularity. As the months went by, the plant actually grew taller, resembling that bean stalk in the fairytale. But, since my life is rooted in reality, not fiction, my daily preoccupations superseded the needs of a simple houseplant. In the following months it thrived but showed little sign of either growth or weariness. Perhaps it didn't require much care, after all. So began my descent into abandonment and neglect.

It wasn't intentional at first—exactly. Some months I was just too busy to notice the lackluster leaves drooping over the parched dirt. Eventually, one of the main stalks leaned over the edge of the pot in a pose that suggested suicide. A shred of sympathy prompted me to tie the despondent stalk to its stronger companion, thus restricting it as one might be restricted by a straitjacket. Another year of sporadic watering brought some healing to the wounded plant, but I seriously considered that its quick death would be a blessing for both of us.

Still, after six years I just couldn't dump it in the compost pile like a limp stalk of celery. In September I moved the plant outside for some fresh air. (At least that's what I told myself.) It even seemed to respond favorably—for a while. But by October it had an obvious case of jaundice. After the first frost, I knew it was terminal. I told myself to bring the plant inside, but in the end, I just left it to its fate. I didn't really kill the plant: I just set it free—sort of.

In the end I gave it a proper resting place over the side of the hill where I also tossed my pumpkins and Christmas trees each year. I only hope it doesn't come back to life in the spring.

Just by the Seat of Our Pants

One article of clothing that has been associated with unflattering metaphors is pants. Most children have been told that they have "ants in their pants," when they can't sit still. And "Liar, liar, pants on fire" is an accusation that has taunted kids for generations. But sometimes the *pants* themselves become the source of embarrassment.

One of the most humiliating predicaments I experienced as a kid was while I was roller skating. I can't count the number of times I had strapped those wheels to my shoes and skated around our block. Of course, I had every crack and broken piece of cement memorized, but no one can predict the occasional stray object. Not only did I fall, but half the neighborhood witnessed it. Despite the pain, my pride got me up immediately. Unfortunately, that move revealed my undoing.

My sister immediately pointed to the spot I had just occupied on the sidewalk and said in a voice that carried to the next street, "Hey, Gail, you wet your pants!" That humiliation would be revisited all summer by the neighborhood gang.

It was Carol who was the next target of shame. It was a typical summer afternoon, and we were running through the neighborhood yards, climbing and jumping over anything that got in our way. Ordinarily, a fence wasn't much of an obstacle, but this time Carol didn't quite make it. Her pants were caught on the top of the chain link fence, and, like Peter Rabbit, her fate hung from a torn piece of clothing. Try as we could, the ripped pants were hopelessly hooked—and so was she. It was getting late. Mom might come looking for us—and that meant more trouble. Finally, ignoring any sense of propriety, I tried to convince Carol that removing her pants was the only means of escape. She refused that option. (There were boys present.) But after a long—and uncomfortable—period of contemplation while suspended up-side-down, she agreed to let us tear her pants further so that she could free herself. The exposure revealed bloody scratches from the fence. But the worst was explaining all this to Mom—without being a smarty-pants!

My last story shows that it isn't who wears the pants in the family, but who *knows* who wears the pants. Several years ago my husband and I attended a fundraiser that was being held in a school. The event, which was attended by adults, featured a variety of games and food throughout the three-story building. When Richard and I became separated in one of the crowded halls, and he couldn't find me, he assumed I had gone to the next floor. So, he ascended the staircase in pursuit of his lost wife.

I must add here that Richard has a habit of sneaking up on me and playfully slapping my behind. It is an annoying gesture that I have cautioned him not to do, especially in public. Although impropriety was never reason enough to abstain from this bad habit, a more scalding lesson awaited him on those stairs that night. Ahead of him on the steps was the person—or, at least, the pair of slacks—he was sure he recognized. So sure was he that he quickly moved forward to execute his characteristic slap on the behind. But when the recipient turned around and revealed himself, not only was he not me, he was a man! For a moment they could only stare at each other in shocked bewilderment. Then, as the man's face began to redden in anger, Richard struggled to gather his wits about him, suddenly and stupidly blurting out, "I thought you were my wife!" Realizing the folly (and possible implications) of this remark, Richard abruptly turned and fled.

Needless to say, my husband stayed close to me for the rest of the evening. I could have mentioned that he got what he deserved, but he was suffering enough with embarrassment. Besides, he knew he had narrowly escaped a stronger lesson, if only by the seat of his pants.

Project Is a Construction Nightmare

The leftover cartons of landscaping stones were stacked in the garage for years, and they weighed as heavily on my mind as…well, a box of rocks. I finally thought of a small project that would utilize them: a decorative stone column. After all, I had watched the professionals cement those stones on our house, and I was (sort of) paying attention. It looked easy enough, but I took the coward's approach and waited until my husband was out of town. I'd surprise him.

First, I picked out a spot for the column on a hill and dug a hole for the cement foundation. I fashioned a footing frame out of scrap lumber, which I held together with duct tape. Not the best solution, but I figured it would hold together long enough for the cement to set up. After several trips up and down that hill, I learned two things: bags of cement are deceivingly heavy, and buckets of water weigh twice as much going uphill. (Actually, I also learned a third thing, but you probably guessed about the duct tape.)

The following day I found that the cement had hardened but was slightly uneven. I had erroneously believed that, like water, it would find its own level—which I assumed was *level*. I told myself that those imperfections would be covered anyway and shifted my attention to building the pillar's frame. Once that was accomplished I decided to cover it with a wire mesh, like the pros. But, unlike them, I forgot to wrap the frame with an insulation of treated paper first. Pulling off that chicken wire wouldn't have been so bad if I hadn't been so aggressive with the nails.

By the time I was ready to cover the column in cement—one I was told by the man at the hardware store was a different kind than the one I used for the foundation—it was late afternoon. The thought of hauling those buckets up the hill again was soon replaced with an idea: I would apply the mortar in the garage. In retrospect, it would have been easier to cover my car in frosting.

The next morning I viewed the column's hardened surface with dread. How could I move this sarcophagus up a hill and onto its pedestal by myself? I considered waiting for my husband, but the naked column looked like a failure, while a completed one, even with a lopsided exterior, resembled an accomplishment. No, I would move it myself!

But how? The column was too heavy for me to move alone. But I discovered that if I rocked the structure gently, I could wobble it onto a hand truck and perhaps down the driveway. But the weight was even a challenge for this device, and the effort flattened the wheels and made navigating the hill impossible.

Well, I wasn't going to leave my creation on the curb! I would have to get it up that hill. My attempts included several futile maneuvers with different objects. I tried pulling it with a rope, but the uneven ground resisted passage. I managed to roll it onto a blanket to which I gave mighty tugs, but, apparently, not mighty enough. I even employed a plastic sled, but I would have to wait for winter to make progress that way. I soon realized the folly of using these flimsy gadgets for such a Herculean feat. As I sat panting next to my ton of stone, I wondered how in the world the Egyptians were able to accomplish the Pyramids.

Well, if those slaves could do it, so could I! Fearing that the heavy column would topple down the slope, I finally got down on my knees, pressed my hands and shoulder against the monster, and pushed. It moved, albeit only inches at a time. I tried to calculate how long it would take to go another 20 feet at this pace, but a lack of oxygen clouded my thinking. At last, I rolled the pillar onto the pedestal and, in case of rain, covered it with black garbage bags. It looked like the monolith in the film *2001, A Space Odyssey*.

I was just able to stand upright the next morning so I began applying the decorative stones (with yet another kind of mortar). The manufactured pieces certainly looked like real rocks, but, at this point, I would have resorted to adhering pine cones to finish the job. The process was like assembling parts in an unknown puzzle. In the end, the column's facade resembled Mount Rushmore.

But it would have to do. My back was as stiff as the cement pillar, and I couldn't even stand up when Richard came home. "What do you think?" I moaned from the garage floor.

"Good job," he remarked cheerily. Then, with a nonchalance that *cemented* his ignorance of my ordeal, he added, "You should make another one."

They Always Return to the Scene of the Crime

I don't have a fascination for rocks, but with such an abundance of stones around here, we have found many practical uses for them. We used them to line our pier, create landscaping borders, and make a retaining wall. Last fall I gathered enough to make stone steps, finishing just before the ground froze. But, like a squirrel, I also had my stash set aside for later.

I have reasons for keeping the whereabouts of these stones to myself. First of all, my husband has had it with rocks. Since we moved here he has picked up and transported (with great effort) thousands of rocks, only to pick them up and transport them to another spot when I come up with yet another idea for using them. Not only that, but I have actually added to our rock collection by seeking out bigger and better ones from surrounding areas. These I hide until I figure out how to get them where I want them. That's almost as difficult as moving them.

You would think that I would have learned my lesson a few years ago when I built a stone column and threw my back out. (You might recall my great idea to construct the wood and mortar pillar in the garage first and *then* take it up the hill.) This time it was the rocks that would have to be brought uphill, and I would do it very carefully, one at a time, and out of sight of my husband. (And, yes, I really needed these big rocks because we were redoing a garden wall, and the old rocks were just too small, and…just mind your own business, that's why!)

One of the rocks (okay, boulder) had to be transported over recently seeded, soft ground that could not be safely traversed by a car or even the wheelbarrow. (Frankly, I was worried about leaving my own footprints!) I thought of sliding the rock to its destination on a big piece of cardboard but didn't want to risk having it slide off. Then my former weapon of choice popped into my head. Of course! The sled! I mean, the rock was not as heavy as a cement pillar, was it? Well, it felt like it, especially going uphill. It is amazing how a plastic sled that moves like a rocket over snow can feel like you are dragging a bathtub when it's on bare ground. I pulled in short bursts, catching my breath and assessing the distance in between pulls.

Just a little bit farther, I kept telling myself, until I finally decided it was my last tug: I would roll it the rest of the way tomorrow. But in mid-yank I was startled by the voice of my husband, who had spotted me from a window.

"What are you doing?!"

I don't know why, but my explanations never sound as good out loud as they do in my own head. Anyway, Richard carried the rock to the front yard with the stipulation that this was the last one. Fine. (But I don't recall hearing the word *ever*!)

The Roads Less Traveled Are Never Dull

I was looking forward to a relaxing drive to South Carolina with my sister, Carol. But I forgot that our road trips usually lead to unpredictable predicaments.

There are several reasons why trouble follows us. First, without our husbands along, we can drive hundreds of miles without eating more than a few snacks we have in the car. On a trip last year we delayed getting gas for so long that we were down to fumes and could barely sputter into an old station off the highway. Carol discovered that the washroom was dirty, but when she returned to the car, the more repugnant sight was that of my gasoline-soaked body. The defective pump had failed to turn off when I removed the nozzle. I took off my shoes and just hoped that my clothes would dry as I drove. Meanwhile, we had to hang our heads, like dogs, out the car windows so we could breathe. The truckers thought that we were flirting with them.

We also tend to talk each other into doing things that we might not consider individually. When a washroom in a shop filled with tourists had a long line, Carol suggested that I use the empty men's room. When I discovered the broken lock, she assured me, "I'll watch the door." She must have been distracted by the nearby carrousel of postcards because moments later a man walked past her, opened the men's room door and exposed me to an entire crowd of strangers.

We also love taking the scenic routes. On this trip we traced a faint line on the map and navigated through the Smoky Mountains. What we anticipated was a breathtaking view; what we encountered was a dense fog that intensified as we ascended thousands of feet into the clouds. Clutching my sweaty palms, I leaned toward the center of the car, foolishly thinking that shifting my body weight could thwart a slip off the narrow road that disappeared into the fog.

Our last night was scarier. We found a charming inn from 1789 whose five rooms had accommodated such guests as Abraham Lincoln and Jesse James (who purportedly left bullet holes in the walls). The clerk gave us a warning with our two keys: "This one is for your room; the other is for the front door, which is locked when the staff leaves. You're on your own until morning." We wondered what that meant—until we read the guest journal in our room. Almost every entry mentioned unexplained noises, erratic problems with the lights and hot water, or ghostly apparitions. Our room had a view of an old prison and cemetery. At exactly midnight we were jolted awake by the shrill sound of the clock alarm (that we had not set). We kept a light on until morning when we could unlock the front door and make our escape.

For the rest of the trip we abandoned the rural routes and stuck to the main highway. It seemed a safer bet.

Tasks Test Skills in Math and Patience

I was never great at math, especially those convoluted word problems, but I am somewhat skilled at figuring out how something goes together—unless those devious instruction-writers make an algebraic word problem out of a plastic jungle gym and leave a step out. My father used to say, "The first thing you do before you put something together is throw out the directions!" He was right. Like the pattern for a simple skirt that I needed to sew for some of my cast members. I have followed patterns before, but it was impossible to accommodate this one. Even my sister, my accomplice in this sewing feat, was stumped. We mumbled possible solutions back and forth. "If I double the fabric and place it on the fold and flip the pattern to the other side and—nope, still not enough room for these pieces!" The result was a skirt with an alternating print for a crazy-quilt effect that looked—well, I creatively described it as "fun" to the actress who had to wear it.

One of the most frustrating step-by-step-directions-to-nowhere was via a dog harness. I had to replace the tiny ribbon contraption that no longer fit my puppy. Purchasing a new one presented a challenge: Although I knew her breed, age, and weight, what I didn't know—and is apparently the way they categorize dogs in China—was her chest size. (I don't even know my own chest size.) I tried my best to do the tricky word-problem math: If her head is approximately half the size of her chest, and her jaw opens to half the size of her head, and her tiny baby teeth make marks that reach two-thirds around my wrist, then I just have to approximate the circumference of my arm and multiply it by four, minus one third. Or return the darned thing.

So I went by what looked about right, and, of course, that was wrong. As per the sketchy illustration, I tried putting her head through both loops and squeezing her legs through, which might have worked if she was a stuffed animal instead of an actual dog. I loosened the straps to the maximum length, but it was still too tight. Finally, I unbuckled the strap, but then I couldn't figure out which loop went around her neck and which one was for her chest. It didn't help that my pup was squirming with confusion because there was no treat involved in this trick.

At last I put the blasted thing down and suddenly realized that the contraption was not a dog harness at all but a diabolical Venn diagram. If I had one-hundred percent of my mind when I started, and I used fifteen percent of my brain for every five minutes of frustration, the remaining percentage of sanity is equal to the area in which circle of the dog harness? As usual, it's a trick question.

Paris Is City of Surprises

I was ecstatic when my sister suggested I accompany her to Paris some years ago. Nancy, who had been to Paris before, prepared an itinerary that began with a walk on the Champs Elysees. We watched the promenade from a café table on the legendary boulevard. I imagined the writers and artists of the 1920s observing the same scene from these cane chairs.

Of course, those artists would not have sat on chewing gum. Before I could remove the mess, an apologetic manager whisked me upstairs and into a storage closet, where he attempted to remove the spot with ice. Unfortunately, that's not all he attempted, and I made a flustered escape back to the table. Unnerved, I decided that I better mind more than my purse in this city!

We saw Paris from towers and trains and boats. We strolled through Versailles and rode bicycles to Monet's gardens. We purchased extravagant high heels and drank champagne. Days flowed into nights of late dinners and long walks back to the hotel. But the spectacular week had brought an unexpected feeling of homesickness. Then Nancy cheered me with a surprise.

She knew that I wanted to visit the bookstore, Shakespeare and Company, made famous by the Expatriates in the 1920s. She went on to tell me that, remarkably, a man who actually knew Ernest Hemingway was speaking there that afternoon. Convinced that the bookstore would be overrun with literary groupies, I dragged my sister away from Notre Dame, where she was photographing gargoyles.

At last I approached the bookstore, whose windows gave a teasing view of its interior archives. A small sign indicated that the shop would open at noon, and I planted myself in front of the famous green door, determined to be first in line. But my excitement was distracted by someone who was pressing against my back. Then, suddenly, I felt him kiss me on the back of my head! Not wanting a repeat performance of the "Café Romeo," I was determined to thwart this Frenchman's advances with a readied fist. I wheeled around with a fury that defied any language barrier. But it was I, stopped in mid-swing, who suddenly needed a translation.

For this man—this impostor—was wearing my husband's face! My mind scrambled to make sense of the impossible, but all I could do was collapse onto a bench. Who was this arrogant doppelganger—and how and why did he find *me*?

Then I heard Nancy laugh. But only when I recognized the man next to her as my brother-in-law did the second man come into focus. It was my husband. My sister had concocted a plan to have our husbands fly here for a romantic rendezvous. I was thrilled to have my husband with me, but after the shock wore off, another thought occurred to me.

"So," I teased, "there's no lecture on Hemingway?"

Of course, I forgave her for the subterfuge. As for my husband, this surprise would count for a lifetime of valentines.

Despite Blunders, the Show Must Go On

Some of my most unforgettable moments have been onstage—or backstage—of a play. After years of experience with school and community productions, I have learned that the play must go on—even when the actors are still in the bathroom when the curtain comes up.

That is one example of what happened during the high school shows I directed. Anyone acquainted with teenaged girls knows that they are ready when they are ready—and not a moment before. Such was the case when one of my actresses failed to enter on cue: She was drying her freshly polished nails under the hand dryer in the bathroom.

Another missed entrance was even more haunting—literally. The play was a ghost story, and I gave a boy a small non-speaking role which only required him to show his face in a window, scowl, and disappear. Well, he disappeared all right: During the intermission he decided he was going home and refused to re-appear in the second act. In desperation, I substituted one of the stage hands, whose cameo appearance in the window created even more of a mystery for the perplexed audience.

Blunders are not limited to youngsters, as illustrated by an older woman cast as the housekeeper in a community theater whodunit. Suddenly confused in the opening act, she prematurely opened a closet door, exposing a stage dummy intended to be revealed at the end of the play. The cast, a drawing room full of suspects, pretended that they hadn't seen the corpse, but there was little surprise for the audience when the closet was opened again later with an anticlimactic "Aha!"

Actors aren't the only unpredictable elements in live theater. Props and scenery can also be unreliable. In a school production I directed, a plastic rat was rigged with string so it could appear to run across the stage. Although it worked during rehearsal, the scene brought a wave of laughter at our first performance. The plastic rodent had flipped up-side-down and was moving backwards, feet up, as a frantic crew member pulled it from across the stage.

One of the funniest stage bloopers occurred when I was in a production of Arthur Miller's *All My Sons*. At the end of the play a main character commits suicide by shooting himself. A loud gunshot is heard and an actor comes on stage and informs the man's family of the sad news. But in one performance the prop gun would not go off backstage. Finally, the flustered actor made a hasty entrance but altered his line to say that the man had died—by *hanging* himself. No sooner had he delivered these words and the prop gun went off backstage. The stunned cast froze. The actor then quickly added, "And then he shot himself!"

It may be true that "all's well that ends well," but in some cases it's best when it just *ends*!

Pink Robe Has Life of Its Own

Some possessions have so many memories that it's difficult to discard them. That's the way I felt about my pink terrycloth robe. After all, it had been a companion for years as I made breakfast or curled up on the couch at night. Several children were soothed in those pink arms, and it even comforted me when I was sick. Although tattered from wear, it was destined for more life.

I was delighted when my sister gave me a new robe for Christmas, but my old favorite was not ready to go completely out of my life, yet. The solution was to leave it at my mother's house so I could wear it when I visited. Everyone in the family was familiar with Aunt Gail's pink robe as it always accompanied me when I stayed there.

The problem was that the pink robe resided in my mother's house, and I lived 300 miles away, which meant that I couldn't keep an eye on my old pal while I was home. One wouldn't think that was necessary, but it turned out that such vigilance was the only way to preserve its dignity.

At first the signs were subtle. I would be sipping coffee on the first morning of my visit when I noticed a small stain on the pink lapel. "How did ketchup get on my robe?" No one had an answer, but I noticed that a few eyes were suspiciously averted. The next indications of skulduggery were not blatant on their own, but my sense of violation was heightened. The final straw came when my pink robe was mysteriously strung up on a bedroom window to block the sun. That was it! A proclamation was issued: "No one touches my pink robe!"

I was teased for a while, especially by my siblings, but I was satisfied that my pink robe was safe. Then, on my next birthday, my sisters made a book for me. On the cover was written the title, *A Secret Life*. Inside, each page featured a photograph of different people wearing my pink robe in a variety of settings: on my brother-in-law in a fishing boat; on my brother as he shoveled snow; on my mother as she rode her motor scooter. It was draped over my pregnant sister on a doctor's examining table, downhill skiing on the back of a stranger, and posing on the shoulders of a hunter beside a rifle. It even was worn by a bulldog that slobbered beer over the counter of a local bar. Was nothing sacred?!

My sisters confessed. They had "stolen" my robe for the purpose of having people pose in it for this book. Very sneaky. The pink robe now hangs in my own closet at home.

At least I think so.

Revenge Is a Stinging Situation

Don't let that rhythmic hum in the summer air lull you into thinking that danger is not lurking at your feet—or, as in my case, one hand and two knees. Getting stung by wasps proved to be a frightening affair, and I was determined not to let it happen again. First of all, it was very painful. But I also broke out in hives. That prompted me to consult a doctor who determined that I had an allergic reaction to the stings and gave me a prescription for an EpiPen, which administers a dose of epinephrine to avert a possible life-threatening reaction. In case you're wondering, that only buys you fifteen minutes of time to get medical attention, and I don't mean the kind my husband administers in the form of ice cubes. I got a little woozy reading how to stab myself in the leg with the auto-injector. I assured myself that if the situation arose, my fear of needles would be superseded by my fear of dying.

Future bee stings may not prove to be that serious, but I was suddenly paranoid about being outside. When we had guests soon after my incident, I declined to join them on our deck by the lake (where I was stung). Instead, I sat on the patio near the back door, where one of my girlfriends and I stayed on high alert. Suddenly, we heard shouts from near the lake.

It wasn't long before we heard shouts, followed by the appearance of victims as they ascended the hill. "They got me!" Karen said. Behind her was my son, limping from the fresh bite on his "good" ankle. (The other one was just healing from the previous week's attack.) I was administering first aid in the form of antihistamines and meat tenderizer when I noticed my husband and Tom preparing to return to the scene of the crime. I used the calmest voice I could muster. "What are you doing with that baseball bat?"

Tom offered a quick explanation as he followed my eager husband in his hot pursuit of the winged culprits. "Richard's going to pound on the boards to bring them out, and then I'm going to kill them with this bug spray."

My girlfriends and I recoiled in horror. The other men went to watch. This is what I call the "poke-it-with-a-stick syndrome." It's how men react to a dangerous situation that could just as well be left alone. But, of course, they can't just leave it alone.

The confrontation sounded like a fight scene in a movie that is played off camera: You hear threats, warnings, thuds, whoops and running, and then the victors emerge and begin their boasting. So did ours. "We must have killed fifty of them!" "I used the whole can of spray!" "We'll go back down tomorrow and get the rest of them!" Of course, there's no such thing as "getting the rest of them." In fact, the wasps and their multitude of friends are probably planning an intricate plot of revenge right now. Meanwhile, in our camp, it's "hunting season."

I'm Not the *Only* One, You Know

Two people may be company and three a crowd, but the way I see it, the more people involved, the less likely you are to appear foolish. It just goes back to that old excuse that's used to cushion you from sole responsibility, "I'm not the only one, you know."

Not that you want to go running off with a crowd of imbeciles carrying torches and pitchforks, but it does help to have a posse of companions to support you sometimes. I learned that lesson in high school when my cohorts drew me into a situation that seemed innocuous enough at first, but when I was left holding the bag, I saw the enormity of my folly. We had a substitute teacher for drama class that day. (That always *sets the stage* for trouble, doesn't it?) We convinced her to let some of us rehearse scenes in the boiler room behind the theater.

Of course, we resorted to shenanigans, like climbing up rungs in the wall that accessed a metal platform above the furnace. Then someone gave a signal that the teacher was approaching, and everyone scrambled out. Except me. I was trapped near the ceiling. Even worse, two music teachers soon entered and became engaged in conversation just below me. I panicked while my imagination took over. What if the man and woman were having an affair? I considered that if I was discovered, they would be compelled to "silence" me. Several excruciating minutes passed before my fellow classmates, plagued with guilt and concern, sheepishly returned for a group confession. Embarrassed, I climbed down from my perch and slipped past the teachers before their dropped jaws could form words of much-deserved condemnation.

You might think that as an adult I would know better than to let peer pressure lead me astray, but you'd be wrong. Let's see…well, there was the time I assisted my neighbor in a late-night escapade to transport discarded sections of sod we had targeted earlier that day—perfect for patching our own ailing yards. We figured that no one would question two young mothers pulling a rusty wagon of pilfered lawn down the street (besides our husbands).

One menacing situation that I initiated on my own involved the confiscation of an old plywood sign from a property that was being bulldozed for new construction. (We weren't stealing; we were "aiding in demolition.") All I needed was the cloak of darkness and two co-conspirators: one to assist in the removal and another to drive the getaway car. If during the caper anyone questioned us, I was prepared to say we were merely fumbling through the grass for a lost car key. If that didn't fly, I could always point to my partners in crime and resort to the usual excuse: "I'm not the only one, you know!"

Getting Attention Backfires

When I was in school, most girls didn't take athletics too seriously because there were few opportunities through those achievements. The real competition among the girls was for the attention of the boys. For some of my classmates, it was important to be viewed as the prettiest or funniest or most charming. I guess I wasn't competitive in that regard, either. Boys asked me out, but I wasn't willing to pretend that I wasn't as smart or as clever as they were, and that put my name at the bottom of the list of girls a boy might call for a second date. The attitude I had regarding boys is best summed up by the lyrics in a popular show tune from *Annie, Get Your Gun*, "I can do anything you can do better; I can do anything better than you." It took me a long time to learn that if you try to show a guy up, he is likely to never *show up* again.

Blame it on my youth, but I did just that on one of my first dates, which was a bicycle ride and picnic. There were four of us, including my best friend and her boyfriend, and our destination was the lake although it was not intended as a finish line.

For some reason—probably nerves—I pedaled so fast that the others had to struggle to keep up. It didn't take long before it turned into a race, and my sense of competition kicked in with a rush of adrenalin. Unfortunately, winning was a hollow victory that steadily deflated, like my bicycle tires, on the way home. In addition to learning that out-riding someone you want to impress can backfire, I should have heeded another lesson Annie Oakley discovered in that Broadway musical: "You can't get a man with a gun."

Not that I went that far, but much of the time I wasn't sure if I wanted to corral some guy for my own—or hang his head like a trophy on the wall. I had a hard time deciphering an invitation from a challenge, the result of which was usually shooting myself in the foot.

One young man I met in my college calculus class seemed to like me, and we shared our woes over the course's difficulty and helped each other cram for tests before class. I discovered what a thin bond that was when I received a higher score on an exam. He covered his wounded ego with some sarcastic remarks about me, the gist of which was that I liked to complain that I was poor in math just so I could show off when I did well. I perceived that as laying down the gauntlet. No one, especially some dumb guy, was going to tell me that I was faking stupidity! From that point on I studied like crazy, memorizing theorems and doing equations in my sleep. When the next exams were returned, I waved my high score like a victory flag and ended up achieving a very decent C in the class. From then on I had a lot of study time—alone.

However, that didn't mean that I didn't use some choice weapons from my personal arsenal to gain the attention of another young man who struck my fancy. In retrospect, a gun would have been a more subtle option than some of the methods I used that backfired. I had heard that the best way to a man's heart was through his stomach, but I should have also heeded another bit of advice: There's a first time for everything, but it shouldn't be served to someone you want to impress. I can add another adage to this rule: Don't trust every recipe you see in a magazine.

My recipe-for-disaster was called "pizza loaf," an intriguing combination of two favorite foods: meatloaf and pizza. The name alone should have been a red flag, but I was a novice at cooking, and I really wanted to make an impression on this guy. So I spent my hard-earned money on the ingredients that probably started arguing with each other in the grocery bag on the way home. By the time they were in a bowl, I was mixing chaos and anarchy with my bare hands. The American classic, meatloaf, was reduced to an Italian version of mush, which lost semblance to both *meat* and *loaf*. By the time I served my international dish to my hungry recipient, it was a toss-up as to whether it should be eaten with a fork or spoon—or at all!

My next kitchen debacle was intended to satisfy several hungry men, including my father and a few friends. With my mother out of town, I took on the role of Julia Childs for what I planned to be a memorable dinner. Well, it was, but for the wrong reasons.

Not since Macbeth uttered those ominous words had there been so fair and *fowl* a day! My only excuse is that the bird in question *looked* like a chicken! Okay, the neck was rather long, but all the fowl at the store looked pretty much the same covered with plastic wrap. If I had known better, I never would have purchased a duck—or whatever greasy imposter this was.

And I wouldn't have stuffed it—like one does to a turkey or any other respectable bird. This creature had more skin than meat, which was quite obvious when I presented it as the main feature at my table. Dad tried, but extracting more than a couple forkfuls of meat was about as tricky as removing sand from your shoes with a tweezers.

"And what's with this neck?" someone asked.

"Yeah!" chimed in another. "And why is it so rubbery?"

Although the stuffing was soaked in grease, they fought over it like wild dogs. "Well," Dad exclaimed with more than a touch of sarcasm, "at least there's cottage cheese!"

Never underestimate the value of good side dishes.

Lawn Ornaments Come to Life

Once that huge propane tank was removed, a perfect place for a garden was revealed. Even after we fenced off an area for vegetable beds, there was a place for flowers and a little bench. This was a dramatic contrast to the alien spacecraft that occupied that spot for so many years. But, even with plants, my green space still needed something—something colorful, cute and fanciful—that the deer wouldn't eat. In other words, lawn ornaments.

These decorations can make the difference between plain green stalks—that used to support flowers before the bunnies loped off their heads—and eye-catching, giant petals fashioned from metal and reflective paint. Throw in a few battery-operated lights glowing through translucent butterflies or sunflowers, and even the birds do a double-take.

The problem with anything this cute and fun is that it is difficult to stop accumulating them. It is not an intentional habit: It is a psychological trigger that is pulled each time I see something that would be just too adorable next to my fake rock or artificial mums. Or, for that matter, my real trees along the paths I made in our woods. I was pleased with my little trails, but they needed something more, something *whimsical*.

The solution came about unexpectedly. I was attending an estate sale in our neighborhood and approached a box of statues that I first thought were Santa's elves, as each had a red stocking cap. But when the bidding started, I suddenly recognized that they were little gnomes—and the perfect accent pieces for my nature trails. So, yes, I bought all eight.

A few days later I carried them down to an area just beyond the creek's footbridge, leaving them there while I proceeded along my paths to find just the right spots to place them—under trees, on stumps, behind rocks. But when I returned to the bridge a half an hour later, the gnomes were gone. My first thought was that I had left them somewhere else. But as I looked about, other thoughts occurred: Elves make toys; trolls guard bridges; maybe gnomes play hide-and-seek!

Suddenly, I noticed one of them posed on the top of a post. A few steps later, I found a pair of them playing chess. These discoveries continued until I frantically left the paths and hurried into the house.

When I began to express my astonishment, my son leapt from the couch with a mischievous cackle. "Did I fool you, Mom?"

Sure. I never imagined that in addition to eight gnomes, there would also be a "six-foot leprechaun" in the woods.

And, if you think these fanciful statues were all that I purchased at that auction, well, you don't "gno" me!

Park Is Anything But a Small, Small World

Vacations appeal to many of our desires, providing opportunities for relaxation, adventure, learning, and fun. Certainly Orlando, Florida offered all of those, but we learned that having a good time is a lot more tiring than it used to be.

We planned this trip to Disney World as a graduation gift for our two nieces, one of whom was graduating from high school, the other from college. Although Richard and I had been there years ago, Katarina and Annalise had not, and their excitement for this experience fueled our own for sharing it with them.

We started the first day with energy and enthusiasm as we boarded the hotel shuttle for Disney World. Thirty minutes later we pulled into Epcot's parking lot and boarded yet another bus bound for the Magic Kingdom. That journey ended with a mass exodus that continued on foot. Finally, like a beautiful mirage, the outline of the fantasy park appeared—on the other side of a lake. Still enthusiastic (but a little less energetic) we crossed the waterway via ferry and reached the park entrance—that is, after we waited in line for security checks, and then another line for our tickets, and then another line to get our "fast passes." Finally, we stood before Disney's All-American Main Street with its marching bands, quaint shops, and…a bakery, which was our first stop. We were hungry!

My nieces were fluttering with excitement and navigated the streets with savvy from one attraction to another. The first was Space Mountain, an appropriately named ride that simulated space travel with projected images of stars and planets while your rollercoaster car "launched" into the sky and then sped into a dark hole. It was at this point in the journey that I closed my eyes, only slightly aware of the voice from the control room back on Earth giving out desperate instructions to return. Wait a minute! That's not Cape Canaveral! That's Richard! Everyone on board could hear the weary astronaut wailing, "Let me out! Enough, already!"

That comment became his mantra for much of the week. In Frontier Land we climbed the tree house steps just as we had years ago with our children. But this time the Swiss Family Robinson's retreat seemed as distant as Mt. Everest. Even the log ride on plummeting rafts felt like the *long* ride on the African Queen that sent Humphrey Bogart over the falls. And a realistic tropical heat at Animal Kingdom had us limping through the Moroccan streets and bazaars of Casablanca in search of shade—and the letters of transit.

The girls and I learned that the best way to maneuver Uncle Richard through Disney World was via indoor attractions that featured air-conditioning. So we alternated experiences that provided thrilling effects with those that had *chilling* effects. Richard even became a fan of the Little Mermaid after spending a cool half hour "under the sea."

Not that ten hours of strolling through enchantment doesn't take its toll. It's enough to make Cinderella take off her glass slippers. We could have used a pumpkin-carriage—or even a ride in a tea cup—to view the wonderful world of Disney that is anything but a small, small world.

Sometimes "Old School" Is Cool

As my nieces and nephews would say, I do things "old school." What they don't realize is that old school can be cool—like when my siblings and I extended our recent trip to the Lake Superior ice caves and added two days of skiing in Minnesota. Our middle-aged coolness kicked in soon after we settled into our lodging, and my brother plugged in his iPhone so we could listen to some oldies-but-goodies while we enjoyed wine and conversation. Imagine our surprise when the management called to say our music was disturbing other guests outside the rental unit. Oops! It's been a long time since we were told to "Keep the noise down, kids!"

But the tone was already set for the weekend. Just because we are all over fifty doesn't mean we are old. To prove that I pretended I wasn't afraid of heights and rode a gondola up the mountain to a breathtaking (as in "I can't breathe!") view of Lake Superior. I clicked into my skis and selected innocuous-sounding trails like "Snow Bunny" and "Kittens' Mittens." But before I knew it, these comfort zones had diverted me onto black diamond runs, and

I was flying uncontrollably down slopes with terrifying names like "Out of Control," "Tree Slam," and "Wet Your Pants."

But I held on. Actually, I did better than that, and a new feeling of power even had me changing the music in my head. I always sing while I ski. Sometimes it's just in my head, and sometimes I say the words out loud. It just makes me feel good. But, instead of my usual Sinatra-style standards, I felt a sense of adventure that had me humming the "James Bond Theme" all day. That's just the way I roll: old school.

After dinner that night I strolled over to the restaurant's gift shop. I'd like to think that it was my new-found sense of adventure, but I suspect it was a commonality of friendliness that resulted in a conversation with two skiers. Soon my sister and nephew joined us, and we learned that the men were Canadian and here on a group ski trip. Unfortunately, our friendly banter caused them to miss the bus back to their hotel. We watched as they scurried across the parking lot in pursuit of the eluding tail lights. Their hotel was a long, cold walk away. Of course, we offered them a ride.

There was barely room for the two men in the backseat, but I was squeezed between them on a pile of ski gear. The good-natured fellows reminded me of boys I knew in high school, especially the ones that Carol and I hung out with so often in our old neighborhood. I jokingly said that for Canadians they spoke English very well, and our laughter led to one pun after another. The fun reduced us all to giggling sixteen-year-olds. They expressed their gratitude for the ride, but we all felt lucky to have shared each other's company that night. Upon exiting the car, they thanked us again. Then, while extricating himself from the tangle of poles and helmets, one leaned in and remarked, "I didn't think I'd run into a hot chick tonight." Whether it was the dim light, the numbing cold, or their intake of beer, I appreciated the compliment but couldn't help joking back, "Just how remote *is* it in Canada?"

After a second day of skiing, we middle-aged siblings soaked our weary bodies in the hot tub. Simultaneously, an idea gleamed in our eyes. We rushed outside in our wet bathing suits and threw ourselves into the snow while my nephew captured the spectacle on his camera. Some onlookers thought we were crazy, but they weren't familiar with our old-school cool. It's just the way we roll.

Best Shot Is Not in Best Interest

Of all the creatures that inhabit our neck of the woods, I have had the opportunity to see all of them up close, except for one of the local black bear. It's not that they aren't around. One pulled my bird feeder down in search of breakfast after a long winter's nap. I even spotted one of these elusive creatures lumbering down near the lake once. But never up close—until recently when my sister and I were driving along Highway 29 on our way to Minneapolis to visit my brother. We were talking when, suddenly, something caught my eye along the highway, and in a moment's flash I realized that it was a bear.

While seeing a bear at this time of the year may not be unusual, these circumstances made for an unlikely spotting. First of all, the speed was pretty fast on that highway. Secondly, the animal's location was in the snow-covered area that divided the four-lane highway. But what made the sighting most coincidental was that I happened to glance at the median just as the bear's head was emerging from the opening of a metal culvert. The outline of that black head, with its distinct ears and nose, was unmistakable—even from a passing car.

"That was a bear!" I said excitedly to my sister, whose head spun around in a futile effort to see it, too. Of course, I *had* to go back to show her. So I turned around at the next opportunity, scanned the location from the other side of the highway, made another U-turn, and parked on the shoulder. Our mission, naturally, was to get a picture of that bear.

This involved opening the trunk and finding the cameras among our luggage. But we soon realized that it was nearly impossible to get a good shot through the constant stream of cars and trucks between us and the culvert. In addition, the bear seemed camera shy and put his nose down at the precise click of the shutter. We had enough sense to remain where we were, but I was determined to get a good shot. I just needed a better angle—a *higher* angle. All I had to do was get up onto the roof of my car so I could shoot *over* the traffic.

So, up on the trunk I crawled, but just as I attempted my ascent to the roof, a highway service truck pulled up behind us. Halted there on my hands and knees, I couldn't exactly feign car trouble. As the men approached, I quickly explained our intention to photograph the bear. But they had assumed that and had already contacted the DNR. Apparently, this was not an uncommon situation—bears often took winter refuge in culverts—although my precarious position on the car was a safety hazard that was attracting more attention than the animal.

In the end we only had a few blurry images of a large black head. But we sure had an interesting story about how we got them!

Chapter 5

Sentimental Journeys

Trains Take a Sentimental Journey

The post-war housing expansion gradually increased traffic in our Chicago neighborhood, and we eventually grew accustomed to the perpetual noise of cars and busses in the street.

However, there was one welcoming sound that permeated the din occasionally, especially at night. I would turn in my bed, alerted to the low rumbling of a passing freight train. The tracks were only two blocks away, high above the backyards that bordered it. The trains rumbled over our busy boulevard by means of a viaduct that separated our neighborhood from the commercial setting of 95th Street. One always walked quickly through that dark tunnel, avoiding the litter and puddles that collected there. And there were many of us who nearly ran out of the viaduct at the sound of a train overhead, fearful that the trembling cement pillars would collapse.

Yet the trains held an exotic mystery, too. Hands waved from the engine and caboose as their journey to places unknown sped out of view. Sometimes a vagrant jumped from a car and scoured the trash cans in our alley. Somehow, in the decades since the Depression, these sojourners had forgotten the terminus they so desperately sought when they first embarked on these moving vestiges of hope.

The tracks, too, stirred our young imaginations and sense of adventure. We placed pennies upon the gleaming rails and waited in the prairie grass, hopeful that the mammoth cars would soon crush our coins into faceless medallions. We carried out this activity near our grandparents' home in Michigan, too, where we also gathered iron ore pellets that had spilled from loaded cars.

When we moved to the suburbs, I could walk to the tracks that took me to my first job in downtown Chicago. Even the commuter train held an air of romance as an array of passengers contemplated their missions of business or pleasure at various stops along the line. The bustling crowds in Union Station were a stark contrast to the quiet journey home that gently rocked along rails and into vanishing horizons.

In the fifties, when the passenger trains still ran between Chicago and Iron Mountain, my mother took advantage of the convenient means of travel so that she could bring my sister and me with her to the lake cottage. The train seemed so luxurious and exciting to the little girls who watched the city slip away with the sunset as the tracks disappeared into the cool, dark woods.

I have returned to the lake for good. In winter the exposed landscape permits a view of the same tracks that bordered my childhood world. Every night I am beckoned by a familiar call. Beams of light flash across the pines as clashes of iron and steel crescendo and recede into darkness. The sound enters my sleep, haunting my past and promising dreams to come.

Car Is Uncool at Any Speed

The ideal car for large families like ours was a station wagon. That's what we had when we took a trip out West in the summer of 1968: a black '67 Ford station wagon, powerful enough to pull our new camper, but, of course, it didn't have air-conditioning.

The West is a beautiful place in the summer, but its temperatures are better suited to rattlesnakes than humans. Still, we were excited about this vacation that would take us from our home in Chicago all the way to California. Only three of us could comfortably occupy the backseat so a tiny area for one more kid was cleared among the luggage and camping equipment in the back. My siblings and I grudgingly took turns there, wedged between a suitcase and a Coleman cooler. One of us would switch places when the current nominee threatened to throw up from the heat and exhaust fumes.

But my father had a plan to make this car trip more comfortable. He was a solution-finder who delighted in finding economical and ingenious ways to improve a situation. Shortly before our vacation was to begin, he arrived home with a box containing what he claimed would provide air-conditioning for the car. This device, known as a "swamp cooler," was a window-mounted, evaporative air cooler for automobiles. The gadget was a metal cylinder that was attached to the car window with clamps. The operation was simple: outside air passed through the cylinder and over a water-soaked filter inside, thus creating a cooling effect as the air flowed throughout the car. The passenger—which, in our case, was my mother—merely had to pull the attached cord occasionally to douse the filter into the reservoir of water in the bottom.

But Mom was skeptical. How could an eighteen-foot long vehicle traveling through the desert with its windows closed be cooled by a damp wick the size of a cotton sock? Dad assured her that it would work: It said so on the box. As the designated cord-puller, she received her instructions and merely scowled at the metal contraption that rattled over her right shoulder.

By the time we got to Mesa Verde, Arizona, the temperature had reached 103 degrees. Dad insisted we keep the windows closed. "Give it a chance." By Lake Mead, we were panting like dogs. Still, Dad was optimistic. "I think I feel something. Pull the cord again."

Mom tugged, and drops of water spilled out and rolled down her arm. "Look," she finally said, "the only one feeling anything is me because it's leaking." (Those of us in the backseat swooned; the passenger in luggage mumbled incoherently from the tailgate.)

When Dad finally surrendered, we rolled the windows down and gratefully felt the hot wind on our faces. Thankfully, that was the end of the air cooler for the rest of the trip. Nevertheless, our ever-hopeful father vowed to try the invention another time—just maybe not in the hottest part of summer.

Personal Objects Connect Us to Our Past

The plate simply cracked in half. Granted, it was jarred in the sink when a pot slipped out of my wet hands, but the fault line was already there. The plate was one of the last of my original set of white Ironstone dishes, the remaining few of which I had given to my son when he moved into an apartment. Now I was washing them in my son's kitchen—and apologizing for the breakage. "It already had a line in it," he called out.

A line, indeed. It also had a chip. That's what happens over time. I have had other sets of dishes since these, but the white ones were a wedding gift from my parents, and I am a little sentimental about them. Silly, but they have held more than food over the years. They also hold memories of my first cooking efforts as a new wife, all the daily meals I served for my husband and children, and even the special occasion dinners we hosted for family and friends.

Isn't it funny how simple objects carry stories about your life? Maybe that's why it is sometimes difficult to part with the things that have been part of our lives for so long. If nothing else, these items can take you back to another time and another place that is really another you. It's a long ride from where we started to where we are right now, but when something triggers a memory of a stop along the way, well, those objects become the souvenirs of life's journey.

Like the white dishes. Other pieces had broken over the years, and one by one I replaced them. But I noticed subtle comparisons between the newer pieces and the originals, an almost imperceptible difference in the weight and color. Eventually, the dishes developed their own identity with tiny chips and hairline cracks while still reminding me of those early days.

I was so excited to set up housekeeping when I was newly married. I remember how much fun I had arranging my new dishes on the kitchen shelves of our first apartment. I took such pride in stacking the bathroom towels that I had received as shower gifts (in my coordinating colors of blue and brown) next to the carefully folded bedsheets with their bright floral pattern. Everything was fresh and new—just like that phase of my life.

The towels are long gone, having also served to wash cars and clean up oil in the garage. The sheets, too, had other functions before their patterns literally faded away, including makeshift tents for the children, improvised covers for the backseat of the car, and as drop cloths for painting projects.

Very few material things survive the years of everyday living. But just like my white dishes, they say a lot about how we have lived.

Clotheslines Make Natural Connections

I grew up in a neighborhood of tiny city yards hedged in by fences, garages and alleys. But a bird's-eye view would have showed that they were all connected by a series of zigzag lines: These were backyard clotheslines, and everyone had one. Once a necessity, the clothesline is nearly extinct in modern America, but the simplicity of hanging laundry outside was a fulfilling experience in ways that could never be matched by a machine drier.

My mother would carry the wash up from the basement in a vinyl-lined wicker basket and set it outside in the middle of the yard.

The clotheslines stretched the length of the yard, from the house to the garage, and were supported in the middle by portable aluminum poles, forked on one end and anchored in the grass on the other. A bag of clothespins bobbed from one of the lines overhead, but my mother always carried a few in her hand, apron pocket, and mouth as she secured each wet article to the sagging line. The process didn't take very long, but it often served as an invitation for a neighbor's conversation. Sometimes it was just a greeting from across the yard or alley, but one neighbor, a good friend of my mother's, would lean over our picket fence with the same purpose that one expresses over coffee shared at a table. Laundry day was an occasion for socializing, too.

My sister and I often played tag among the hanging lines. As we ran, we touched the walls of drying sheets and laughed when the other popped out to surprise her sister and end the chase. Wooden clothespins were also toys, and a popular game, especially at birthday parties, was seeing how many you could get into a glass milk bottle by dropping them from a kneeling position on a chair. Two clothespins could by attached at their slots in such a way that they served as a gun when I pretended to be a cowgirl. Outlaws lurking behind wet towels were no match for Annie Oakley.

Even after an automatic drier was installed, my mother continued to use a clothesline. After all, it was foolish to use all that electricity when the sun was shining and a warm breeze was blowing. And there were those items for which a drier was not very effective. Blankets and jeans, for example, were just too bulky to put in a drier. Then there were those winter things that, just released from storage in mothballs, needed airing. But the sweetest smell of all is that of sheets just in from the line.

Some cities now have ordinances against hanging laundry out in your yard. I lived in such a suburb, but I often ignored the rule. My small stretch of line served a loving tradition. Nothing else could duplicate the fresh scent of grass and clouds and sun. When spring arrives, there is a yearning to capture the fragrances of happy memories. The answer, my friends, is blowing in the wind.

Old Desk Holds Memories

The fascination that people have with antiques, particularly objects of their youth, is understandable. We all love a reminder from the good old days, even when the item is a little nicked and battered. After all, that toy—or book or chair—is over fifty years old. Wait a minute! Does that mean that some of us are also a little nicked and battered? Could we, too, be described as "worn around the edges and showing some age?" Hmmm.

That thought occurred to me as I cleaned up an old desk that had been in my mother's basement for so long that I forgot it was there. My parents had purchased it around1950 from a resale shop, which means that the desk is probably several years older than I am. Still, I couldn't help making a comparison, albeit strange, between the condition of that old desk and myself.

We have both survived several decades and had more experiences than showed on our exteriors. From a distance—or at least in the dim light of the basement—the wood desk looked pretty good. (I prefer to be seen in candlelight, but one does have to go into the light of day, doesn't one?) My mother accommodated me with soap and a cloth with which I cleaned away the dirt from years of storage. Beneath the surface was a truer story. Isn't that always the case?

The desk had belonged to my father, whose familiar image seated there with head bowed over papers is still easily and vividly recalled. I can also see the green desk blotter, the marble clock, the black "Records" book, and a brass letter holder. The desk remained with him through the years and his moves to other homes. It's the only piece of my parents' furniture that still exists from my earliest childhood. I half-expected to find an old stamp or yellowed envelope or— better yet—one of my Crayola creations inside a drawer. But, alas, those were gone. Even the papers from more recent business had been cleared away. Yet, it was not exactly *empty*.

As I moved my hands across the desktop, I felt the familiarity that had endeared it to me. Then I went to work. Touches of wood stain restored the color to the worn edges, and some polish highlighted the pretty tones of the mahogany. Even the brass handles, darkened with age, revealed their gold once again. And a crack in one foot could easily be fixed with glue, couldn't it? After all, a desk this old should have some flaws. That's what gives it character.

The desk is being given to my son, who just purchased his first home. He will use it for many more years, I'm sure. He appreciates things that have some history, sentimentality, and character associated with them—things that are, I guess, a lot like his mother.

What Comes Around, Goes Around

While visiting a used bookstore in an unfamiliar town, we encountered a vast assortment of record albums. Apparently, these vintage gems are being rediscovered. In an age of technology that supersedes itself every day, such anachronisms seem an unlikely choice for the computer generation.

But, not being part of that category ourselves, we enjoyed the nostalgic trip afforded by the albums. Our fingers flipped over the worn edges of albums whose covers were often familiar. "Oh, remember this?" "I had this one in college." "Don't we still have this one?"

Indeed we did. We still have most of the records from our combined collections. Some of Richard's albums date from the fifties. It is an eclectic assortment of his musical taste that feature popular singers like Doris Day, Frank Sinatra, and Bobby Darin, as well as the soulful voices of Nancy Wilson, Dakota Station, and Dinah Washington. His albums also include the music of Broadway hits like *Oklahoma* and jazz by such musicians as Dave Brubeck.

My own albums were first purchased after I could save enough babysitting money to afford the luxury of owning my own music, like the Beatles' *Sergeant Pepper's Lonely Hearts Club Band*. I must have driven my parents nuts with those songs.

After all of these years, a particular song will take me back to a specific experience. There is the song that was played over and over at school dances and stayed in my head the next day. There is the one that played on the radio when my boyfriend kissed me for the first time, and another that reminded me of him after we broke up. There are the tunes that a neighborhood garage band practiced all summer long. There are the songs that my girlfriends and I always sang together, and the ones that I sang by myself when I was alone.

Last Christmas my brother gave my sister a vintage album by a group called Harper's Bazaar. It was identical to the one we owned and listened to over and over. Carol immediately brought out her record player—yes, that machine that plays 33 1/3 vinyl discs—as well as some of her old records. She put the oldies on, and we were suddenly transported. "Remember this song?" We were teenagers again, listening to our favorites in our bedroom and singing along.

It's funny how the words come back to you. Many of the selections are rarely heard on the radio anymore. But the past was coming back with the familiar, albeit scratchy, renditions that we heard a hundred times in our youth from groups like Blood, Sweat and Tears and The Association.

"*Cherish* is a word I use to describe…" *all* the music of those good old days.

Letter-Writing Is a Lost Art

Most of the showers, weddings and graduation parties I have attended in recent years have a distressing factor in common. The gifts that are given are not acknowledged by the recipients. No thank you note, no phone call, no e-mail—not even a quick click of a text message. Apparently, as I was once informed, "Young people don't do that anymore." Oh. Since when did the thank you note go out of style?

When I was in grade school, letter writing was an important skill that was taught with the same discipline that was applied to handwriting. Just as perfectly executed cursive was stressed, the etiquette of the friendly letter was just as valuable. "Remember," my teacher told us, "you will be judged not only for *what* you say, but *how* you express yourself." I have never forgotten that lesson.

At home written responses were an expected responsibility. Gifts that were sent to my sister and me were shortly followed by our neatly written thank you notes. Following the guidelines provided in school for these "bread and butter letters," we kept the word *I* to a minimum, inquired about the recipient, and included pleasant and interesting news about ourselves. Not only did we thank the person for the gift, but we expressed our appreciation for their thoughtfulness. Finally, we proofread the letter for errors and recopied it on pretty stationery. Stationery was always a welcomed gift. An aunt once gave me pages embellished with the words "Gleanings from Gail." (The personalization was even more appreciated once I consulted the dictionary.)

There is something artistic about the process of writing with a pen on attractive paper. The flow of words from one's imagination to the physical application of the hand is more deliberate than that which is executed on a computer. While words that are typed present a conventional interpretation, handwritten words suggest subtleties of a more intimate nature. For what is more personal than the individuality of one's handwriting? The flourish of a letter, the emphasis of an underlined word, even the size and slant of the words on the page add meaning that is unique to the correspondent. They are one-of-a-kind exchanges that may last a lifetime. After all, who has not kept a special letter as a memento? Aren't love letters really souvenirs of the heart?

In this age of computers and cell phones, communication is fast and brief. Text messaging reduces the English language to abbreviations. Each year of my teaching career I noticed that my students' writing revealed an increased use of these shortcuts (*w/out, b/c,* etc.). I emphasized that there is a difference between subway graffiti and love letters. The former requires a can of paint, the latter requires poetry. Cyrano de Bergerac knew this when he penned letters to the beautiful Roxanne. And children know this when they write heartfelt, handwritten messages on Mother's Day cards.

Beautiful letters are worth writing and keeping.

Fashion Trends Come Back to Haunt You

The older we get, the harder it seems to keep up with the latest fashion trend—or to pull off wearing it without looking foolish. If you are like me, you have already committed enough fashion faux pas to fill a closet. When I look back on some of them, I have to ask myself, "What was I thinking?"

The answer, of course, was that I wasn't thinking. I was simply trying to be in style. It wasn't my fault that some of those fashion trends were ridiculous. My responsibility for following them began when I was old enough to pick out my own clothes. One of the first articles I selected was a pair of white culottes that I pleaded with my mother to buy for me. If I could have seen myself from a distance I may have noticed that I looked like a walking pyramid. Yet, even at a closer viewing, I didn't seem to notice that I resembled a circus tent with a clown head on top (my hair was the result of several bad permanents).

In high school all the girls tried to duplicate the exaggerated eyelashes of British model, Twiggy. Mascara and pencil sufficed, but the use of false eyelashes became very popular. I tried them—once. I was going on a date and wanted the "Twiggy look." It didn't take long before the only *look* I cared about was the one that required my vision. I had to tilt my head back so I could see under the heavy fringe that kept sliding around my eyelids. By the end of the evening, my eyelashes had moved around so much that I felt more like Mr. Potato Head than a model from *Seventeen*.

Sometimes the name of a trend should be warning enough. The prettiest blouse in the world could not distract from the widest pant legs in the world, appropriately called "elephant pants." Ironically, at the same time, the miniskirt was popular. Apparently, a skirt that showed your knees was just not short enough. I can remember rolling my skirt up at the waist after I left the house for school (lest my mother know). But the skirts got even shorter in college, and sitting down became a challenge—as did getting in and out of cars, bending over, waving...

Women aren't the only victims of fashion foolishness. Some of those polyester leisure suits from the '70s could have served as flotation devices on boats. And who convinced men that it was masculine to wear shirts with floral or paisley prints? Although my husband has no memory of it, he actually wore a bow tie a few times. I bought it for him when we were first married: It was maroon with gray polka dots. It seems clownish now, but at the time I thought it was cute. Well, what do you expect from a girl who once believed that her circus culottes and Bozo hairdo were in style?

Home Movies Show Glimpses of Past

The box of home movies had been stored in the basement for years. Clearly labeled by my father, they covered family events since my early childhood. However, the old projector was broken, and it had been decades since any of us viewed those films. When my brother brought a working projector with him for a family visit, we all settled in for an evening of memories.

The faded images that flickered across the screen stirred immediate recognition. A time capsule had opened, and our younger versions bounced in and out of the camera's lens. There were my sister and I opening Christmas presents. "Of course!" I suddenly remembered. "That was the year I got my Shirley Temple doll!" As the camera panned the room, the faces of relatives turned and smiled. There were my grandparents, looking much younger than I remembered them. And my uncles, merely teenagers, performing silly pantomimes. Others, long gone from this world, returned for fleeting moments as the film rolled on.

These glimpses did not satisfy. No sooner did I utter a word of recognition, and the loved one disappeared into the receding frames. My great-grandmother reached for something out of the camera's view. But I could almost see her red nails and hear her lilting voice. The slender figure of my mother paused long enough to acknowledge my father behind the camera, and then moved away toward some unknown task.

The scenes changed with jerking transitions from birthday parties to Thanksgiving dinners to Christmas morning. Suddenly, the film jumped to the lake at the cottage, and my father came into focus. With head submerged in the water, he circled the rowboat with powerful strokes. Then, with a final splash of his rubber fins, he turned on his back and flashed a grin toward the boat. And, for a moment, I was there again, watching him from my seat at the bow. But these images on the film were so brief, and I yearned for more.

That feeling intensified as the film unraveled its final scene, a gathering in our living room. The camera revealed the familiar setting but failed to focus on the details. I longed to revisit the room and see it up close: the patterns on the wallpaper and drapes, the arrangement of furniture, the view through the windows. If I could just walk through the rooms, I might know again the nuances of the house that I knew then. If I could pause on the objects and faces, I might revive the times they occupied and feel, once more, their presence. Such is the foolishness of sentimentality.

For film cannot replace that which has been lost. Although its images bring the past to mind, it is memory that must preserve them in the heart.

Family Adheres to Remedy

As much as we are taught to avoid getting a wound dirty, there's a rumored remedy for injuries that contradicts that notion. Apparently, if you are alone in the wilderness and sustain a deep flesh wound, applying mud to the area can serve as a healing poultice. Of course, in the area I live in, you'd have to make a poultice out of sand and rocks.

However, there was a poultice that was commonly used in our family years ago. My grandparents always had a can of black salve in the medicine cabinet. It was purchased at the drugstore and came in a small metal container that resembled a can of chewing tobacco. The inside was filled with a black, tar-like substance that was usually heated before use so that it could be applied more easily. The purpose of this gooey salve was to draw out the infection in a wound. Anything from a deep gash to a stubborn sliver was usually slathered with black salve. Since the results were generally positive, its application became as standard as Vicks Vapor Rub for colds— although it would not be out of the question to *substitute* black salve for the job.

Although the use of black salve was common practice in our family, it drew stares from those unfamiliar with the ointment. That's why we covered it with a Band-aide. My mother also became an advocate of black salve, and it became a coveted item when its availability waned. Eventually, only my grandparents could acquire the magic potion from a local vendor where they lived. The contents of our last can were carefully doled out for the more serious afflictions.

That final occasion arose after my brother stepped on a nail. My mother cleaned the puncture wound thoroughly, but within a few days the area became red and swollen. Out came the match for warming the can, and on went a generous glob of healing ointment. However, it wasn't long before a red line of infection snaked up his leg. Soon my little brother was limping into the doctor's office alongside my mother. The doctor removed the gauze from my brother's foot but stopped abruptly at the sight of the oozing, black goo.

"What," he snapped, "is that!" My mother's dissertation on the wonders of black salve failed to impress the doctor. He scraped the sticky substance off the wound and told her sternly, "Don't ever use this again."

My brother's wail echoed down the hallway as he received a tetanus shot. His cry of defeat ended an era. Modern medicine had won. Black salve joined the ranks of mythical miracle cures. Except for those of us who just might have an old can of the stuff tucked away in the medicine cabinet. You never know when you might need it.

Backyard Becomes Outdoor Theater

There are occasions when no one wants to end the fun. That was the case when my family celebrated my nephew's graduation. After the food was cleared from the tables, a full moon rose above the trees, and the garden glowed with lantern candles. My sister suddenly bounded up with an idea. "Let's watch a movie—right here in the backyard!"

The concept of an outdoor movie is one with which we are all familiar. Outdoor theaters were all the rage in the fifties and sixties. Although we had to drive across the city, the attraction was worth the trip. With names like *Starlite,* a drive-in theater turned a Chicago suburb into Shangri-La.

From couples in convertibles to young families in station wagons, the audience-on-wheels was varied. Parking spots were selected by personal preference: true movie buffs took first rows, lovers took the back rows, and snack fans stayed close to the concession stand. (Sometimes parents had to move their cars after discovering that their children were more interested in watching the romantic show that was taking place in the next vehicle.)

Drive-in movies often had a general appeal. Romantic comedies were not sexual romps then. Horror flicks had more suspense than gore, and comedies were funny without being offensive. Humorous scenes were punctuated by the muffled laughter in cars across the lot.

The slam of car doors was another familiar sound at the drive-in. Who could resist the smell of buttered popcorn that wafted over car roofs? Just to make sure that you were aware of the assortment of treats available, giant hot dogs and talking candy bars appeared on the screen. Consumption of those foods necessitated the purchase of drinks, which eventually led to the stumbling procession of children to the restrooms. But children rarely saw the end of movies. The station wagons left first, their sleeping cargo already in pajamas and curled up under quilts.

I can't even remember the last time I experienced a drive-in theater. But my sister's makeshift screen on the back of the garage brought back Starlite memories. Again our family huddled together under the night sky to enjoy a movie together. True, the images were slightly distorted on the sheet held up by duct tape, and we had to lean forward to hear the tiny speakers attached to the short wires of the projector. But it was just as much fun as I remembered at the original theaters.

That is, until the end. Nancy, who was holding her dog's shock collar, forgot that the movie equipment was set up outside the invisible electric fence. That oversight resulted in giving her quite a jolt when she got up during the movie credits.

However, her shock was only temporary. Besides, that was a small admission price for the experience of an outdoor theater.

Ice Cream Memories Never Melt

The ice cream truck made a daily excursion through our Chicago neighborhood on hot afternoons. No matter what we were doing, the sound of those tinkling bells made us stop in our tracks. Half the fun was watching the wrapped treasures emerge from vapors of dry ice.

Sometimes my mother brought cartons of ice cream home from Walgreens. In order to satisfy our family's varied preferences, the flavor compromise was always Neapolitan. The square pints were sliced like cake—actually a perfect base for the other dessert on special occasions. My father was fond of pop floats, which was reason enough for my mother to buy a bottle of root beer to make black cows. For several years, Friday was designated as "pop float night," and we looked forward to enjoying this treat while we watched *Twilight Zone* on television. There is an art to sucking ice cream through a straw—and it's a noisy one.

But it was always more fun to go out for ice cream—or more accurately, frozen custard. Our favorite source was Tastee Freeze, a drive-in stand that lured customers from all over the South Side. Swirls of vanilla never tasted so good.

Summers in Michigan were highlighted by ice cream in the regional flavor of "blue moon." My grandmother treated us to huge scoops of the aqua-colored creation that quickly became our favorite. My sister and I have had countless discussions about the flavoring that may have included anything from vanilla to lemon to almond—individually or in any combination. Regardless, it was delicious down to the last lick of our blue tongues.

Evening walks at the cottage were usually excursions for ice cream. The lakes' small grocery store (the proprietors lived on its second floor) had a freezer near the door stocked with frozen treats. My selection was always a Dreamsicle, and I savored each creamy bite as we strolled back home. The orange sherbet coating disappeared with the last orange streaks of sunset. It was the best way to end a perfect summer day.

Some years ago I was watching my son's little league game when the action on the field came to an abrupt halt. The pitcher held the ball, the batter turned his head away, and the outfield gazed into the distance. We on the bleachers were confounded at first. Then we realized what it was that had given the boys such a sudden and dramatic pause: the music from a passing ice cream truck! The melody held the boys in a momentary trance as they heeded the familiar call to the universally beloved treat.

I have always loved ice cream. As it did when I was a child, it can turn an ordinary day into a "two scoops" special occasion.

Sundress Was Summer Glamour

Most of us look forward to warm summer days when our clothing of choice consists of shorts, a t-shirt and flip-flops. This comfortable outfit is standard fare for everything from working outside to entertaining. But it wasn't always.

There was a time when even backyard entertaining had a dress code. I'm not talking about hot dogs and Kool-Aid with the kids. I mean cocktail parties with invited guests. Men wore long pants and seersucker sport coats, and women wore pretty sandals and sundresses. They sipped cool drinks served in tall glasses. Conversations drifted across a patio illuminated by strings of paper lanterns. There was always soft music in the background, and couples danced under the stars. Well, at least that's how it's depicted in the movies. I might have romanticized a little, but not about the sundress. I know all about the sundress, and I remember it well.

The sundresses I wore as a little girl were sleeveless and adorned in rickrack. Our Grandma Signe sewed some for my sister and me, which we wore for summer occasions like birthday parties, Sunday picnics, and out for dinner. We even put them on for company, like Grandma Rose's cocktail parties at the lake. After swimming all day, our hair dampened the back of the dresses, and our sunburned shoulders were exposed, but we were appropriately attired, and we felt pretty.

Grownup versions of the sundress were much more elegant— and more daring with styles that included off- the-shoulders or spaghetti straps, as well as backless and strapless versions. Walking in heeled sandals and full-skirted dresses necessitated a more feminine movement in which women seemed to float with the gentle fluidity of long-stemmed flowers in the breeze.

That's how my Barbie doll (via my imagination) entered a catered soiree on the lawn of a spacious estate. With one hand holding a tiny clutch purse and the other waving to catch handsome Ken's attention, she was the epitome of summer couture in her flowered sundress. (In the Barbie catalog the outfit is named "Garden party." Need I say any more?)

Some film stars have given the sundress its sex appeal: Marilyn Monroe in *The Misfits*, Deborah Kerr in *From Here to Eternity*, and Kim Novak in *Picnic*. Would Novak's provocative dance with William Holden have had the same effect if she was wearing jeans instead of that off-the-shoulders pink dress? I don't think so.

It is believed that the growth of suburbia had an influence on creating a more casual lifestyle. Shorts and t-shirts certainly make life easier and more comfortable. But I also have a sundress in the back of my closet, perfect for a "moon glow" picnic. It may not be William Holden, but *someone* just might ask me to dance.

Sentiments Are Preserved in the Heart

The large, blue plastic box had been moved several times: from our home in one state to our new home in another, and then from various rooms for storage. Now it was time—a cold winter afternoon—to go through the years of correspondence that belonged to my daughter.

The blue box was a someday task whose time had come. So I lugged the heavy container into the hallway, sat down on the floor, and began going through hundreds of pieces of correspondence one at a time. Emily kept every communication sent to her from about age thirteen—not a surprise to those who knew her.

And she knew a lot of people. There were letters from her eighth-grade pen pal from Australia, postcards from friends on vacation, and correspondence that followed her to college and around the globe. She used to say, "You can never have too many friends."

Of course, it was an emotional review of moments in Emily's life: birthday cards with rainbows and unicorns (that she loved); get-well wishes for a broken arm and a case of pneumonia; greetings from Santa and the Easter Bunny; and graduation blessings that wished her a lifetime of dreams-come-true. Many of these were sent from loving family members.

But there were also many notes from her friends: their anticipation of parties and school events; private jokes they shared; boys they liked (and the girls they didn't); and expressions of encouragement ("Hang in there!"). From her best friends since childhood to the sorority sisters she had in college, correspondence often included heartfelt sentiments of loyalty and affection. Sympathy cards sent after Emily's grandfather died comforted her with the words "I'll be there for you," and "love you." How much that means to an eighteen-year-old away at school!

I recognized my own notes, many of which had been inserted into cards or packages I sent and all addressed affectionately to my "Baby Girl." Each one had a variation of cautionary advice, encouragement, and anticipation to see her again. Some cards contained my husband's handwritten greetings with wishes for her to enjoy herself. And there were cards from my son, uncharacteristically admitting that he looked forward to her coming home soon.

These latter sentiments I would keep, along with the several albums I already have of Emily's mementoes, among which are photos of her with friends and family—always smiling, if not laughing with the joy she shared with them. But it was time to let go of the rest of these from the blue box. I can do that knowing that these dear sentiments given to my daughter will now be preserved in my heart.

Birthday Card Documents Years of Wishes

It began in 1977 with a cute birthday card that my sister, Carol, gave to me. She jokingly wrote inside, "Unsigned. Now you can use the card again." The following year on her birthday I gave the card back with my best wishes and permission for her to use it again. By 1979 we were writing inside the card in a manner that permitted yearly comments while conserving space for future greetings. So began our traditional birthday card.

For several consecutive Februarys, I resurrected the card for Carol's birthday. She reciprocated a few weeks later for mine in March, making me the caretaker for most of the year. Then, occupied with raising our children, the card was forgotten for seventeen years. I surprised my sister with its reappearance in 1999. And, although the card has resurfaced only a handful of times since then, the handwritten sentiments inside make this a shared treasure.

Our alternating exchanges in various inks express the simplest, yet fondest, memories of our adult lives. Early entries referenced events we attended together, celebrations at home or at a favorite restaurant, and some milestones along the way, especially the birth of our children. Meanwhile, the card was kept in a file box I have for greetings and stationery. We even had intentions to start a shared card for our young daughters, but that idea was tucked away in the less reliable file of "good intentions."

Although our special card only appears sporadically, much is expressed in our succinct comments. Carol spent one birthday in Vale, Colorado, where she skied next to a favorite movie star. "Robert Redford only skis with the best," I wrote later. My forty-ninth birthday was spent getting a colonoscopy. "I'm sure the doctor will get to the 'bottom' of it," was Carol's quip.

Life's transitions are noted briefly but with significance. "I can't believe you're thirty!" Carol wrote the year she helped arrange a surprise party for me. Two years later, after a crisis in her personal life, she recorded, "Thank you for all the love and support you've given me."

I was nine-months pregnant with my daughter when my sister first gave me the birthday card. Decades later I used it to record our recent retirements from teaching and relocation to Michigan. The card's back page scarcely allowed room for Carol's final sentiments about moving into her new home across the lake from me. Her last line pays tribute to our childhood memories of all the summers we spent here between the winter birthdays: "Our dream comes true."

That seems a fitting caption for the card that has kept a lifelong wish for two sisters.

Address Book Is a Family Record

It had been in bad shape for years: The tabs were worn, the pages were loose, and most of the information inside was scratched off, written over or simply obsolete. My excuse for not replacing my address book was that I could still use it. In truth, I was a little sentimental about it.

After all, a lot has changed since I first began putting entries into the little red address book in 1984. We had moved to another suburb with our two small children, and it was a busy time getting acquainted with new people and different services. These changes were all reflected on the pages of the book, but the contents hold more than names and numbers: They tell a story—my family's story.

The quick reference list on the opening page is a hodge-podge of services that includes everything from emergencies to conveniences: pediatricians, music teachers, babysitters—most irrelevant over time. But it is on the rest of the pages, the alphabetical list of people we knew during those years, that there has been the most dramatic change. The transformation was certainly not sudden. Every year I altered addresses for friends who moved. We lived in a transient area whose houses had an average occupancy of five years, so that was to be expected. There were common situations of a husband being transferred to another state or a growing family seeking a larger house in a different subdivision. Still, that doesn't take the sting out of losing playmates for your children or saying goodbye to neighbors with whom you had become close friends.

And there are other loses, too—people we had known for years and shared in the experience of acquiring a home and raising children. One family followed a husband's many jobs across the country, moves noted above scratched-out addresses. Other friends had divorced, going different ways that also separated them from us. Another couple had their first child one week after ours, and we cherished their friendship. Though I sadly had to omit the husband's name on a Christmas card after he passed away, it remains on the page of my book as a reminder of him.

Even among my own family, changes are marked in lines that eradicate one address and add a new one. College addresses for my children occupied space in the book for several years, and my son's many rental locations are covered and recovered in White Out. But those who are no longer here haunt the pages every time I open the book: relatives whose names adorned invitations for family celebrations and holiday parties; addresses that are absent from my Christmas card list; and numbers I knew by heart for phones that no longer ring.

No, I can't get rid of that little red address book. It holds too many memories.

County Fair Keeps Fond Traditions

Perhaps it is the nostalgia that brings many of us back to the county fair every year. It hasn't changed much since we first experienced it as children. As with much seen through those innocent eyes, the fairgrounds were a place of enchantment. Its flashing colors and moving parts resembled a giant kaleidoscope. Anything was possible.

One of my first memories of the fair was eating cotton candy. I leaned from my mother's arms to the heap of spun sugar held before my face. The encounter was unpleasant, and I promptly announced my reluctance to eat something that "feels like hair."

I also recall that my grandfather wore a hat and tie for the occasion. He sat on a bench in front of the concession building and watched the parade of strangers wander down the midway. As he mused over a bottle of cold beer, he must have recalled his own memories of fair days.

The women had other interests at the fair. As the last days of summer yielded the final harvest, they entered their prized produce into competition. Whether showcased with leaves and flesh still firm and bright, or preserved in jars of special recipes, the best of their garden crop was displayed as a tribute to themselves and the blessings of summer.

Other entries that celebrated a season of growth were the livestock. For a city girl like me, the barns were filled with wonder. I marveled at the scale of the horses and the girth of the steers. But my favorite animals were the newborns, curled and sleeping on mounds of hay.

The fair was filled with enchantment: the smells of fresh popcorn and fermented hay, the sounds of calliope music and barnyard animals; the sights of colorful arcades and exhibit buildings that beckoned crowds. They are all still there. They were there when I was a child, a time that surfaces afresh each year. I can still feel my stomach thrill to the lift and drop of a brightly-painted horse, a memory revived through the years with my own children. A third generation now grips the brass pole, smiling and waving to the watching adults with each revolution. They are all still there.

So on Labor Day weekend, as summer slips beneath an early dusk, I return to the county fair to recall the wonders that captivated me as a child. That little girl is still there, ascending the Ferris wheel and leaning over the safety bar to glimpse the midway beneath a swaying chair. Music from the carrousel drowns out the voices of the crowd as the spectators blend into groups at the game booths and rides. Some look up with distant, expectant faces at the little girl who is already flashing past them to a place where anything is possible.

Chapter 6

Sass and Sensibility

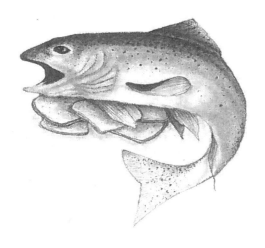

Normal Is Subjective

While waiting for our meals in a local restaurant, I couldn't help but notice the orders that were delivered to the next table. The man's sandwich was too ordinary to remember, but his companion's plate held a unique lunch: a towering stack of unadorned toast. I didn't want to stare, but I did sneak a few glances. No butter or jelly. No accompanying soup or salad. Just a dozen slices of dry toasted bread. Discreetly, I asked my husband, "What do you think of that?"

I immediately realized the folly of my question, but I went on to explain as surreptitiously as I could while he located the jelly and slathered it on his own portion of toast. "Maybe she just likes toast," he mumbled.

"But," I protested, "that's all she's eating. And not even the crust, just the inside. Don't you think that's odd?" He just shrugged and dipped his toast into his eggs.

The real question, however, is not whether the young woman's selection was odd, but why *I* considered it odd. There isn't anything strange about toasted bread. It's not as if she ordered squirrel or jellyfish or—oh, boy!—now I am going to reveal *myself* as the weird one with strange food aversions. Not only do dislike toast, I hate butter. Furthermore, I avoid the traditional Friday fish fry because I abhor seafood. So who's the odd one here? Me, I guess.

Unless you agree with me, and then we're both normal, right? That's the way it is with feeling normal. Everyone else is crazy, strange, weird or just plain odd if they don't have the same tastes, preferences or opinions that you do. Case in point: My husband and I can't help offering critical comments when listening to a politician speak on the television, even though we know it is an inanimate object (the television, not the candidate, although...). If those who hold different opinions than ourselves qualify them as crazy, then even the two of us deserve that label, for my husband and I don't agree with one another, either. But we are used to that and can discuss our differences intelligently. Besides, he knew I was crazy when he married me.

Normalcy tends to run in families. What some people might observe as bizarre behavior is simply genetics to others. So if your brother likes to remove his clothes in public places, that's because hyperventilation is a family trait. So is exhibitionism, probably, but your relatives might call it an "outgoing personality." The rest of us just think you're all nuts.

In fact, anyone who does not conform to your definition of normal is just, well... my mother likes to use the phrase "a little different." We always know what she means. The person could be the nicest, friendliest, most normal guy in the world, but, well...he's not like *us*.

You Can't Use That for *That*!

My son's interest in bugs included grasshoppers, some of which he captured and brought home for my approval. I would stare at the insect whose world was now a few blades of grass in a plastic container that Grant had punched with air holes. I admired his thoughtful gesture for the grasshopper, but, unfortunately, it ruined another piece of my precious Tupperware.

The idea that some objects are not meant for certain purposes is a concept that eludes the people in my family. From digging in the dirt with tablespoons to cutting cardboard boxes with my sewing scissors, my children have shown misguided resourcefulness. I have caught my husband in the act of polishing his car with a bathroom towel. I guess the soft and fluffy texture appealed to his feminine side. But his masculine side received an angry lecture on the stupidity of ruining what had been a good towel. My voice always reaches a screaming pitch when I remind him that, "No, it won't just wash out and look the same!"

That illogical reasoning also prevails in the misuse of other so-called "washable items." I don't care how long it takes to find something in the garage, if you can't find your funnel then change the oil in the car after you buy a new one. Do not use my kitchen funnel. Vegetable oil and motor oil are not "basically the same."

Apparently, I didn't specify that the rule also applies to drinking glasses. While liquids such as milk and orange juice are quickly washed away in the sink, there are some restrictions concerning other things that might be placed in a glass. At the top of my list—and I don't think I'm being oversensitive here—would be rusted tools or corroded metal. It took several washings before I could return a glass to the cabinet after I found it filled with old coins soaking in a solution of disgusting, gray sludge.

Before I am judged as unreasonable, I want to point out the merits of a wonderful invention called the flyswatter. It is designed to kill insects, and it is effective in this intended function. It has no other use as, say, a spatula or back scratcher. So when a fly lands on the table, it should not be smashed with a magazine, especially one that I have not yet read. I may be overreacting here, but I lose both my appetite and my interest in reading when I see splotches of insect parts and blood on the cover of *Better Homes and Gardens*.

That being said, I do make exceptions for emergency situations, especially if an unwelcomed creature enters the house. In those cases my husband has my permission to throw my shoes at a mouse or use the bed sheets to capture a bat. Can't find the flyswatter for that hornet? May as well use that Tupperware lid—it has holes in it anyway.

Thoughts of Retribution Best Left Undone

A general rule of growing up is "live and learn." And though most of us make a lot of mistakes along the way, the consequences and our own moral integrity teach us not to make them again. But what about the grown-ups who never learn—the ones who continue to behave badly and feel they are exempt from rules that govern the rest of us? It's these adults who can really get me riled up, and I find that the older I get, the less patience I have with them. In fact, I harbor a secret desire to personally dispense the appropriate consequences for these adults.

Like when adults use foul language in public, especially when children are present. I don't buy the excuse that swearing is accepted now among adults. I also don't excuse this behavior on the premise that alcohol makes someone who knows better spew four-letter words because his ability to formulate phrases in polite English is incapacitated. A remedy that I recommend is filling their mouths with dirt (a symbolic gesture) and sealing them shut with duct tape (which facilitates listening) while a severe lesson in civilized communication skills is given. Or simply rapping them on the head.

Next on my list are crazy drivers. I'm not talking about the person who innocently cuts into your lane and then offers an apologetic, uplifted hand because he didn't see you. I'm talking about the "dog's behind" who doesn't bother to look before he pulls out in front of you, and doesn't care that you have to slam on your brakes to avoid hitting him—which, by the way, is a tempting fantasy in itself. Instead, you imagine giving him a good piece of your mind, but only after you have tied him up with the bungee cord that is holding his rusted door to his car.

While I'm on a roll here, let me add litterers to the list. There is no reason why anyone should throw garbage out his car window and onto the street—unless he can't tell the difference between garbage and everything else that he has in his life. The fast-food containers that blemish the countryside could easily wait to be carried to a trash can, but these scoundrels have no respect for anything but their selfish impulses. I have an impulse myself. Well, actually it's a creative action that would elicit an immediate and memorable form of discipline. But my husband says that I can't because I would be arrested—even though I explained that I wouldn't use real bullets.

Although I have more on my hit list that fulfills my need for dispensing fanciful retribution, don't worry: I (probably) won't act on these desires. But if I did and I was held accountable for being "still crazy after all these years," well, as the songwriter Paul Simon wrote, "I would not be convicted by a jury of my peers."

Silence Is a Refreshing Change

I awoke during the night with an immediate awareness that something in the house was beeping. At least I thought I heard a beep. Maybe I was dreaming about trucks backing up. I knew it wasn't the smoke alarm, whose impossible-to-ignore, air-raid sound has gone off on more than one occasion to let us know the batteries are low, usually in the middle of the night.

As it turned out, the intermittent beeping was from my cell phone, which needed to be recharged. I wish it would just shut up and let me find out for myself the next time I wanted to make a call. I know that sounds (pun intended) intolerant of me, but the truth is that there are too many gadgets in my house making beeping, buzzing, ringing, or other annoying noises. I also know that most of these sounds are intended to make life easier and more convenient. For example, when the clothes have completed the washing cycle, the washing machine buzzes—the same, annoying buzzer sound that the dryer makes when the clothes are dry enough to remove—and then a few minutes later it buzzes again to tell me that they are *really* dry and it is turning off, disgusted with my lack of attention to the first buzz.

Maybe this wouldn't be so bad, but my husband often confuses the laundry signals with the sound of the timer on the oven, which he associates with eating, therefore setting off his own "yummy" sounds. Adding to this cacophony is Bella's high-pitched whimper in anticipation of her dinner, which she thinks has just been heated in the microwave. All of this, of course, is met with my response: "That's not anyone's dinner. The clothes are dry."

We recently replaced our old refrigerator with a fancier model from which ice and water may be obtained without opening its doors. That being said, the doors are still routinely opened to get the food. But it seems that closing each of these French doors is not done so routinely. I know this because an alarm beeps if the door remains ajar for more than a minute. This also occurs when someone doesn't close the freezer after helping himself to ice cream late at night when the other person is sleeping—until, of course, she is awakened by a refrigerator alarm.

Fortunately, our house phones have a traditional ring, but our cell phones are only distinguished by the music that mine plays and the buzzing sound that my husband's phone makes. In the event that Richard gets a call, it is a toss-up as to whether I go to the laundry room, Bella goes to the microwave, or Richard begins to salivate.

The next time I purchase an appliance, I will forgo all the bells and whistles. Sometimes, silence really is golden.

Women Want Romance for Valentine's Day

As Valentine's Day approaches, men squirm with the burden of getting their special ladies something special. Regardless of how many times you have heard that such holidays were created by the greeting card companies, you are not getting off the hook with that excuse. Not because I am an expert on gifts, but because I am a woman, I will try to shed some light on what women want—and don't want—for Valentine's Day.

Before I go any further, let me emphasize that anything that can be remotely defined as a power tool is not an appropriate gift for Valentine's Day. Even if she is the tree-cutter in the family, you better save the chainsaw for her birthday. Next on the list of non-romantic gifts are household appliances. Most wives don't mind doing housework, but they don't want to be reminded of chores such as vacuuming and mopping on a day that means "hearts and flowers." I know that you just want to make her life easier, but that was too late the day she married you.

Even practical women don't want practical gifts on Valentine's Day. There are two reasons for this. First, society has ingrained in her mind that this is the day when a man shows how much he really loves her. The second reason is less obvious, but it has to do with bragging rights. In other words, when her neighbor gets a delivery of flowers, or her co-worker receives a box of candy the size of the copy machine, she wants something splashy, too. No matter how much you appreciate her, she won't see it that way if your surprise for her is a pizza coupon you stuck on the refrigerator. Now, a diamond ring stashed *in* the pizza is a different story.

The gift doesn't have to be expensive, but it does have to be thoughtful. For those of you who are still wondering why a set of new tires is not an appropriate present on the big day, let me make clear the difference between romantic and merely thoughtful. A three-course meal at a restaurant is romantic; a supply of three-ply toilet paper is merely thoughtful. Tickets to a concert are romantic; bags of manure for her garden are merely thoughtful. Well, you get the idea.

The standards of candy, jewelry and flowers never fail, but you don't have to be traditional. Making her dinner or even making a card with your real sentiments can mean more than a dozen roses. If nothing else, use the popular sentiments expressed on those conversation hearts candies that still say it all: "Be mine" and "I love you." Those words work every time.

Perfect Picnic Is Worth a Thousand Words

Summertime—and the living is easy. Or so it is depicted in the current issues of home and garden magazines. They make elegant backyard suppers ("for eight to ten of your closest friends") look so casual that any fool can pull it off effortlessly—except, it seems, this one.

The articles make the parties seem so appealing. A glossy cover sucks you in with an attractive outdoor setting in which a festive table is adorned with garlands of flowers (that you pick that morning and weave together with raffia). The table's centerpiece is a fourteen-layer cake containing the surprise ingredient of lavender. Apparently, all that garden work is also effortless because the only sweating shown in the photographs is on the glasses of cool drinks held by the smiling guests.

But something is wrong with those pictures—or rather, too right. First of all, all the guests are wearing clothes that just happen to coordinate perfectly with the party's theme of pink roses. Variations of that hue do not stray farther than pink-tinged orange, worn by one female who fashionably poses next to a man who is wearing a contrasting pair of pants in dark pink. I'm not sure what the man in the bow tie is laughing about—maybe he just heard the host tell them that the cocktail table is a "mix-it-yourself-free-for-all." Either that or his tie is a trick one that squirts water.

By now I find myself reading the description of this engagement party. I wonder which couple are the bride and groom-to-be. It could be the *pink-orange* and *dark pink*, but the bow tie guy looks pretty happy. According to the host, the festive occasion began with everyone joining him in a merry jaunt across his estate for berry picking. *Berry picking? Really?* Those women in cocktail dresses and high heels just came from the berry patch? Maybe they brought extra clothes and changed for the party? Were their berry-picking clothes also pink? All I know is that when my husband returns from a morning of picking strawberries at a nearby farm, the last thing I want to do is celebrate. He is so berry-stained, he looks like he ruptured an artery.

I move on to the section with recipes. Sure, I'd like to serve "lemon-thyme-peach lemonade" in a crystal pitcher, but that would mean another trip to the garden for fresh thyme, and I know I would be too exhausted from making a fourteen-layer lavender cake that morning. Instead, I would "save thyme" by making yellow Kool-Aid in my brown Tupperware pitcher. My color scheme would mimic the wasps and ants that eventually invade my picnic. I suppose I could host a sophisticated outdoor party. All I need is the setting of the Biltmore Estate, the culinary finesse of Martha Stewart, and an assortment of attractive friends, one of whom wears a bow tie. Well, maybe next summer.

Don't Heed Signs of the Times

As a child, growing older was affectionately described by well-intentioned relatives as "getting *so* big!" Maturing isn't as cute as it was then. In fact, the signs of getting older can be downright annoying.

I got one of those early signs when I found my first gray hair. At first I questioned what I saw in the mirror. How could that be? I was barely thirty-one and had just given birth to my son. I decided to blame it on him. (As it turned out, he was probably responsible for a lot more gray hairs through the years.)

There are less subtle indications, too. Years ago a teen-aged clerk in a store asked, "Can I help you, Ma'am?" I turned around, expecting to see the older woman he was addressing. It took a few seconds to realize that he was talking to me. That's the way it happens. One day you're a "Miss," and the next day you are offered assistance to your car by an adolescent.

Birthdays don't really count as indicators of aging. You are usually celebrating with people who love you, and they all tell you that you look great. After all, that's what friends do: lie so that you feel good. If you're smart, you'll surround yourself with people who are much older. If nothing else, you'll seem young by comparison.

But there's no way to hide the reality of a changing body. Although I weigh less than I did in my forties, the distribution is a lot more—well, "creative." I adhere to an exercise routine and diet that would qualify me for a spot on the cover of a muscle-building magazine—if I were in my twenties. Unfortunately, that regime is a few decades late and now only has the slow-release effect of a single raindrop sliding down a mountain—which, by the way, is how I feel after my workouts. My eyesight isn't what it used to be, either. I recently spent several minutes trying to grab a stray hair from my face, only to discover it wasn't a hair at all. It was a wrinkle.

Maybe these signs aren't as unpredictable as I thought. My sister is a little younger than I am, and what happens to me usually hits her two years later. I give her plenty of warning.

"Your favorite foods will soon require a chaser of antacids."

"Squinting won't work anymore. Get the glasses."

"The Bogeyman we feared is real. Although invisible, he will grab at your body and pull it downward. His name is *gravity*."

Still, I'm not giving in to the laws of nature without a fight. Besides, I have a powerful weapon against aging that requires no gym, no deprivation and no sweat. I simply *think* young. After all, age is merely an attitude—and I've never outgrown having one of those!

Wireless Means "Connected to Disaster"

All we wanted was to watch television in our new home, but the dynamics of acquiring service resulted in our having to install a satellite dish. A few years later my husband decided to switch providers, and I arrived home one day to find a second dish next to the house. We still get the same stations, but now we can also communicate with aliens via the spaceship beacons in our yard.

We also have a gadget called a "modem" that, when turned on, produces a magic power that connects us to the internet. It doesn't work well or consistently, but it is the wireless option of choice for people like us who apparently live in what is referred to as a "dead zone." Moving here from the city, I naively assumed that power was generated through the ground, and all you had to do was plug yourself into it. Now I know better. It is magic—*bad* magic.

Let me present some evidence to support my hypothesis. I can have a normal conversation with my husband in the car or the kitchen, but if I attempt a discussion while he is watching television, something happens to his ability to think and speak. It's almost as if the television is putting out a type of magnetic field that insulates him from reality. The government may or may not be using high-definition television to deliver subliminal messages. (You don't have to believe it. I'm just sayin'.)

Meanwhile, I'm losing brain cells with the microwave. A chef told me that he wouldn't use a microwave because it changes the molecular make-up of food. Since we are pretty much composed of the same elements as the very dinner we put on the table, couldn't *our* molecular structure also be changed? I mean if there was a crack in the microwave or you stood too close? (You don't have to believe it. I'm just sayin'.)

I read a few years ago that paranormal activity is decreasing because of the increased use of cell phones. It seems that all that wireless activity is polluting the air and making spiritual communications harder. Even ghosts have bad reception.

Power now comes from the air, not just the wall sockets. Handheld devices come alive at our bidding. Sooner or later we all become "connected," but maybe there's a price to pay for this wireless life we lead.

I have a theory that in the future everyone will have a micro-chip inserted into his forehead. No need for money or charge cards. You will just get your head scanned at the store by a robot who will know everything about you from a wave of a wireless wand. It will nod as a monotone voice tells you, "That loaf of bread is ten dollars. You are also due for a colonoscopy."

You don't have to believe it. I'm just sayin'.

Just Push That Button on the Top

One of my favorite lines is from an *I Love Lucy* episode in which Fred Mertz is trying to take a picture of his wife. "Look at me and smile," he tells her. Ethel retorts, "Make up your mind. I can't do both."

Taking good photographs requires more skill than simply taking aim and pressing a button. That's why so many vacation pictures have people with monuments growing out of their heads. As impressive as Mount Rushmore is, a photograph that features the four presidents sitting on your children's shoulders simply does not do justice to either group.

Then there are those who want to get everything they can into a single photo. They're known for walking backwards while directing everyone to stand as close together as possible. The result is a panorama of sky with a tiny group of fused humans in the distance that are later mistaken for a flock of birds.

Of course, close-ups can be worse. My mother's class reunion was captured in an interesting photo some years ago. While her classmates lined up against a wall in a restaurant, the photographer leaned over the table for the group shot. But instead of featuring the smiling faces of the alumni, the photo was dominated by a giant ketchup bottle in the foreground. The classmates looked like they were in a hotdog advertisement.

The reverse can happen when humans block the camera's intended focal point. Shots taken through car and bus windows while sightseeing often reveal nothing more than blurred images behind blobs of flesh. The explanation later is always more interesting than the photo itself. "You can't see it in this picture, but there is a herd of buffalo between that man's elbow and that woman's armpit."

Trusting someone else to take the picture is just as reckless. How hard can it be to operate a camera? Nearly impossible for some—but they seem to be the ones who agree to do it. They begin by twisting the camera like a Rubik's Cube. You offer the simplest direction you can verbalize, "Just push that button on the top." You pose and smile. They look at the camera and shrug. You tell them patiently, "No, the button on *top*." You pose again—but your smile is a little strained this time. They lift the camera, examining it from underneath. With gritted teeth you mutter, "The button on *top*!" After several agonizing seconds they finally snap the picture, immortalizing you with an open mouth as you were captured in mid-sentence saying: "Just push that button on the *top*!"

For many people, picture-taking is anything but a *snap*.

Confessions of a Jealous Canine

Our dog Bella was a little put out when we took care of my brother's dog for several days. After all, Bella is the queen around here, and Carleigh was acting like a princess. This is Bella's narrative about sharing her throne with the unwelcomed usurper:

"I knew when that pup arrived with her own luggage that she was a prima donna. Her humans unloaded a bag with instructions for meals and play. Her toys have names, like a stuffed alligator that she calls 'Gator.' How imaginative. (I named my water bowl 'Xanadu.' I just never told anyone.) Everything, including her leash and collar, is pink. I wouldn't be caught dead with such girly accessories in my neighborhood. (But I wouldn't mind someone telling my mom where to buy them.)"

"Well, 'Her Highness' is in for a rude awakening if she thinks a few circus-dog tricks will get her any special privileges around here. First of all, there is no begging at the table. Standing on your hind legs will only give you a backache, so don't even...wait a minute. What is Dad doing with that piece of meatball? Are you kidding? That's the oldest trick in the book!"

"Sometimes Mom takes me on the frozen lake, and I run to each ice shack. I just peek in each fishing hole and then pee next to it. I don't know why this irritates the fishermen. I've seen them do the same thing. Of course, we can't take Her Highness on the lake because 'We wouldn't want little Carleigh to fall into a hole in the ice.' *Oh, wouldn't we!*"

"Finally, *Wheel of Fortune* is on! That's my cue to cuddle on the couch. Hey! What's Miss Priss doing on my Mom's lap? Playing the sympathy card again, is she? In my obedience class I was wolfing down the reward treats before the lapdogs even hit the floor. And just who took first place in the Halloween bobbing-for-bones contest? I'd like to see a little 'poop-a-poo'—or whatever she is—master that trick! Apparently, no one around here seems to remember my achievements. In fact, they don't seem to remember me at all!"

"At the moment I am trying to get some sleep, and I am not sharing my comfortable bed with Her Highness, no matter how much she cries. Apparently, my mom is not onto her little game. That last whimper was a pitiful sigh that landed her in bed with my parents. Just the way she curled up between them makes me grind my canines. I hope they all catch fleas."

"Post note: Her Highness returned to Minnesota, and things are back to normal. Right now Dad and I have the couch to ourselves, and Mom is cooking a pot roast for dinner. Me? I am getting ready to deliver the saddest whimper you have ever heard."

Favorite Cup Is for Tea and Sympathy

Look, it's not as if there aren't plenty of other cups in my kitchen. From dainty tea cups to hearty hand warmers, there's a selection of receptacles for the drink of your choice. Just don't take my favorite! It has been clearly identified and placed on the right side of the cabinet with an exaggerated amount of space that's separates it from the ordinary mugs that anyone is welcome to use at any time. I shouldn't have to go over this again, but I will.

My mug has a large red heart on one side with the words "I Love Lucy" scripted in white. The other side of the cup has a photo of Lucy and Ethel. There's an inscription on the inside that reads: "It's times like this when you know what friends are for." This mug cannot possibly be confused with those that have a Cubs logo, a birthday cake, or my dentist's name. So why does my family have such a hard time remembering this?!

I suppose you are wondering why I have such a passionate allegiance to a simple piece of ceramic. Well, I do like this cup. Lucy makes me smile. I've had it for a long time, and filling it with my coffee or tea gives me comfort. The cup is like an old friend that is always there when I need it. At least, it should be.

But, alas, it is not given the reverence it deserves. Instead, it is jerked from its position on the shelf (with Lucy and Ethel always facing out), filled with Kool-Aid or Pepsi—*Really? Cola in a cup?"*—and then abandoned somewhere in the house like a…well, like an ordinary cup. There is absolutely no consideration for it being dropped, knocked over by the dog, or left to absorb stains from drinks that don't belong in it in the first place.

Sometimes I catch the culprit in the act. It could be a nephew, slurping away with a mouth full of cookies—or one of the adults, carelessly swinging the cup during an animated conversation. It can even be my own husband, who will drink out of almost anything short of the dog dish. Recently he enjoyed water from something he told me was "a great cup." He continued gulping joyfully as I walked away. It was a soup bowl.

I suppose I could just give in and join them. It doesn't really matter: Lucy cup, sugar bowl, measuring cup, tin can… No, I can't do it! Instead, maybe I should put a lock on the cabinet—or hide my favorite mug in a safe place. Or maybe *I* need to go to a safe place.

Yeah, like England. Now there's a place where tea cups and coffee beakers are given the respect they deserve!

Fashion Is a State of Mind

With two upcoming weddings I planned to attend, I reassessed my special occasion dresses. There was the little black dress that might now be *too* little and the strapless cocktail dress that is best disguised by holding two cocktails. I've kept these items in case the right occasion to wear them again would arise. I just can't imagine what that occasion might be.

More accurately, the occasions are there, but the etiquette has changed. The problem is that people just don't dress up much anymore. I lament the loss of party dresses almost as much as I do the youthful figure I had to wear them in.

I wore a sparkling, sequined dress one night on a cruise and noticed that people were staring at me as I stood next to a grand piano. I finally realized that they thought I was the entertainment and were waiting for me to break into song. That is still better than the embarrassment I suffered while accompanying my husband to a hotel where he, as a school administrator, was chaperoning the prom. The little black dress I wore was short, and the heels I tottered upon were very tall so after watching teenagers sway back and forth under a mirror ball for a couple hours, I was ready for a break. I strolled about the lobby for a while and finally took a seat at the bar. After several minutes I was approached by the hotel security and asked to leave the premises. Apparently, sitting alone at a bar in a nice dress aroused suspicion that I was a prostitute!

But formal attire was once the expected attire at social events. Even at cocktail parties men wore ties and women wore fancy dresses. There was something elegant about holding a martini from an arm dripping in costume jewelry. Music from albums with titles like *Cocktails for Two* played in the background. Trays of canapés were paraded through a room of suits and plunging necklines. Very *James Bond.* Very *Breakfast at Tiffany's.*

When did we lose this form of elegance? How did "casual Friday" become a fashion statement? When did "dress jeans" become a substitute for a nice *dress*?

I fantasize about the days of sophisticated style at a cocktail party. Instead of listening to the pop of beer cans, I will hear the tinkle of ice in highball glasses and the instrumental music of Mancini on a hi-fi stereo. Conversations about abstract art and astronauts murmur through a penthouse apartment. Two men study a painting of a nude on the wall. "It's a Picasso," one says with confidence. "It's a fake," says the other. A woman overhears them and interjects, "It's real." Then, as she walks away, adds nonchalantly, "I ought to know: I posed for it."

I notice my glass is empty and saunter to the bar. A man in a white dinner jacket half-turns toward me as he utters to the bartender, "Shaken, not stirred." The handsome stranger and I share a knowing smile. Of course, he notices my dress.

Feed a Cold, Starve a Fever, and Pull the Plug

How did I get this virus? I didn't even have any symptoms, or at least I didn't recognize them. And I couldn't figure out where I had been that would have given me this bug. It was my son who diagnosed it. "You know, Mom, you have a virus," he said with hands poised over the keyboard. "That's why you can't do anything online." I didn't even know my computer was sick.

I tried to sound more like a savvy, computer-literate woman of the modern age and less like the technologically-challenged product of the mid-century that I really am. "Oh," I said. "I thought so when I tried to view pictures of reindeer and images of naked people came up instead." Then, using a tone that a really hip mother might use, I said, "Would you just fix that, dear?"

Then, with the same tone that his father uses when he doesn't want to waste his time explaining something to me, Grant mumbled a response, waved me away, and proceeded to click away for about an hour. Programs that indicated they were "checking," "starting" or "fixing" something came up so fast that I don't see how he could even focus on what the screen read. "What does that mean?" I would interrupt, but he just gave me that "eh..." response that he picked up from his father.

When he finally admitted that he couldn't get rid of the virus, I said matter-of-factly, "Well, then I will take it somewhere and have the sick part removed."

That's when he gave me the real diagnosis. "Look, Mom, your anti-virus service expired a long time ago, your battery won't hold a charge very long anymore, and your programs are outdated. Your computer is old. It might just be better to get a new one."

I knew he was right, but part of me was thinking that this is the person who might be standing next to my bedside someday making life and death decisions for me. I hope he gives me more consideration than he does my computer. I could just hear him: "Well, her battery's weak and her programs are pretty outdated. Best to just pull the plug."

I dismissed that scenario from my head and replied to his suggestion as much like a cool, modern mother as I could portray in the face of defeat. "I guess you are right. I will get a new computer."

But the other woman—the inept, real me—couldn't help thinking that things were sure easier with an old-fashioned typewriter. All I had to do was change the ribbon once in a while. And any information I needed could be done with a phone book or encyclopedia.

Life was a lot less complicated when things had no strings—or cords—attached.

Favorite Aunt Needs to Make a Big Splash

Being a special aunt requires a lot of love. Being the *favorite* aunt requires a lot of manipulation. It isn't an easy position to attain, and the possibility of slipping to the number two spot is an ongoing threat.

About the time that my own children were outgrowing their toys, my youngest sister was beginning her family. I rekindled my play skills for this new audience of babies and wove my magic spell. Special toys, sugary treats, and scary bedtime stories were my best attractions. My sleepovers rivaled a weekend at Disney World.

However, it didn't take long before I realized that I was not alone in my quest. My sister Carol was also vying for best aunt. As an elementary teacher she had an unfair advantage. She could build a realistic pirate ship out of cardboard and create constellations out of flour and water. My leaning towers of pizza paled in comparison. Of course, the real winners here were the nephews and nieces. Their aunts' goodhearted rivalry provided a lot of attention and fun. Their parents also enjoyed the benefits of two adoring babysitters.

My move to Michigan was accompanied with a promise to continue my role as special aunt. In the winter the children came to ski and sled; in the summer they played in the water along our shore. I always kept a jar filled with my chocolate chip cookies, which had taken first place in a baking contest. When Carol moved into her new home across the lake from me, it was fun to share the children again. Until she upped the ante with something called Splash Island.

There I was, preparing a seven-course potpourri of snacks and planning my scariest bedtime story, when I heard familiar laughter across the lake. I hurriedly got into my kayak and paddled toward the sounds of unrestrained glee. And there they were, bouncing with delight on a large inflatable raft called Splash Island. Even the adults were enjoying the new purchase. If I had known that a plastic water toy could dethrone me, I would have kept that leaky Slip-n-Slide. I could have tied it to the pine trees and told the children it was a giant slingshot.

The echoes of joyful play and laughter subsided with the setting sun. Shortly, they were all at my door, dripping and hungry. "What's for dinner?" "Can we play a game later?" "Will you tell us one of your stories tonight?"

I opened a container of my "Blue Ribbon Chocolate Chip Cookies." They are my best weapon. Nobody beats them.

Special Occasions Have Expiration Dates

A friend asked how my dog enjoyed the treat she had given to me for her. I thought about the special dog bone wrapped in plastic. "She hasn't had it yet," I said. "I'm saving it for a special occasion." My friend looked confused. What, for a dog, is a special occasion?

For that matter, what is the special occasion that justifies anything that I put away for another time? The answer to that is simple: Some things are too nice to *waste* by using right away. There always seems to be a reason to reserve it for a better, more appropriate time. Unfortunately, that time usually never arrives.

I think this condition is more prevalent among women. Men are less concerned about preserving the newness of their "good" jeans. Instead, they indoctrinate every pair of pants with splattered paint so that all of them have equal status. However, women will wait years for the suitable occasion to wear expensive jeans, only to discover that they no longer fit.

Most women have good dishes and fancy stemware that can only be used on very special occasions. However, even Christmas can be a dangerous time for those delicate wine glasses. It's wiser to give old Uncle Charlie the juice glass and keep the heirlooms in the china cabinet. No, the good stuff is just too good for the family, and that includes all of your clumsy relatives.

In fact, a lot of items are reserved for company—the right kind who appreciates the fact that you've been saving that embroidered hand towel just for them. A friend of mine did just that when she hosted our study club's members in her home. The next week she told all of us how disappointed she was that none of us had used that pretty towel. We confessed that it was just too fancy so we opted for the one hanging on the back of the bathroom door. "That," she exclaimed, "was the one we use on the dog!"

Finding the right occasion has kept many things in their boxes. I love pretty cards and stationery, but I have to have just the right person to whom I might send my special ones. After several years I still have my favorites—*I Love Lucy* and Barbie note cards— tucked away, safe from casual use. That affliction also includes ridiculous high heels that will only adorn my feet if I am stepping into the ballroom of a royal castle. I have nightgowns of satin and lace that are just too fancy to wear to bed. (Besides, they put too much pressure on my husband.)

How long will I save something? I imagine that just before my funeral one of my loyal relatives will say, "No, she can't be buried in that dress. She's saving it for a special occasion."

Rainy Day Projects Never Get Done

A windowsill is an interesting piece of real estate. Nothing lives there, of course, but objects can occupy the space for months—even years—with little regard from human occupants. It begins innocently, like putting batteries there until you have a chance to install them in the flashlight. You only remember that they are there when you need the flashlight.

Take the button I placed on the windowsill of our laundry room, for example. I intended to sew it back on the skirt from which it came, but that opportunity never arose. Sometimes, when I was folding laundry, I'd glance at the button and say to myself, "I really should put that button back on. It would only take a few minutes." There's the rub. Although I will set aside an entire day for large projects, small ones are usually pushed aside with the excuse that I can always do that later. Meanwhile, the button remains on the windowsill, and my skirt has a permanent safety pin.

What I need to do is set aside a rainy day for all the little projects I have literally set aside. Like the extra photographs that I need to organize and label. And the scraps of fabric that I intended to sew, and the pieces of wood I saved for my scroll saw, and the craft items for making Christmas ornaments, and the unframed prints that are rolled up in a corner of the attic.

It's not that I don't want to do these projects. I have very good intentions when I set them aside to use later. When I was first married, I began collecting miniatures for shadow boxes. I made a few as gifts and incorporated the tiny objects into Christmas-themed, single-room "houses." I made the last one, an ice skating shack, for my niece several years ago. The problem is that I still have enough miniature accessories for a dozen of these themed structures. I stumble upon them in the basement when I am looking for paint or sandpaper. Yes, I feel a little guilty that all those tiny elves and toys are waiting for another Santa's workshop. Maybe if I have grandchildren someday…

Despite my pattern of procrastination, I have brought an occasional recipe home with me from a friend's. It usually remains in my car for several days before it is carried inside and left on top of the dryer. Although the kitchen is only steps away, the doomed recipe is moved to the windowsill of the laundry room. Then, one day while I am folding clothes, I will see it there and think about putting it in my recipe box above the refrigerator. But that would mean dragging over the kitchen stool so that I can stand on it to reach the cabinet and sorting through the stacks of yet-to-be-organized recipes. Better leave it for now. I'll do it when I sew on that button.

Household Task Is a Pressing Issue

Like most little girls, I loved to play house and recreated household duties that were acted out with toy-sized pots and pans and tiny plastic clothespins. So when I married, I was excited to set up housekeeping for real—with one exception. "I'm not fond of ironing," I told my husband, which he soon realized meant that I would find any reason to avoid it.

Oh, I would iron on occasion, but those occasions were few and far apart. Then I read an article that suggested a method to cut time at the ironing board down significantly: storing pants between the mattresses. That's right, my husband's folded slacks kept a perfect crease while they "slept" in bed. Too bad it didn't work for his shirts.

It's not that I never iron, but I have found ways to minimize my time at this chore. Like waiting at the dryer for that precise moment when the clothes are just dry enough to be wrinkle-free but haven't yet crinkled under the weight of the entire load. I also love wearing a sweater over a blouse, which only necessitates a quick pressing of the cuffs and collar. But my favorite convenience of all time is the miracle of Permanent-press. (By the way, the person who invented this product could have made a fortune by putting these ingredients in a face cream.)

In case you suspect me of being lazy, let me assure you that I can be pretty fastidious when it comes to my home and personal appearance. From the hems of curtains to the seams of a dress, I meticulously apply an iron for that smooth finishing touch. But if I have a choice between a linen tablecloth and one that is wrinkle-free, I guess you know my preference.

Some people find the act of ironing a relaxing activity. I wish these people would "relax" at my house. (I could also introduce them to the soothing benefits of a mop and bucket.)

Maybe attitudes regarding general housework have changed over the years. Most adults don't have the time or inclination to scrub their floors until they see their faces reflected in the shine, and most wives have more going for them than the distinction of having the "whitest whites" in the neighborhood. Frankly, my husband's undershirts are filed in his dresser under the following categories: "Appropriate to be seen in public," "Passable peeking out of a shirt," and "Bottom drawer." This is my own version of *Fifty Shades of Gray.*

By the way, this aversion to ironing is not hereditary. My son takes his ironing very seriously, even pressing his undershirts for a smoother look under his crisp dress shirts. But then, he is a single professional so he wants to *impress.* Me? At my age I am entitled to my wrinkles.

Better to Bite Tongue Than Speak Mind

It was an instinctive habit of pouring the contents of the carafe into his thermos, but the moment the lid was put on, the coffee spilled over onto the counter.

"Oops," my son said, explaining that he was used to making the exact amount for his thermos each morning and forgot about the extra coffee for me. I bit my tongue and resisted adding, "That wouldn't happen if you had a wife."

I'm surprised I have any tongue left after all the biting of it I've had to do. It's hard to be a good mother when I have to dole my advice out in crumbs while I have a feast of wisdom to serve up when the occasion arises—which is quite often, by the way. On the morning of the coffee incident, I had already spent my two-cents' worth by telling him that he could offer that pretty friend of his a place to stay overnight when inclement weather makes it too dangerous for her to drive home. This time he only gave me a strong look, which I guess saved me from eventually telling him that no *respectable* girl would so capriciously spend the night anyway.

It's not so easy being a mother who knows best. But it's even harder not to exploit this gift. I learned when my son was little that my advice is best administered in small amounts, lest it cause an unintentional overdose, in which case he would simply not listen to me at all. For example, "If you did all your homework tonight you would have time to clean your room tomorrow so that you could have your friend over early enough to have him help you pick up all the Lego pieces before he has to go home." (I lost him at "homework.")

I also found that giving an exaggerated description of the worst scenario can ruin a mother's favorite weapon: telling him something for his own good. For example, "I heard of another little boy who wanted to play in the flooded street, too, but then he got sick from the contaminated sewer water and had to go to the doctor and get a shot." Those scare tactics don't have the same impact on a grown son. So I stop myself from saying, "I heard of another carefree bachelor who thought that a good income, nice house, and fancy car were enough for him—until his Corvette broke down, and he didn't have a girlfriend to give him a lift home."

Sometimes I am tempted to express my opinion at a moment when it can be accommodated by that precarious opportunity of "while we are on the subject." Say he is commenting on a nice home-cooked meal that I have prepared for him, and I say something like, "You know who can really cook is that nice single teacher in your department at school." But I say instead, "Don't forget to eat your vegetables."

Sometimes it's best just to bite your tongue before you open your mouth.

Chapter 7

Close-ups of the Heart

Dad's Photograph Albums

The earliest photographs of my father reveal him as a young boy growing up in Norway, Michigan with his parents and two younger sisters. These pictures are carefully mounted on black pages and labeled with silver ink in my father's meticulous printing. His albums continued the chronology of his life as he entered the Navy, married, and raised a family of his own. They document the life I knew, as well as the one I could only glimpse through those early lenses.

Over the years the old albums were stored in the basement, where they succumbed to a gradual decay. After my father passed away, I took his albums from their musty boxes. My intention was to remove the old photos and place them in new albums. I would then present them to my mother as a special Christmas present.

The task was simplified by my father's accurate documentation of dates, names, and places. As I pulled the black and white images from the disintegrating pages, the story of my father's life unfolded in the succession of captured moments. There he was posing in graduation gown, bathing trunks, or Navy uniform, smiling from a world that time could not breach. In another his arm reached about the waist of a dark-haired girl. She looked up at him, smiling. Over and over again—at a picnic, the beach or a dance—I recognized that girl as my mother. The photographs provided a surreal progression from which I watched my parents fall in love, marry, and bring four children into their world. Yet these pictures brought a depth of understanding that words alone could not, as well as a yearning that comes with all that is loved and lost.

My father's picture-taking resulted in a family history that included all of my relatives. There are pictures of his sister's ranch in North Dakota and our smiling faces as we posed on horses or tractors against an endless blue sky.

There are holidays and celebrations with both sides of the family, posing at tables of food or in front of decorated Christmas trees. And there are the pictures of us in everyday life, smiling in bathing suits at the cottage or bundled up in winter coats in the backyard.

My father had specific advice for taking photographs. "Throw out the ones that are not in focus or just not good." He also said, "Bring the camera close to people so that you can see their faces. Years later you'll want to remember exactly what they looked like." I came to know how valuable that lesson was in preserving the images of those I love.

The restored albums now are kept in my mother's living room, where they are easily accessible. The entire family takes them out periodically and revisits my father's past, as well as our own.

Another year has passed without him, and on this day, his birthday, it is difficult to imagine that the man I knew as so full of youth and vitality would now be a great-grandfather in his eighties. I can picture him as he was on so many other birthdays, smiling over a cake into the lens, offering us yet another close-up of the heart.

Account Book Reveals Life of a Family

Recently I came across a record book that my father began when he purchased his first home. His neatly printed account of monthly expenses tells more than the cost of living. It details the life of our family in the house where I was raised.

The first page of the book is labeled on the top line with the address of our first house in Chicago. My parents purchased the frame home in October, 1953, just as my sister was outgrowing her crib in our small apartment. Although I was only three years old, I have a memory of my introduction to this new home. Underneath the front porch I found a toy telephone made of red metal that was apparently left by the previous owners. In my childish curiosity, I wondered why any little girl or boy would leave behind such an intriguing toy. The house itself would be my home into adulthood.

The record book stirs other memories. My grandparents, who lived with us for the first several years, loaned my father some of the money for a down payment. Each month entries revealed my father's reimbursement to them along with household expenses. I see now how valuable this family commitment was for all of them. All I knew growing up was that the house was shared with loving people who contributed to my happy childhood.

The pages of the book tell a story of our house. It begins with the down payment on a new stove. Each purchase had a significant impact on the monthly budget and was identified with an exact price:

"Snow shovel, $2.03;" "Five tons of coal, $85.20." (I can only vaguely recall watching the men shovel coal into a basement window from a truck in the alley.)

The first major remodeling was done in the sloped recesses of the narrow upstairs. Because my father did the construction of new walls with complete rewiring himself, the total cost was only $64.08. Dad mastered his carpentry skills with other projects over the years, including a patio for barbecues, a garage for his antique car, and dormer bedrooms for two more children. Walls were knocked down for a larger living room, and the house was jacked up for a brick foundation and a finished basement. Finally, new siding and a beautiful entrance greeted those who entered over the years.

My father was proud of his home. At the end of each year he wrote the total cost of home improvements. By 1970, the year we moved to a suburb, the total was $7,015. The last entry in the book reveals the sale of our beautiful home and a profit, after seventeen years, of only $1,435.

That figure probably disheartened my father, but I would disagree with its relevance. The love, work, and sacrifice that my father put into our home made it priceless to his family.

Mom Enriches Family's Life

My earliest recollections of my mother, Virginia Mae (Foster) Sundstrom are vivid pinpoints from which the broad backdrop of my childhood was illuminated. Although she has continued to be the vibrant matriarch of our family, her maternal influence was first experienced by me, her oldest child. And those early images and impressions are still clear in my mind.

Decades since I have toddled into her arms, I can see her smiling face as we sat opposite each other licking ice cream cones on a blanket at the park, or as she held my hand to steady me on the sand along the beach. Her eyes mirrored the same blue-gray of the water, her dark wavy hair a contrast to the blond shore. She was striking and lean, her legs appearing even longer in a bathing suit, which she wore often, especially at her parents' cottage. There she swam across the lake with the same strong strokes that marked her athleticism in high school. Still a girl at barely twenty-one, a favorite photo shows her pulling the oars of the old rowboat with her baby girl on the seat in front of her, a scene that she could not have imagined a few years earlier when she dreamed of going to college and becoming a physical education teacher.

She did not pursue that dream for financial reasons, but her future was also shaped by her love for my father, for whom her affection was rekindled each summer of her teen years in Michigan. Their marriage would bring my father to Chicago, a destiny that included their home and four children. The fact that we were a happy family, of course, was the result of two loving parents, but each shared gifts that have stayed with us. Because my mother always appeared to be so confident, we not only learned from her example but admired her, as well.

My mother was proud to have a home and worked tirelessly to maintain and beautify her nest. She was always busy, and I have several images of her doing household tasks: ironing Dad's police shirts; running clothes through the ringer of the old washing machine and then hanging them on the line outside; rolling the wallpaper with balls of blue cleaning putty; and washing dishes while she viewed busy Jeffery Boulevard through the kitchen window. Any boredom that was expressed by us kids was always met with the same comment: "Do something constructive." I have learned to do that to the point of feeling guilty if I neglect my duties.

But my mother also knew how to have fun and created situations from which joyful memories are still recalled. Quite suddenly on a hot, muggy day she would announce that we were going to the beach, packed lunch, and directed us into the car. On one of these occasions she brought paper and water colors instead of sandwiches, and we sat on a blanket and painted Lake Michigan under a cloudy sky. I learned that having fun is often spontaneous and doesn't have to cost anything.

However, money is something for which I have learned a great deal of respect from my mother. Despite a tight budget, she managed to provide us with all we needed while still finding opportunities to give us things we also wanted. New clothes for school were supplemented throughout the year with outfits that she sewed for us. Not only did she make some beautiful wool skirts for me to wear in high school, she also created party dresses for dances and special occasions. And when I opened boxes with a pretty robe or soft sweater or even (and especially) a typewriter on Christmas, I appreciated the sacrifice and love with which they were given.

And there were other gifts, those of time and effort: the birthday celebrations with homemade cakes, the Halloween parties in our basement, the sleepovers in the backyard tent, and the Girl Scout outings with Mom as leader. Our friends were always welcomed into our house, and I learned that home is a place where love creates happiness for all who enter.

But Mom created happiness away from home, as well. Many times she packed the station wagon with food coolers, suitcases, and diapers for a family trip. There she was, cooking spaghetti on the little stove of our "pop-up" camper and hanging towels on a makeshift line—all so we could see the Grand Canyon or the Badlands or wherever she and Dad led us on these wonderful family vacations. She doled out baloney sandwiches and cups of hot chocolate in the car so we could enjoy ski trips in Michigan. With Dad at the wheel and Mom at the helm, every trip was a vehicle for adventure and lessons in life. I learned the value of seeing beyond my little world into the broader one, especially with those I loved.

The greatest gift I learned from my mother was what matters most—family. It meant making the effort to see relatives, whether traveling across the city to visit aging aunts or packing up the car on Christmas morning for an eight-hour trip to see our grandparents. It meant hosting family gatherings and honoring traditions. On St. Patrick's Day Mom's Irish family was treated to a traditional corned beef dinner. In respect to my father's heritage, she also made Swedish meatballs, rice pudding, and *pepparkakor*, all of which were served to both families on Christmas Eve. I, along with my siblings, maintain these customs because our mother showed us how family traditions keep us connected to each generation.

I am fortunate to have a mother who has not only enriched my life but given me gifts that I might share, continuing her legacy for our family and those whose lives she has touched.

Antics Show Humor and Heart

My father became a policeman in Chicago, and he often came home with outrageous tales. Two of my favorite stories reflect his compassion and sense of humor.

The paddy wagon was a familiar sight in many neighborhoods. It patrolled the streets, hauled away drunks, and delivered babies. Ambulances only served customers who paid; consequently, the policemen did a lot more than fight crime. Some of their duties included delivering the deceased to local funeral homes. One of these common calls resulted in unusual circumstances. Dad was driving with a rookie whose enthusiasm for the job did not include "special deliveries." Putting handcuffs on an inebriated punk and tossing him in the paddy wagon was one thing, but a cold cadaver in the back gave the young cop the willies.

In many instances the victims were quickly proclaimed dead and whisked out to the alley and waiting paddy wagon. That was the case for one old woman whose last ride was accommodated by Dad and his partner. The younger man moaned with complaints for having such a creepy burden in the back. Dad commented that, "At least they go along quietly."

Just as he said that, the vehicle hit a pothole that made both men jump, further distressing the spooked rookie. Suddenly a soft groan came from the back, and the two men looked incredulously at each other. Then, as the corpse sat upright, a scream erupted from the young officer, who bolted from the wagon as if death itself was chasing him. For Dad, a veteran, it was just what happens when things—and paddy wagons—go bump in the night and wake the dead.

The other incident shows another side of my father's personality. On most nights of his shift, he passed the same homeless men wandering the streets. Sometimes they slept on the sidewalk or the entrances to buildings. Although most of these men were harmless, vagrancy was a crime, and the police were obligated to get them off the sidewalks.

One man in particular never ventured far from the same corner, seeking shelter between the crumbling brick buildings of a hostile neighborhood. The old man's tattered clothing offered little protection from the encroaching Chicago winter. One snowy evening Dad stopped his police car at the familiar corner and sternly beckoned the old man to get in. Despite the vagrant's frantic remarks that he wasn't doing anything wrong, he acquiesced. Dad drove slowly, ignoring the old man's tearful pleas from the backseat. After circling the block, he stopped the car and ordered the man out. Then Dad reached over and tossed something into his arms. It was one of Dad's coats, one that would see the old man through the winter. Then, without saying a word to the bewildered figure standing at the curb, Dad just smiled and drove away. The memory of this deed would warm both men all that winter—and beyond.

Just Be Quiet and Let Your Father Drive

One of my earliest memories is squeezing into the back window shelf of our 1950 Ford. It was a cozy refuge that afforded me a view of a world that was new and intriguing. My parents assumed their positions in the front, and I slid down to the upholstered bench behind my father. It didn't matter where we were going. I felt safe. My father was driving.

In those days many women did not have a driver's license. But younger and more independent women, like my mother and her friends, did. Still, they usually only drove short distances on errands. Significant journeys like vacations always required a man at the wheel. So my mother, like most good wives, sat on the passenger side of the car and made sure that the children behaved themselves.

And we did, of course. My sister and I were both excited and appreciative of these family excursions, and we sat patiently while watching out our windows. But over the years our backseat became crowded, and Dad eventually purchased a station wagon to accommodate his four children. The rule in the car, dictated by my mother, was always the same: "Just be quiet and let your father drive."

Driving was something that my father did well. From the moment our car left our alley, we trusted that our father's knowing eyes and competent hands would guide us to places near and far. Requiring no more than a thermos of cold water, butterscotch hard candies, and a map ("You know I took a class on map folding!"), he always got us to the right destination. No emergency could thwart his plan. Flat tires and broken radiators simply caused minor delays.

Bad weather only intensified my father's concentration, and, if we became antsy, we were reminded by our mother to "Just be quiet and let your father drive."

Despite all the glorious places that my father took us, I cherish most the *getting there*. Those hours in the car—no air-conditioning, car sickness, squabbling siblings, and bag lunches—were the best of times. We shared the single mission of going somewhere as a family. My father was driving, and we were together and safe.

In the decades since, I have done a lot of my own driving. Of course, my husband took the wheel when we took our own children on vacations. Now that we are alone, I find the responsibility of driving to be just another necessary chore in this busy and complicated world. Sometimes I wish I were that little girl again, anticipating all the new and exciting things that were just outside my window and down the road. Oh, how I yearn for those earlier days when all I had to do was heed my mother's words: "Just be quiet and let your father drive."

Relatives Celebrate the Green Promise

Despite all the "wearin' of the green," St. Patrick's Day often dons a coat of white. At the very least, it is a cold day toward the end of a winter that often just doesn't want to let go. Still, celebrating my Irish heritage in Chicago was never hampered by the weather.

The Irish are a hearty group of people. Their suffering, especially throughout the potato famine years, resulted in mass immigrations to the United States. Some of my own relatives arrived here at that time. The first of them happily served in the Civil War, being paid to take the place of a wealthy man. No job was beneath the dignity of an immigrant for whom America offered a decent life in exchange for hard work.

As long ago as that time appears, it is not so distant that I can't come close to touching it. This first relative settled in Indiana. His granddaughter was my great-grandmother, the "Wild Irish Rose" of our family throughout my childhood. I now realize that behind those sparkling dark eyes was the knowledge of the suffering that her grandparents carried from their homeland. It lingers through the generations as an unspoken reminder of the sacrifices made for freedom. There is a dignity in how the Irish silently carry that burden.

Not that I was aware of any of this growing up. My mother's family, like many on Chicago's South Side, had lost more than their accents over the years. Scarcely a trinket from the old country had survived, and contact with relatives in the Emerald Isle ceased to exist over the generations. As far as my relatives were concerned, Ireland was a distant memory, revived in sad ballads that haunted funerals and neighborhood saloons.

But on March 17 we celebrated being Irish. The city held a grand parade downtown and crowned an Irish queen. Bagpipes played. Pretty girls danced a jig. The Chicago River flowed green, and so did the beer in the local taverns. The teachers put shamrocks on their bulletin boards, and we all wore the color of the day, Irish or not.

St. Patrick's Day was the only time our family celebrated our Irish heritage. My grandparents and uncles came over for a dinner of corned beef, red potatoes, and cabbage. My mother made yellow cake with green frosting and served it with tea. There was no talk of that long-ago Ireland. But there must have been thoughts of those struggles. Even now, I think how much this day in the gray of winter must have meant to those who clung to such a green promise.

Home Was Where Everyone Was Welcome

The neighborhood kids often played at our house when I was growing up. My parents made them feel welcome, and the tradition continued through my college years. Much to my sister and my delight, this list of drop-ins included boys. However, we weren't fooling ourselves about their motives. We had a ping-pong table in the basement—and a very entertaining father.

On a typical Friday night friends congregated in the rec room and took turns with the paddles. But after rotating out, they soon found their way to the other end of the basement: Dad's work area. With his tool bench as a podium and a dangling bulb as his spotlight, he related the outrageous experiences he had acquired as a policeman. No one had a more popular father.

And no one enjoyed people more than he did. It wasn't enough to invite them in the front door and offer them food and drink: They had to be entertained. Whether it was leading adults to a punchline or leading children to a toy, Dad made sure that everyone had a good time. They were also led downstairs for a narrated tour of remodeling ventures, clever gadgets, and antique oddities. Everything had a story.

He was also a good listener, encouraging the anecdotes of his guests with sincere interest. Farewells were always delayed, and return invitations were always extended. One day my father came home and told my mother that he had just bumped into our minister and invited him over. He barely got the word *now* out before my mother—who was in the throes of housecleaning—gathered up the clutter, tossed it in the bathtub, and closed the shower curtain—just in time for the doorbell.

Collections and passions have a way of spilling out beyond their boundaries. When my father bought a restored 1929 Model A, the garage became a new arena for him. The unique sound of that motor chugging through the alley was recognized by all the neighbors. If the garage door was open, many of them wandered inside to watch Dad puttering under the hood. It was as much a conversation piece as it was a mode of transportation. As he spoke of the good old days, he was also creating the best of times from the present.

When I think of my house in those years, it seems lit from within. The lamplights, where so many gathered, glow in memory now. The conversations still echo where my father stood. The shadows encircle him with love. I can still hear his voice. Dad, your spirit has never left.

Dad Shows Taste but Not Discretion

Like most men, Dad loved food and appreciated a good meal. But, as his sense of taste grew keener, his sense of propriety seemed to diminish. Here are some "recipes for disaster."

As much as Dad enjoyed eating, he really was not a good cook. But he did have a flair for creating skillet meals with leftovers. This mix and match method was achieved by taking an assortment of leftovers from the refrigerator and heating them up together—even when they had no business being on the same plate. This unique medley of partially burned cuisine included a chicken leg from Sunday's dinner under a slice of Monday's meatloaf, which was topped with Tuesday's spaghetti. All was subjected to Dad's secret ingredient: a dash of Tabasco sauce.

But he seemed to like the leftover concoctions as much as he enjoyed their individual premieres at previous meals. If they were eatable once, they certainly could be revived in a repeat performance. No food was exempt. Even if it was frozen. Even if it was frozen for several months and looked exactly like the top of a wedding cake that a certain daughter was saving there for her first anniversary. (He ate it as a *very* cold treat after work one night.)

In a worse scenario, Dad ate something that no one should have eaten—except our dog. Despite the image of a large canine on the box, Dad mistook the dog treats for beef jerky (a favorite of his). His defense was that the word on the label, *Pup-O-Roni,* looked a lot like the word *pepperoni.* As for the taste? He said it wasn't bad.

If you are thinking that Dad had no sense of taste, you'd be mistaken. He definitely had preferences for certain foods, many of which he purchased at preferred restaurants around Chicago. Most policemen know where to get the best hot dog, Polish sausage, barbeque pork, and fried chicken. Dad also loved Chinese food and sometimes took us to his favorite places in Chinatown. Of course he had to tease us with his old joke: "Do you know why there are no dogs in Chinatown? …" The answer always gave us pause over our chop suey.

He was also vocal about what he didn't like, and we were all aware of that short list. But, if a new recipe was introduced, he wasn't going to hold back his opinion. Once, when I invited friends to join us for Easter dinner, I tried out a sweet potato soufflé recipe that sounded good. Well, Dad didn't think so. And he let everyone else know it. He just put down his fork and bellowed, "This taste like monkey vomit!"

Needless to say, that was one leftover that would not be added to Dad's skillet meal the next day.

Family Photos Are Out of Focus

You have probably picked up one of those humorous greeting cards on a store display that features an awkward or unflattering photo of someone. Most of them are old pictures that may have been meaningful to the original owner at one time, but to the rest of us, they're just weird. But don't you have some family photos of your own that are—well, just weird?

Getting everyone together for a family photograph is difficult enough, but when children are involved, it takes the patience and timing of a bomb expert to get it done before everything blows up. One of our gems shows three of us smiling, including my ten-month-old son, whom I am holding on my lap. But my daughter, standing next to us in her little sailor dress, is anything but a sweet addition to the happy family image. Her eyes are red from crying, and she has an angry pout on her face that is a result of a temper tantrum she threw because we wouldn't allow her toy in the photo. In retrospect, the bug-eyed E.T. doll was less distracting than her scowl.

I admire families who can pull off a group photograph in which everyone strikes a dignified pose. You know, the kind where even Grandma got the memo and is wearing the same colors so that the entire clan looks like a patriotic flag. My brother and his wife had a similar idea for their family, except they dressed in black. I guess the photographer forgot about the background, which was also black. Consequently, the photograph has a disconcerting effect: while their bodies have completely disappeared into the background, only their heads are visible, eerily floating like the faces of ghosts. Along with their two children, their black cocker spaniel was also in the picture, but we have to take their word for it.

For several years my mother had a photographer come to our house to take pictures of my sister, brother, and me. One of the last professional photographs we have was of the whole family. But that was before my younger sister was born, and it has become a family joke that she thought she was adopted because there are so few pictures of her. Some years ago I made a copy of that last family picture—but with one unprofessional touch. I pasted a picture of a baby monkey wearing a dress and bonnet onto my father's lap so it appears that he is holding my infant sister. Nancy proudly displays that framed photo. Oh, she knows it's a monkey, but you'd be surprised how many people assume that *she* is the baby in this family photograph!

It's funny how family photographs stir memories. One taken in the late forties shows my grandparents smiling with their three teen-aged children. My aunt still remembers when it was taken because she hated her hair and had been crying before it was taken. Ah, memories!

Long Weekend Highlights October

Aside from my favorite fall holiday, Halloween, there was another day on the calendar that made October special. Chicago always celebrated Columbus Day, and we had the day off of school. It was like getting an extra Sunday to enjoy the early autumn weather and peak of color.

Of course, we learned all about Christopher Columbus in school, and his construction paper image adorned classroom bulletin boards for the few days between autumn leaves and jack-o-lanterns and ghosts. One has to be awed by such bravery. I wonder if there were any moments when the explorer doubted himself. Maybe there *were* monsters in the sea that ate ships. Maybe the world *was* flat. Fortunately, he persevered and returned home to a delighted king and queen.

While I recognize the achievements of this great explorer, Columbus had a less than royal reception in our house. You see, I am half Swedish. Leif Erikson is something of a god in my family. Scandinavians know that the Vikings discovered America first. (My Irish side of the family didn't really care who was here before they were.)

Several years ago a tradition of celebrating Scandinavian heritage was adopted by my father's hometown. The town of Norway's businesses and local organizations offered ethnic foods and entertainment. The day was kicked off with a parade on Main Street. It was led by my father, who proudly assumed the role of Leif Erikson. While his attire of muslin and fake fur was designed by my mother, he created the elements that most characterized his hero. He carried a shield that he had cut out of plywood and painted with Viking designs. He fashioned a helmet from pieces of metal and deer antlers. Finally, he brandished a homemade sword. With my brother at the wheel and the top down, my father stood proudly in the back of his 1929 Model A "fiord" that rolled past the enthusiastic crowds.

This festival usually coincided with Columbus Day so our entire family could enjoy an extended weekend here. We left right after school on Friday so that we could get ready for the parade the next morning. Even the little ones walked behind Grandpa, Swedish flags in hand.

My parents eventually retired here, and for several years, rain or shine (even snow flurries), my father continued to portray the Viking hero that is the admired ancestor to all Scandinavians. One year the event was held on an especially cold day, and although my father displayed his characteristic charm, he looked chilled and tired. Just two weeks later, he was gone.

In the years since, my brother has taken my father's place in the backseat of the Model A, brandishing the homemade sword for the little Vikings who wave along Main Street. It is a weekend our family still celebrates, but in honor of our real hero, my father.

Thank Heaven for Little Girls

Some of the children in our family have created humorous memories that continue to make us laugh year after year. One of these situations occurred while my daughter and I were traveling to Michigan with my parents. My father played some tapes that featured music from the forties. Although Emily was only three, she sat quietly and seemed to enjoy the music.

As it grew dark, Emmy (as she was affectionately called) watched the full moon out the window as a crooner's voice sang the song "Moon over Miami." It was not a song she was familiar with, but it seemed to entertain her as our own moon danced along outside. She pressed her face to the glass and grew thoughtful as she listened to the lyrics. Suddenly, she looked around the car with a sense of wonder as the words "moon over Miami" repeated. Still puzzled, Emmy glanced once more at the moon, then at the radio, before she leaned over and whispered, "Mommy! That man is singing to *me*!" My parents and I erupted in laughter. How, indeed, did the voice coming from the car radio know that there was a moon over *my Emmy*?!

Another favorite story involves my niece Kate, who loved dressing up and was especially excited whenever my sister took her shopping for new clothes. On one occasion, despite Carol's guidance toward more practical outfits, Kate was fascinated by a rack of white, frilly dresses that resembled bridal gowns. Her mother explained that these were First Communion dresses, but Kate was determined to have one of these dresses that abounded in satin and lace. Finally, Carol said, "These are for little Catholic girls." Disappointed, Kate paused a moment and then inquired hopefully, "Then where are the dresses for little Lutheran girls?"

A final incident that illustrates a child's innocent misunderstanding occurred with another niece. My sister was waiting in her front yard for the school bus to drop off her six-year-old daughter. It was difficult for Nancy, who was nine-months pregnant, to walk to the corner to meet Katarina. Instead, she stood next to their huge Great Pyrenees dog and waved as the bus pulled up to the curb. The massive but gentle animal stood at an eager attention for he knew that Katarina would soon emerge from the opened door and rush toward them. But on this day Katarina paused on the bottom step to respond to the driver, who called out a comment that even Nancy could hear across the yard.

"Wow!" he said, pointing to the huge dog in the pink collar. "She's as big as a horse!"

"I know," Katarina replied matter-of-factly. "My mother is having twins."

Out of the mouth of babes.

Mother's Day Gift Gives Reason to Smile

Several years ago my daughter gave me Lucille Ball's autobiography *Love, Lucy* for Mother's Day. She knew that I was a fan of the television show *I Love Lucy* and had often watched episodes with me. I put the book aside in anticipation of reading it soon. But just two weeks later my world collapsed.

Our beautiful Emily was in an accident that took her life. Many of you have also suffered personal tragedy that defies description. You will also understand that as a result of this loss, it seemed that nothing else could matter again.

For months I stumbled through a numbing routine. One day a pink flyer arrived in the mail. It advertised a course at the local community college. The class was entitled "I Love Lucy." For the next few days the paper was moved about the kitchen until my husband said, "The class might be good for you."

Further encouraged by my son, who was attending the college at the time, I agreed to inquire about the course. On a bitter cold morning in January, I drove to the school and asked for the class application. The description promised a study of what made *I Love Lucy* a success. Still unsure and hesitant, I suddenly noticed the course number and stared at it in disbelief: *33077*. It was my daughter's birth date: March 30, 1977 (3-30-77)!

Over the next ten weeks I attended the safe haven of the 1950s via *I Love Lucy*. The class presented a background on the show that introduced groundbreaking techniques in early television. We students researched the show's writers, directors and wonderful cast.

But my favorite part was when the instructor dimmed the lights and showed scenes from the best episodes of *I Love Lucy*. Understanding how those comedic bits originated and were executed only enhanced the magic for me.

However, the majority of my classmates were half my age, and they were a reticent audience. Perhaps waiting for a crude punchline or vile insult, they missed the greatness in this endearing— and wholesome—show. *I Love Lucy* endures because it expresses the value of life's precious gift: sharing love and laughter with one another.

Soon after the course ended, I took the book *Love, Lucy* from the shelf. I opened it to the inscription my daughter had written the previous year: "Happy Mother's Day, Mom." Once again, my daughter had found a way to make me smile.

Son Provides Humor

Now that my son is grown, I can laugh at some of the embarrassing situations he created. I'm not sure that he has adopted the same attitude, but, as I continue to tell him, "That's life."

The first incident occurred when my son was still a toddler. One evening I put my two-year-old son into the car and headed to the local doughnut shop. Once inside I set Grant down behind two stools that were occupied by a couple of female teenagers. But no sooner did I place my order when I heard the girls squeal. They immediately whirled around, prepared for combat. Someone had patted them both on their behinds. But, instead of the adult molester they had imagined, their eyes readily fell upon the toddler who was looking up at them. It was my two-year-old, who had merely yielded to a sudden impulse to express his admiration. Although they were disarmed by his adorable smile, I grimaced with a premonition of what *his* teenaged years might bring.

He exhibited the same gesture in a restaurant. I had taken my daughter to the restroom and left my husband at the table with Grant. That's when the waitress brought our food. Standing between their chairs, she leaned over to reach the middle of the table. Grant couldn't resist the opportunity to show his appreciation for the young woman's figure, and she quickly snapped upright with indignation. But, instead of turning to the cherub in the booster seat, she faced my husband with an accusatory look. Understandably, she wasn't buying his explanation that his son liked to slap women on their butts. We ate dinner in a hurry and left.

Not that my son hasn't had his share of embarrassments. He was about eleven years old when a meal at a relative's home brought out his sense of modesty. My sister-in-law asked my son which piece of chicken he would like. Although she repeated the question several times, Grant refused to take any. On the way home we asked him why he wasn't hungry. "I was," he said self-consciously, "but I didn't want to say *breast* in front of everyone."

Another word triggered a worse scenario a few years later when I accompanied him to a medical clinic for some x-rays. My teenager wanted to fill out the information sheet himself at the desk— the pretty, young receptionist might have had something to do with this—and I took a seat. But after a couple minutes, he elicited my help.

"They want to know when my last period was. I don't remember."

I told him to stop joking. After all, there were other people in the waiting room.

"No, really, Mom," he said, annoyed at the question. "I don't remember what time my last period was."

I suddenly realized that my student-son was confusing a woman's menstrual cycle with his last class. I quickly walked over and whispered a brief explanation into his ear.

"Oh!" he said, dropping the paper as if it were on fire. "I thought…"

"I know," I said with as much sympathy as I could while suppressing a giggle.

Grant swiftly took a seat on the other side of the room, where he suffered a long wait. Meanwhile, neither he nor the girl at the desk dared to look up at the other.

My last anecdote illustrates another humiliating experience. This occurred when Grant was in Acapulco on spring break with a group of college friends. He decided to purchase a shirt from a local vendor on the beach. Once back in the rental unit, he unfolded the t-shirt, slipped it on and headed toward the door. His buddies burst into laughter.

"Hey, Grant! What's up with that shirt?"

In that moment Grant realized that what he thought was a man's t-shirt was really a swimsuit cover-up for a *woman*. Needless to say, he took a lot of ribbing for the rest of the week. He ended up giving the shirt to me. Of course, I wear it over my bathing suit.

Pictures Capture Treasured Moments

Family albums highlight moments through the years, but they are not the whole story. When I look at the pictures of my son as he grew up, I fill the gaps with memories.

Some of the earliest pictures reveal Grant as a baby, flailing his arms with excitement at something just beyond his reach (although it seemed that nothing ever was). Later photos capture him in suspended motion as he looks up from play: pushing a toy bulldozer, pedaling down the sidewalk in his fire truck, and mastering a two-wheel bike. Not shown are the deep holes he dug in the yard that were large enough to accommodate him and his toys. I am also reminded of how he constantly wore out the knees of his pants, the toes of his shoes, and two sets of bicycle tires.

There are pictures of him with missing baby teeth and later a chipped front tooth (playing basketball on the cement drive). There's a rock star pose with an imaginary microphone, and later a broken nose (breakdancing in the kitchen). There are several pictures that capture him running around, and others that reveal the various wounds as a *result* of running around. I have no pictures of the emergency room, but we both remember that very well.

A holiday photo shows an excited five-year-old holding up cowboy boots. He wore them on our trip out West that summer. That's when he sneaked off to a corral, determined to ride a horse. He climbed the fence and balanced one leg on the rail while swinging the other in an attempt to mount the saddle-less horse. (We rescued him just before he met his fate in a pile of manure.) There are poses of him making a funny face in a Halloween costume and beaming proudly in his Boy Scout uniform. My mother snapped a photo of him in my father's Navy uniform (worn over his pajamas) and captured Grant's impromptu salute.

In another, the lens caught his impish grin, but I know that he had just teasingly provoked his sister by poking—or hugging—her. In others, when he swam or skied for the camera, I can still hear his voice shout repeatedly, "Watch me, Mom!" But I also know other things beyond the pictures' borders: the hours of practice on the trumpet prior to a band concert; the strikeouts before hitting one—finally!—out of the park; the nerves behind the smile in the prom photo.

Years later the camera captured proud moments of a young man in cap and gown, but it does not show the personal tragedies he bore or the strength he found. Nor does the photo of a mother embracing her adult son reveal her depth of love and pride.

With each year's birthday, another picture will be added to a story that seems to have begun only yesterday.

March's Arrival Is Bittersweet

It seems that most years March lives up to the adage "March comes in like a lion and out like a lamb." The month that often introduces spring-like weather usually has an occasional bout of snow to remind us that winter is still not over. The juxtaposition of these seasons in March has a personal meaning for me as my daughter and I were born at opposite ends of this month.

I couldn't say that *lion* or *lamb* adequately describes either of our personalities, for each of us exhibited some degree of boldness and gentleness. It was in our differences that the allusion to March is most apparent. I, with the earlier birthday, was shy as a child and somewhat wary of strangers. Emily, whose birthday ends the month, had an outgoing personality that drew people to her. No one could resist her charms as a baby, a child or a young woman.

I grew up admiring people who possessed natural talents and was convinced that I possessed none. For that reason, my daughter's achievements astounded me. She played several musical instruments, excelled in numerous sports, and created art in many mediums. She compensated for her few weaknesses by working harder, practicing more, and believing in herself. From Girl Scout badges to college scholarships, Emily proudly earned everything she received. Her self-discipline defined her philosophy that "If you want something, you have to go for it."

While I usually approached situations cautiously to avoid embarrassment or failure, my daughter was nearly fearless in her approach to life. She dove into her interests with an enthusiasm that was dazzling. With a love of the outdoors, she enjoyed biking, running, skiing, and climbing. With a love of travel she ventured to Australia and Europe. While studying in Italy, she often traveled alone to other countries, experiences she told us about after-the-fact because "I didn't want you to worry." Of course we would have, but we were so proud of her.

While my Scandinavian looks resemble the pale colors of winter, Emily's beauty was as brilliant as spring. Flecks of sunshine glinted in her large brown eyes. Waves of long dark hair—that I used to confine in braids—flowed about her face as if lifted by a gentle breeze. Her smile literally stopped people on the street. There was such kindness in her face that children eagerly approached her with open arms. She loved children and planned to become a teacher.

It is been many years since there was a reason to celebrate the end of March, and winter never really leaves my heart. Although spring arrives as a reminder of promises made and broken, March's fierce winds cannot extinguish the candles I light each year in memory.

A Tree's Growth Marks Son's Changes

A few years after we moved into our house in Naperville, Illinois, my seven-year-old son brought home a seedling from school. The tiny tree leaned precariously in the few inches of dirt that secured it to the bottom of a milk carton. "For Arbor Day," my son said. We planted it together beneath his bedroom window. "It will grow," I promised.

And despite a series of dry summers, bitter winters, and the trampling feet of children and dogs, the little plant did survive. In fact, it managed to thrive and grow at a rate that surprised me. Within a few years the leaves of the little tree fluttered outside the kitchen windows, making speckled shadows on the window seat. The curtains I had hung there to block the sun were now aided by the branches of the young ash tree.

Because we lived in a new housing development, the few trees along the parkways were small and immature. Unshaded lawns burned in the summer, except on the side of our house where my children enjoyed their Slip-n-Slide, which was hooked up to the hose and provided hours of wet fun. As it turned out, the water benefited Grant's little tree, too. It continued to grow, eventually providing a lush canopy that also offered privacy.

"Remember when you brought this tree home in a milk carton?" I'd ask Grant while he was playing outside. He'd look up at the tree, smile, and then return to pushing his toy trucks through the grass. Sometimes in the evenings he would reach out and capture a lightning bug from under the tree's branches, oblivious to the new growth that summer. But I noticed it—in both the tree and my son. As time went on, I had to trim lower branches so that we could walk under the tree, but it continued its steady climb upward.

The tree became part of Grant's view from his bedroom window. Its leaves tempered the summer sun and caught the rain and snow with soft, upturned hands. They held the moonlight during bedtime stories and revealed the stars on which wishes were made. Many a storm that frightened my little boy shook those boughs, and many a bird hidden there awakened my sleeping teen. The years passed, each season revealing change for both the little tree and my son.

But time, marked by the growth of that tree, has taken us to other places. Now Grant is beginning a new phase of life in a house of his own, one that will hold memories for his future family. Perhaps he will plant a small tree there so that he might measure, in some tangible way, the growth that roots us in both heart and home.

As Children Change

My nieces arrived at our house for the weekend and quickly settled in. "I made cookies," I told them. But one had already found them in the pantry. My other niece reached for the familiar pitcher of Kool-Aid that I had just filled in anticipation of their visit. They had made themselves at home, and that's just the way I wanted it.

These occasions of being together are infrequent and all too brief, therefore, all too precious. Yet, there are familiarities that we have shared since the girls were little, and they give us all comfort. How we cuddle together on the couch and look at the scrapbooks (and see how much they have grown each year). How we tell stories at night to scare one another (and end up in the same bed with the nightlight on). How we swim, kayak, skate, and ski together (and I pretend I am a lot younger than my body tells me). How we stay up late to watch a movie (and have heart-to-heart talks over cups of hot chocolate).

Children grow up. I know that I will not be taking the Barbie dolls and My Little Pony castle out for them anymore. Nor will the craft box that still contains their earliest crayon drawings be brought out for play. Instead of hugging a stuffed toy before going to sleep, they attach their phones to chargers. But they still get a hug goodnight from me.

Will each of the girls carry the special memories I have of them? Will Annalise remember the fun we had when we took her with us on vacations? Will she remember that it was Uncle Richard who carried her on escalators because she was afraid of them? And will she recall that it was I who reassured her from the other side of the door when she was inadvertently locked in the bathroom of an old building, even as the manager broke the second story window in order to rescue the terrified five-year-old. It was one of many times that she sought comfort in my waiting arms.

Will Katarina remember going to Michigan with me each December for the Christmas parade and decorating Grandma's tree? Will she remember the walks we took and the secrets we shared? Will she remember staying alone with us for three glorious weeks the first summer we moved here? And how it broke all three of our hearts to say goodbye?

The girls are in college now. There will be new adventures for both of them as they become young women. And I will continue to watch their progression with love and pride. But there will always be a special place in my heart for the little girls, too.

Moving Forward with Loving Shoves

My brother and I were riding up the ski hill together on a chairlift when he mentioned a discovery he made a few years ago. "I still have Dad's lift ticket that I found on his jacket. The last time he skied was..." But I finished the sentence for him: "In March of 1995." I knew the date because I skied with my father that day.

The impressive part of this memory is not that I remembered the date, but that our father was so ill that year. That October we lost him. The fact that he skied one last time that March is a testament to his belief that sometimes one must push himself in the pursuit of enjoying life.

I think about that lesson every time I ski. I think about how each one in our family was introduced to this activity that challenged us, taught us skills, and gave us wonderful memories of being together. We still have many of the old skis that show the change in style and technique over the years. My first skis were made of wood with a simple strap and clamp that were adjusted over ordinary snow boots. My sister and I had to share the single pair of skis, and we took turns on the bunny hill, practicing the snowplow technique that Dad had showed us.

There are photos in our family album of my mother's early attempts to ski when she was a teenager. The black and white images of a young woman laughing and reclining over a pair of crossed skis were taken by my encouraging father. Those images would be repeated over the years by each of his children as Dad put us onto the slopes for the first time. Eventually, we got the hang of it, inspired, no doubt, by the graceful silhouette of our parents on a distant slope.

But the most cherished aspect of these skiing memories is being together as a family. That was a priority of my father's, and he made it happen whenever he could, especially when we visited our grandparents in Michigan. But there were also times we drove long distances in the station wagon and stayed in motels. I know now what my father had to sacrifice to give us these ski trips, as well as how happy it must have made him to share this activity with all of us.

I thought of all this as I slid off the chairlift with my brother, and we joined my two sisters for the final run of the day. John led the way with a swaying motion that resembled that of my father's. We followed: first Nancy, the youngest, who used to toddle after Dad on tiny skis; then Carol, my bunny hill companion so long ago; and then I, the oldest, always keeping the others in sight. And now, as the afternoon light made long shadows of the pines, our four silhouettes wove across the snow, retracing the indelible tracks left by our father.

Family Continues Going Home

Change is inevitable in large families, but moving away from relatives can be especially difficult. I am fortunate that my siblings and I settled near our parents. We could summon each other with a phone call, and my parents were used to seeing us and all of their grandchildren frequently. So when they decided to move to Norway, Michigan, it was an emotional ordeal for all of us.

Although returning to live in his hometown had always been a plan of my father's, much had changed in the forty-five years since he left. For one, his parents and most other relations were now gone. While it is true that there were still people in Norway who remembered him, in a sense he would be starting over again as he had when he left for the Navy and eventually settled in Chicago. Of course, my father had returned to his hometown frequently over the years, but living there would be an adjustment, especially being so far from his children.

"I just hate to leave all of you kids," he told us. I reassured him that all of us would visit often. And we all kept that promise. Holidays, vacations, long weekends—we saw each other throughout the year.

When Richard and I retired from teaching, we built our home at Hamilton Lakes, just minutes from Norway. As I drive from the lakes through town, I often think of my relatives who made the same excursion over the years. With one set of grandparents in town and the other at the cottage, I went back and forth between two places that both felt like home to me.

It did for my siblings, as well. Carol moved across the lake from us a few years after we did, and my brother and his wife are retiring to the home they just built near us. Nancy will join us here at Hamilton Lakes in a vacation home that will, undoubtedly, be filled with her large family throughout the year. So, as my father used to say, "We all come home to roost."

Home was important to Dad, and this was expressed in a special request. He asked my daughter to design his gravestone with the following depiction: the back of his antique car heading toward the horizon with a setting sun. Underneath would be the words "Going Home." Of course, Emily's drawing met with his approval, and he smiled with satisfaction that this final expression would serve as his lasting epitaph. A year later Dad would pursue that other "home," but his family still feels his presence here where he grew up and returned throughout his life.

When I think about the sacrifices that my father's parents made to come to this country from Sweden and leave loved ones behind, their strength amazes me. Many of their siblings eventually joined them here. Their joy of being together was best illustrated in an old photograph that shows my grandfather surrounded by his brothers and sisters who were playing musical instruments, singing, and laughing in their impromptu family band. Most of them remained in this area, and their children grew up in the same small town with their cousins. Although some made their eventual departures to live elsewhere, a distance bridged by letters, the cousins remained close to one another.

But the stretch of that physical distance can strain the ties that bind. When our children were young, they and their cousins played in each other's yards, shared birthday celebrations, and opened presents together every Christmas Eve. They see each other far less frequently, of course, now that they are grown, and there have been relocations due to college, jobs and marriage. Fortunately, most of them now reside in the Chicago area.

Each of my nieces and nephews has a special place in the family, as well as in my heart. It seems only yesterday they were all children. I can see Kate giggling with my daughter in the backseat—or anywhere they were together; Allison making crafts at the kitchen table, long before art design became her career; Lee, who refused to take off his shoes at the pool but then tumbled in with all his clothes on as calmly as he now deals with finance at a bank. Douglas, always wiser than his years, now shares his wit with students who, no doubt, appreciate his sense of humor. James was the little boy we indulged with late night movies and scary stories—a background that is not unlike what he may encounter now as a lawyer. Katarina and Annalise were the little girls sprawled on the floor with Barbie dolls and My Little Pony Castle. The twins were always running—Rutger in one direction and Gunner in the other—but they have found their own paths as they approach college.

In a way, we are all still children, attached to the family that may be near or far, but always with us. Siblings and cousins are the slender roots that inevitably find their own routes. But the strongest roots are those from which they grew. With love to ground them, they might nurture the connections they share in their ever-spreading family tree and, in one way or another, continue *going home.*

Chapter 8

The Creek Never Freezes

Winter Walk Ends with Icy Plunge

When the Ides of March arrived, the ice was thinning along the shore, and I knew I had better beware and end my snowshoe ventures on the lake. I also knew better than to walk on the big creek that flows into the lake. Even in the coldest part of winter, its deep springs keep this water open.

Still, rumors of a beaver dam on this creek piqued my sense of adventure, and I took Bella with me to check it out. The lake's shoreline was precarious so I crossed through the wetlands, taking heed of where I stepped. The ground is essentially made up of tiny "islands" surrounded by water. One misstep can send you into a hole of water, some of which are very deep. Now that it was winter, these islands were encircled in ice. It crackled under my boots where I had to make longer strides. Soon I was jumping over the distances to make a sound landing on the next tuft. When I got to the creek, I balanced myself on the bank's edge and scanned the water. Uninterested, my four-footed companion leaped off into the brush.

I leaned out so that I could see where the mouth of the creek fed into the lake. There was a narrow trail of flowing water where the ice had opened, but no beaver dam. I then turned my head in the direction of the creek itself. A thin glaze revealed the bubbling water beneath, but the deepest parts, swelling from underground springs, remained hidden. Although the winding creek only afforded a limited view, I craned my neck in an effort to see any trace of a dam. Satisfied that there was not, I turned for home. But the abrupt move made me slip onto the creek's ice—and I broke through instantly.

The plunge caused me to scream, but it was futile as I knew that no one would hear me. The water was already up to my chest, and I could feel my boots filling up as I sunk lower into the muck. Bella appeared, her head lowered with fear. As the icy water penetrated my clothes, I was imprisoned by their weight—a realization that terrified me. But as the water seemed to rise around me, I reached desperately toward the bank.

Finally, I managed to grasp the tips of tall brush that peeked out above the snow and with painstaking effort was able to very slowly pull my legs upwards. Eventually, I secured enough leverage to crawl onto an island. Despite my panic, I trudged gingerly back across the wetlands for fear of falling through again. Home seemed so far away.

When I finally reached our yard, my husband spotted me. I shivered as he pulled the heavy boots from my frozen feet. My clothes, stiffened by ice and mud, clung painfully. A hot bath thawed my body, but a cold lesson left its mark: The creek never freezes!

Planting Trees Is Digging for Trouble

Some of the skills I have acquired come from a tedious process of trial and error. This has certainly been true for planting and caring for trees. However, I think I now have the formula, and I'd like to share my steps for acquiring and planting a tree.

One: Take your husband with you to a nursery to buy tomato plants. Comment to your spouse how beautiful the trees for sale are and how wonderful one of them would look in the front yard. Offer positive images of a green canopy of shade and privacy. Do not mention the word *raking*.

Two: Take the tree home right away so that your husband doesn't have time to think about it. Say things like, "Of course it will fit in the trunk of the car." On the way home compliment his driving skills in order to keep his mind off the appendage that is extending an additional ten feet beyond the car bumper.

Three: Plan where to put the tree before he starts digging. If you change your mind and fill in the hole while he is taking a break, he may come back and notice. My experience is that most husbands who do a job they don't want to do usually like it even less if they have to do it twice. I'd advise learning to like the tree where it is originally placed. However, if you really can't abide the location, just tell him that the hole is too close to the electric or gas lines.

Four: Have the phone numbers ready for emergencies with the electric and gas lines—and phone lines, television cable and underground sprinklers.

Five: Have the correct tools. A shovel is the obvious necessity, but not the only one. In our case, anything from a pick axe to dynamite is appropriate. Once the rocks are removed from the hole, the remaining sand will not be enough to cover the roots of the tree.

Six: Add black dirt. This is a substance that comes in bags from other states.

Seven: Add mulch. This is another substance that also comes in bags from other states.

Eight: Stake the tree. Pound metal posts into the ground and lasso the trunk as if it were a wild bronco. Apparently, trees like to escape in the wind.

Nine: Mark the tree by covering the trunk in white paper or by placing a sign next to the tree that says something definitive like "Tree." Otherwise, your husband will knock it over with the riding lawn mower or cut it down for this year's Christmas tree.

Ten: Water and fertilize the tree for one year. If it is still alive next spring, you have won. If not, take your husband shopping for more tomato plants.

Unlikely Hero Answers Call for Help

The lake seemed quiet that afternoon in July. I was gone for the day, and my husband had just given Bella her dinner and settled into his favorite chair. Yet, even with the noise of the television and the distance of the lake, he distinguished a voice calling from the water. Richard opened the door and listened. Someone was shouting, "Help!"

Richard hurried down toward the shore and spotted a speedboat in the tall weeds. It was empty, but a voice from afar now targeted him in a desperate plea. He scanned the lake and could just make out a head bobbing above the water. Richard considered the distance to the middle of the lake and knew he had to move quickly: The man was drowning.

The only boat we own is a kayak, an unwieldy vehicle for rescue. With few people on this undeveloped part of the lake, there were fewer options for help. Richard rushed along the shore and activated his only choice, our neighbor's old rowboat. Richard knew that the oars were in their boathouse and ran to get them. With some effort he flipped over the heavy boat and dragged it to the water. All the while, the heart-wrenching voice urged him to hurry.

Crisis often calls upon the unlikely hero. When Richard first spotted the man, he hoped that someone more qualified—younger and faster—was already en route. Instead, he was the victim's only chance. His heart pounded as he rowed against the challenge of a strong wind. He checked his progress over his shoulder and then pulled mightily on the oars. Finally, he was close enough to see the man, who was slipping beneath the waves as he choked out, "I can't hold onto him much longer!" Clinging frantically to the man's neck was a small boy.

Their efforts in the water had depleted their strength to the point of exhaustion. Richard was able to hoist the young boy into the boat, but the man, who was too weak to lift himself, could do no more than hold onto the side. Richard rowed as best he could while periodically glancing at his desperate passengers. Both the man and the boy threw up multiple times, expelling more water than Richard thought humanly possible. Still, the man repeatedly told him, "You saved our lives."

It was a slower journey back to the shore. The man's story unfolded as they rested on the dock. They had been swimming when their unanchored boat got away from them. Attempts to swim to shore failed when the child panicked and both of them grew exhausted. They were moments away from tragedy when Richard appeared.

On an ordinary day another boat might have come along, or someone else might have heard the shouts for help. But on this day, as Richard puts it, "It's almost as if that call was for me." Unlikely hero or not, he feels proud to have answered.

Shirt Optional in Short Race

I don't claim to be a runner because I am not. What I am is someone who accepts something before I know what I am getting into. In this case, it was my brother-in-law's suggestion that we do a simple two-mile "fun run" together for a town fund-raiser.

My second mistake was made while registering for the race at the local bank. I quickly scanned the form, ignoring the specifics for the 10K race. Although it sounded cute—like the fancy steps of a square dance—I was not fooled by metric terminology. The only way I could finish a six-mile race would be if I was driving a car. The two-mile race seemed closer to my low expectations so I checked that box on the form. Next to it, in parentheses, were the words "No shirt."

I have a habit of speaking some of my thoughts out loud, and, unfortunately, this was one of those occasions. From the counter in the middle of the bank, I projected the rhetorical question, "Why can't I wear a shirt when I run?"

As soon as the words left my mouth, I realized my stupidity. But, if there was any doubt, the echoes of laughter from the bank tellers were a strong indication of my misinterpretation. What the phrase meant was simply that racers in the two-mile race would not be receiving free shirts. 10K participants would. Oh.

That was okay. Instead of purchasing a shirt with the race logo, I decided to wear my *I Love Lucy* shirt. Although the numbered patch I was given had to be pinned over part of the Vitameatavegamin logo, I still felt Lucy's power. Wait a minute. Didn't she usually screw up and make a fool of herself? Too late. A gun was fired, and everyone started running.

My feet were moving, but everything seemed to be in slow motion. The serious contenders disappeared in a blur of shiny spandex. Some teenaged girls gossiped beside me and proceeded up a hill. *Hill?* It's funny how I never noticed that the town was built on a mountain range. I considered getting down on all fours and crawling when some children bounded alongside. *Oh, no! I have my pride!*

I must have run out of air after the first mile because everything was a little hazy after that. When I crossed the finish line, someone shouted out my time: nineteen minutes and some-odd seconds. I thought they were guessing my date of birth. Either way, I felt like a winner that day—or, at least a survivor.

Superstitions Follow Us from Childhood

Do you remember believing that if you dug a hole deep enough, you'd come out on the other side of the world in China? I have a suspicion that parents used this warning to keep their kids from digging up the yard, but the myth plagued me for years, even after I understood the impossibility of such a feat.

What is not easy to explain is that I still have an aversion to digging deep holes. I no longer believe that a Chinaman will poke his face up from the bottom of my post hole, but I experience a bit of anxiety with such projects because I'm not sure just what I'll find down there. From what I've read about archeology and what I've seen on television, the earth holds a lot of secrets just beneath the surface. That is exciting for some people—buried treasure, valued artifacts, etc.—but I'm afraid I'll find something I don't want to see— like a human skull. Maybe it's best just to leave the past buried.

In a similar way I fear "black water." Although I can swim like a fish, I don't like being in water that is so deep that I can't see the bottom. With my feet lost from sight in the shadows, I am less afraid of what I will find than I am of what will find *me*. Fictional accounts of water creatures and ghosts influenced me as a child, and I always imagined there were unearthly faces floating among the ambulating seaweed.

These superstitions are silly, really. Grownups are supposed to be adept at separating myth from reality. For example, I am confident that I can swallow as many watermelon seeds as I want, and I will not ever grow the fruit itself inside any part of my body. I know that gum will not stick to my ribs, and that colonies of spiders cannot take up residence in my ear (at least, I hope not).

Still, the lines between fact and fiction aren't easily distinguished when they are associated with dangerous outcomes. Whether it is true or not, I avoid waving my arms about in the dark on a summer night because my grandmother told me that this action beckoned bats, who gravitated toward movement. When they entered our lake cottage, she drove them outside by shaking a broom and guiding them towards the porch. But there were nights when my sister and I would lie in bed listening to the ominous squeak in the wall. We were sure that one had come in through the chimney again. We dared not move lest it fly at our heads.

That was a long time ago, but even now I don't tempt fate. I have had to dig some pretty deep post holes, but I don't keep my hand down one of those tunnels very long—just in case an arm in a kimono sleeve reaches up to grab me!

Auctions Indulge Guilty Pleasures

There is something about an auction that appeals to one's sense of adventure. You may not need or even really want a particular object, but when the bidding starts, a sense of competition rises in your greedy soul. ("That woman already outbid me on the antique dishes. She's not getting the chamber pot, too!") Hence, I ended up buying eight garden gnomes, seven Smurf glasses, four dilapidated chairs, and one plywood boat.

As my father would say, "You get what you pay for." He was right, but that never stopped him from bringing home some small treasures from garage sales or auctions. Most of his guilty pleasures were tools, but his biggest purchase was an old tractor. The appeal was in its antique charm and the fun of driving it while a grandkid sat beside him. Mom soon convinced him that the tractor wasn't safe. Eventually—and reluctantly—my father sold it. Was it worth having that tractor at all? I have a photo of my beaming son at the wheel that proves that it was.

My husband, on the other hand, wasn't beaming when he saw the chairs I bought at a recent auction. I assured him that they were going directly to the community theater's storage building for a play I would be directing. He grumbled only a little as he forced them into the trunk and backseat of our car. They were only ten dollars," I said as cheerily as I could before adding quietly, "And the gnomes can fit in the front seat with us."

The boat required a little more convincing. To be honest, I wasn't sure why I bought it. But this little wooden boat had a pretty blue interior, a certain charm, and a low starting bid. Besides, there was someone bidding against me, and that really fueled my sense of competition. So, for only ninety dollars I became the owner of a boat. My sister approached me just as the deal was sealed. "I was only gone for ten minutes!" she said. My retort: "That's all it took."

It also required my husband, nephew, and neighbor to carry it to the water. From there I rowed it to the boat landing. Then they wrestled it onto a trailer so we could get it home. It also took me two hours to scrub it clean (it had been stored for thirty years). It was at this point that I made a crushing discovery: The wood along the keel had rotted, and I could literally push my fingers through the bottom of the boat! I guess a ninety-dollar boat is *a ninety-dollar boat.*

But even this old boat would see another life. My nephew turned it into a bed for a nautical-themed bedroom. So in addition to my ten-minute ride on the lake, the boat was worth the price. Did I also mention that I bought an old motor? Of course it doesn't work, but it will be adorable as a conversation piece. Just ask my husband!

Attraction to Golf Is All in the Head

I have always been attracted to ball games. I mean that literally: My body is a magnet for balls. Since childhood, every type of game involving a ball, from ping-pong to softball, has made an impression on me—usually on my head. So when my girlfriends encouraged me to play golf, I wondered what type of helmet I could wear.

I duck, I dodge, but the balls find me. Some people behave as if they are the center of the universe; my body actually functions that way. Even as a spectator I possessed a gravitational pull equal to that of the moon. I tried to enjoy softball in high school, but I couldn't take being the recipient of the homerun hits to my forehead. Golf balls may be small, but so are bullets.

To be honest, my fear of playing golf goes beyond my propensity for flying objects. I am not naturally athletic. I still cringe when I think of my tennis teacher calling me up in front of my college classmates as an example of how *not* to play the game. At least I am a good sport. Maybe that's why I agreed to try golf. But first I needed lessons. If nothing else, I would learn the proper duck-and-cover technique.

My golf instructor was a young man who was patient and optimistic. I attributed that to his having a minimum of experience teaching middle-aged women, but I was wrong. He knew exactly how to translate a complicated game into the logical steps that even I could understand. There's an advantage to starting out with absolutely no clue about the game: You can only get better. I arrived at the first lesson with an assortment of clubs that my mother had acquired decades ago. My instructor laughed at the vintage set and said, "I'm an expert player, and even I couldn't hit a ball with these things." So, of course, I bought a new set of clubs. (I admit that my selection was based on the pretty, pink golf bag.) There was no going back now.

The first lessons seemed a little overwhelming with so many different things to think about at the same time. There is something sobering about having a man half your age put his hands on your hips and tell you that you are moving them wrong. While I was assured that the process would become more natural to me, I wrote all the instructions down when I got home so that I could practice in my own front yard. Soon I was encouraged to "get onto the course and play."

It wasn't the game that caused my anxiety so much as the course itself, a beautiful vista of green that was lined with large oak trees, like bumpers on a giant billiard table. It would only be a matter of time before I or someone else would hit one of those bumpers and send the ball flying into the number one pocket of my head. Maybe I *would* wear that helmet, after all.

Yard Work Creates Quite a Buzz

If my husband hadn't been using the weed trimmer, I might have been able to hear a warning. But I was cutting brush and didn't hear the forthcoming doom under my feet. The first sign came from three simultaneous stings. All I could do was run.

Of course the wasps followed. I dropped my tool in the marshy undergrowth and leaped along the shore; they followed. I sprinted down our long pier and up the path; they followed. I huffed up the wooden steps in our yard and raced across the patio; they followed. However, they weren't fast enough for the door, and I slammed it shut and ran for the bathroom.

"Antihistamines," I gasped as I opened the medicine cabinet. I was temporarily distracted by the assortment of remedies before me. *Why do I have all these packages that look alike?* Sinus congestion (expired), stomach acid-reducer (empty), anti-diarrhea tablets (for my dog). Ah! Allergy pills! Two kinds: drowsy and non-drowsy. I contemplated for a moment. I might feel better if I took the drowsy pill and calmed down. On the other hand, what if I go into anaphylactic shock and don't recognize the symptoms because I'm too sleepy?!

I went with the latter choice and gulped it down with water like a rapid dog. I checked my tongue in the mirror every twenty seconds until I was convinced it wasn't swelling up. Just in case, I decided that I could use a second opinion. The sound of the trimmer told me that my hasty departure had not alarmed my loving husband enough to stop working. I needed to retrieve my tools anyway so I headed back outside. But just as I got to the path, one of the killer wasps—who was obviously waiting for me behind a pine tree—zoomed over my head with vengeance. My scream elicited a response from Richard. "It's probably just a fly."

For the second time I raced to the house in a panic. Once inside, I threw off my clothes and headed for the bathtub. Maybe the water would sooth my stings. It was then that I noticed a rash developing under my arms. By the time Richard came in, the hives had spread to my back and stomach. His remedy for every ailment is ice and, despite my protests, rolled ice cubes over my blotchy skin. When I could bear it no longer, he went off to check one of his medical dictionaries and returned with a diagnosis: "You are having an allergic reaction." Whereupon he closed the book and asked, "Can you make me a sandwich?"

The hives subsided after a couple hours, but I looked like a freak show attraction ("See woman with bear paw and elephant knees!") As much as I feared being stung again, I knew I would eventually have to face going outside. But next time I would be armed—with Raid!

The Plot Thickens in "Operation Sting"

I may be overly sensitive about bees after my run-in with them this summer, but they seem to be up to something again. This is the conversation I heard between two wasps that were buzzing outside my window yesterday. (Yes, I am fluent in the many dialects of *insect*.)

"I don't know why you're still carrying a grudge against that woman. It was her husband who opened fire with that spray can of poison."

"Don't remind me. Several of my cousins had to relocate after that cowardly attack. However, the woman was the instigator.

She bought the spray. And don't forget that she's the one who went snooping around where she didn't belong in the first place."

"Yeah, but she paid dearly for that, didn't she? Fair is fair." (His laugh is devilish and sounds more like that of a mosquito.)

"What's fair about chemical warfare? And keep it down; you sound like a mosquito."

"I don't know. This sounds like a swarm job, not a simple hit-and-run by two middle-aged drones. I could lose my stinger—or worse. I ain't gettin' any younger, you know."

"Tell me about it! I haven't been in a trash can for weeks. I still take my wife to an occasional picnic or barbeque, but I'm getting too old for all the crowds and noise. I've even lost my enthusiasm for dog poop."

(Buzzing in agreement) "Been there, done *that*."

"When we moved in here, it was a quiet neighborhood. A few yellow jackets, but they pretty much stayed in their own colony. Then these humans built a house and, well, there went the neighborhood. No tolerance for a simple hive in the eaves, and heaven help those of us who live underground! Well, I've had my last mouthful of pesticide! We've got to defend our homes."

"That's what the patio ants said before their houses were washed out with a hose!"

"Quiet! She's quick with that fly swatter. Now, when she comes outside in that swimsuit with the big flowers on it—as if that alone is not asking for it—you attack her thigh."

"Why do I always get the thigh? I hate thighs."

"Because I'm going for the throat. Just a quick sting and then fly away fast. I'll be right behind you. Good luck."

"All right, one last time. I'll be glad when fall is over and we can just hibernate."

Family Takes the Plunge

I could blame the fall mischief on the warm October weather when my siblings and their spouses assembled along our pier to admire the reflection of autumn leaves on the lake.

Suddenly, my sister Nancy said, "A while ago I had half a mind to go swimming. Now I have three-quarters of a mind to do it."

As startling as this remark was, we are all well aware that, as the busy mother of five, Nancy does not even have three-quarters of her mind functioning most of the time. She was confusing the second week of October with the beginning of August. Nonetheless, the challenge was set for her two sisters.

Now, I am not one to back away from an outrageous proposal. Not long ago I skied in my bathing suit, and there was also the sunny Thanksgiving several years ago that prompted a few of us to ice skate in our bathing suits. My mother, Carol and I posed like the Rockettes for a photo that I made into Christmas cards. Under our picture was the caption "Cellulite on Ice."

So it only took a few seconds for me to join and—pardon the pun—follow suit. I loaned swimsuits to my sisters and niece, and we soon formed a procession into the water. My brother cheered us on from the shore. It was alarmingly colder than we anticipated, and the four of us held a brief debate as to whether it was better to enter by slow degrees or simply go for a quick plunge. Since our legs were already numb, we went for total submersion at the count of three.

Our shrieks could be heard down the lake, and a neighbor emerged to see what wild animal might be devouring the geese. We invited him to join us, but *crazy* was the only word of his reply that we could hear. By then we were giddy with a tingling sensation as we dog-paddled in a circle. When my niece announced that she couldn't feel her arms anymore, Carol cautioned us that we were courting hypothermia and could end up like the passengers of the Titanic.

The exuberance dulled as we dried off. My brother reminded us that our Scandinavian relatives routinely dove into ice-covered water before entering a sauna. But I am also Irish and was suddenly craving a hot beverage with a shot of whiskey.

We ended the day with a blazing bonfire, but a slight chill could not be dispelled. As exhilarating as this October dip was, I'm just grateful that my sister didn't propose it in December!

A Unique Emergency Kit

There have been many legendary incidents about travel mishaps that stick in our minds. You know, the ones where a car veers off a bridge and the only way the driver can save himself is to remove his prosthetic arm and use it to break the window. Or a couple whose vehicle stalls in a remote area survives for days by rationing old French fries they find under the seats.

My travel plans are always based on the assumption that if anything goes wrong, I will have something with which to fix it in my car. I don't mean the spare tire and jack in the trunk because I haven't a clue how to use them. I mean the simple objects that can make the difference between life and death. Or at least soaking up a coffee spill before it completely ruins the upholstery.

The contents of my car are stocked for disaster. I know that it is important to carry certain emergency items such as flares, a blanket and a flashlight, but what about more common situations? If you've never had anyone throw up in your car, you've never been a parent, a pet owner or a designated driver. My stash of napkins is not just for wiping ketchup off the steering wheel.

I have a lot of "just in case" items stored in my automobile. Granted, the recesses in the door panels are narrow, but they're perfect for hiding shopping receipts and traffic tickets. I used to keep a steak knife there for protection, but I found that a Swiss army knife added options like a bottle opener. I was once stranded on an island (okay, via ferry boat service) without a corkscrew. That story literally came to blood, sand, and tears before I got the wine bottle open.

Other necessities like Band-aides are kept in the handy compartment that divides the front seat. There's also room for my hand sanitizer (mandatory after touching a gas pump handle), nail polish (that I never have time to apply at home), and expired coupons (that never get any closer to a store than the parking lot). Of course I have an ice scrapper, but since it is usually still "vacationing" in the garage when I need it, I have resorted to using a hair comb on my windshield.

These items may not be part of a traditional emergency car kit, but they have their value. Should I ever be stranded in my car in a desert, I will be able to survive by drinking the water from the radiator. How? I have a straw in the glove compartment.

I know what you're thinking: "What about a cell phone?" You're assuming that my phone is always charged and with me instead of on the kitchen counter. Think again.

A Spontaneous Night Ride

It was supposed to be a casual evening at our neighbor's home—*inside*. After all, it was November, and the temperature was dipping to the low twenties at night. I expected a friendly dinner and socializing in a warm, cozy room that evening. I didn't expect to be sabotaged.

My hostess, Laura, announced, "We're going kayaking after dinner." By "we" she meant the women. I barely had time to protest when my sister, who had just arrived, said nonchalantly, "Don't you have a headlamp?" No, I don't have a headlamp. I also don't own scuba diving equipment because it's not something I ever plan to use. (Do you see what I mean about my family? Now my new neighbor turns out to be just as crazy.)

Well, what could I do but join them? Besides, the men were already gathering up the snack bowls and heading toward the television. I called out to my husband, "If we're not back in an hour, look for us. I think bodies wash up in three days. You can fish me out with that hook we use to pull debris out of the lake."

It didn't take long to go home and change into more appropriate clothing—if there is such a thing for this activity. I slipped into my rubber boots and winter coat and donned a wool ski hat. Once outside I navigated the path to the lake by feeling my way with carefully placed steps, but even the terrain of our yard seemed unfamiliar in the dark. Why hadn't I ever counted the wooden steps before so that I would be prepared for a descent when I couldn't see them?

I could hear Laura and Carol splashing along the shore as they entered their boats. I pulled my kayak to the water's edge and gingerly stepped inside. The addition of my life jacket seemed superfluous as I was certain that if I fell in, I could float for at least an hour in my quilted parka. I lurched forward, scooting the boat into the water a few inches at a time. Once free of the shore, I paddled toward the direction of the giggles.

Although the moon offered some illumination, and we were only feet away from one another, our reflections disappeared in the black water. Occasionally we called out, "Where are you?" and maneuvered our boats in the direction of the voice that answered. It was a strange sensation to paddle forward yet be unable to mark our progress in the dark. Only the isolated house lights gave us a sense of movement.

Before returning home we paused to look up at the sky. In those moments our floating crafts seemed suspended from the distant stars. It was a magical, albeit unconventional, connection to a beautiful November night that I am glad I experienced.

Winter Winds Disrupt Party Plans

My sister invited us to a skating party at her house across the lake. Although my husband was in bed with the flu, I was up for the festivities that included a chili dinner and roasting marshmallows around a bonfire. I felt it was safe enough to walk across the lake, but as I waited along the shore for my new neighbors, a brisk wind brought a mist of snow. "Hurry," I urged them. "We only have two minutes left of daylight." I sounded like a fur trader crossing the Yukon by dogsled.

It was dark when we reached the cleared ice in front of Carol's house. My nephew was attempting to illuminate the area with two work lights that were powered by strings of orange electrical cords connected by extension poles. The children were already circling the makeshift rink while a few adults were donning their skates. I went inside to help with dinner.

But the chili was scarcely set on the table when my brother-in-law came limping in. "Did you fall on the ice?" we asked. Jim's face revealed his frustration. "No! I was just standing there watching, and my son hit a hockey puck into my leg!" No one asked if it was on purpose.

By the time the rest of us joined the skating party, a significant wind was blowing snow across the rink. My sisters and I sat on the icy dock and struggled to put on our skates in the dim light. It didn't help that my fingers on one hand were frozen because the dog had run off with one of my mittens.

Suddenly a gust of wind swept the work light from its pole, sending it crashing down on my already-injured brother-in-law. The light's hook was lodged in his jacket and causing some pain. Fearing he was being electrocuted, my mother's quick reaction to this was to disconnect the other light, thus plunging us all into darkness as we frantically scrambled to free Jim of his electrical appendage. (He now had *two* bruises on which to pout.)

As for marshmallows over the fire…despite efforts to light the logs, the howling wind blew away any promise of a flame—or gooey s'mores! The return trip across the lake loomed far more menacing than the earlier walk at sunset. Using my flashlight as a feeble beacon, I led my neighbors over exposed patches of ice and shifting snow. Gale-like gusts literally stopped us in our tracks. The woman commented that it was an adventure.

"Yes," I agreed sourly. "Like a Jack London story. But they didn't usually end well!"

This one did, fortunately. But as I trudged up my hill, braced against that fierce wind, I was reminded that nature is stronger than man. And even for a woman, survival of the fittest in the Northwoods can be a daily challenge.

Birthday Is a Cool Celebration

I am too old to have a birthday party with a game of Pin the Tail on the Donkey, but I am not too old to have fun—even without a party. So when my day coincided with a club meeting hosted by my sister, I told her I would snowshoe to her house—in a bathing suit—and a party hat.

A few years ago I participated in my own birthday triathlon when I went downhill skiing, cross-country skiing and snowshoeing—all in my bathing suit. It was cold, but nothing like this winter. All I hoped for this year was a temperature in the double digits. In fact, I think that was what I told my husband when he asked what I wanted for my birthday. "I would like my own power sander and a day that reaches twenty degrees." The preceding nights had dipped well below zero, but I am an optimist.

If I was going to do something a little outrageous, I was going to document it. So I asked my husband if he could take a photo of me as I headed down to the lake. I grabbed my camera before heading outside to put on my snowshoes. Richard and Bella followed.

We were moving down the hill when I remembered an important element to my birthday ensemble. "Oh, I forgot my pink party hat." I couldn't very well enter the house in snowshoes so

Richard went back for it. By the time he returned, I was feeling the sting of the cold air and considered for the first time how I would fare on the trek across the lake. Oh, well, too late for that. "We better go now before I freeze to death!" And so the three of us plodded on to the lake.

But I was on snowshoes, and Richard was merely in boots. We hadn't been down this lake path in a long time, and the snow was so deep that Richard could scarcely move. Besides, he was holding my large camera. I finally told him just to take a quick picture and return to the house. Bella had already given up and gone back.

Even on snowshoes navigation across the lake was challenging. I also regretted that I had not worn gloves (a foolish oversight). But a feeling of exhilaration overshadowed thoughts of the cold. Thankfully, the fishing shacks were far down at the other end of the lake. Right now it was just me—in my turquoise, two-piece bathing suit and pink birthday hat. I could have felt foolish, but the truth is I felt liberated. What is a birthday if not a time for celebrating another year of life and doing what makes you feel good about yourself?

But I have to admit that my fingers were hurting from the cold when I finally reached my sister's shore. She had just announced to the group of women that I was arriving on snowshoes, and they were looking out the window as I struggled up the icy hill. The discovery of my modest attire resulted in a general reaction of surprise. Some of them asked why I did it.

"Why not?! It's my birthday!" But I pulled my sister aside, "By the way, can I borrow some clothes to get home?"

Assembly Required, Completion Optional

It is spring, and my mind turns to thoughts of dirt, garbage, and manure. Of course, I am referring to gardening, and unless I plan to grow vegetables on rocks and sand, I need fertile soil. Creating my own compost pile seemed like a good idea until I brought home the handy compost container and read the words on the box that read, "Snaps together—no tools required."

I've been down that road before. Sometimes I am duped by similar promises, such as "simple assembly," "easy directions," or "only takes minutes." I've even put furniture together with a Scandinavian version of a wrench that the Vikings must have used as a weapon. There should be a warning on the box to keep this tool locked in a safe place in case you need to disassemble the furniture and move it out of the room—without taking down a wall.

But nothing beats the complications of assembling something made in China—which includes almost everything. First of all, what is the point of assigning letters to parts and hardware if all the pieces look identical on the printed directions? Putting side *A* onto *B* only helps if you can tell the two apart. You only discover the subtle difference *after* you have screwed them together and realize that they don't fit.

My husband and I once spent an unpleasant afternoon putting together a giant storage box for our patio cushions. Frustration led Richard to the conclusion that there was a devious plot to undermine the American consumer, and a screw was deliberately omitted from our kit. He was too tired and angry later to retract that accusation when I discovered the missing screw in his pocket. His response was the all-encompassing remark, "It's still a piece of junk!"

With that episode still haunting my memory, I tackled the compost box myself and placed the plastic components on the garage floor. I could see evidence of slits and tabs that qualified directions to "snap into place." But the tabs were stubborn and didn't seem to fit properly. My husband entered the garage just as I was attacking the box with a hammer. He offered to hold the sides together while I pushed them into place. But as soon as one side clicked together, the other popped out. I was ready to agree with my husband: Flimsy pieces of plastic and misleading instructions are part of a diabolical plan to unhinge what's left of our sanity.

We finally managed to complete a precarious semblance of the picture on the box. Moving as gingerly as parents putting a baby to sleep, we carefully carried the container across the yard, gently placed it on the ground, and then tiptoed our way back to the house.

If a strong wind doesn't undo it first, the dirt just might hold it together. If not, there's always duct tape.

Sisters Are Still Summer Pirates

There are many reasons why I am happy that my sister retired and moved across the lake from me. After all these years, we are still conspiring together on girlish adventures. One day in mid-October we took our kayaks out for a final ride on the deserted lakes. As we approached the familiar area of our grandparents' cottage, our conversation became sentimental. We recalled our childhood excursions that included building rafts and searching for pearls in clam shells.

I mentioned that my nostalgia for those bygone days has created a yearning for a favorite childhood toy: a painted, metal beach pail. As we skirted the shoreline, I confessed that I secretly hoped to find this coveted item. After all these years the likelihood was ridiculous, but the daydream caused us to gaze absently into the water. Suddenly, a faint shape among the wavering shadows caught my eye.

"There!" I pointed excitedly. The object was only partially exposed and too fragile to free with awkward paddles. We abandoned our efforts, but formulated a plan on the way home.

The next day we put shovels into our kayaks and returned to our destination. This time our journey was hurried with eagerness for our mission. The sun was in our faces as we paddled the length of our lake, down the long channel and across the second lake. Our voices echoed—just as they did years ago—within the corrugated metal walls under the bridge that connected the smaller channel to the first lake. At last we were moving along the familiar shoreline of our childhood route.

With no one in sight, we hoisted our boats onto the shore, rolled up our pants and slowly eased our bare legs into the frigid water. It was enough to make two middle-aged women scream, but Carol and I were now pigtailed pirates scouring for treasure, just as we had so many years ago with the boys next door. Their boathouse, now leaning with decay, was our castle tower, and the shore below was our magic cove. We glanced up at the rotting deck that had been our secret lookout and imagined the "all clear" signal.

We used the shovels to pry and lift our booty through a cloud of disturbed muck. I plunged my arm into the icy water and gently guided the pail to the surface. It was, indeed, very old, but not what we had hoped. "It's just an old bucket," I said with disappointment.

Carol, always the loyal first mate, suggested that the rusted container could very well have been our grandfather's bait pail. This justified our caper. By now our clothes were soaked, and our legs were numb with cold. Still, all the way back, we talked excitedly and reminisced. The beach pail may have eluded us, but there are other adventures ahead. They're on our *bucket* list.

Chapter 9

The American Spirit

Parades March with Youthful Spirit

One nostalgic aspect of the Fourth of July is the parade. A reason for this might be that they are virtually the same as they were when we—as well as when our parents and grandparents—were young. What we love and remember most about parades continues to march down Main Street in our hometowns every year.

Traditions are comforting; they connect us to the past. It is no different with the annual holiday parade. Musicians will step to the beat of a Sousa march. Smiling girls with outstretched arms will wave from decorated floats. Bicycle tires will spin with red, white, and blue crepe paper. American flags will flutter on handheld sticks. Fathers will balance toddlers on their shoulders. Grandparents will watch from folding chairs. The crowds will clap and sing and cheer. These are familiar and endearing scenes of the Fourth of July parade.

I've experienced the parade from two perspectives: one as an observer, the other as a participant. The first time I rode in a parade was in my father's 1929 Model A. His antique car club was invited to participate in the parade of a small river town in Illinois. The overcast day rendered a somber tone to the journey we made down the tree-lined streets. I shyly looked out of the backseat window at the unfamiliar faces along the curb. They seemed expectant, as if someone they knew was about to pass. Their gaze caught us for only a moment before the next vehicle rolled into their immediate view. Our brief encounter was then merged into a single memory of all parades that flowed along the street over the years.

I have also been a face in the crowd. I have been hoisted up in my father's arms so that I could see the spectacle unfold. Between the bands were baton twirlers and an Uncle Sam on stilts and dogs pulled in wagons. Officials in open cars nodded. We smiled and waved as the participants moved beyond us, and a new attraction took its place. How many times I have watched from the same vantage point over the years: sitting on the curb with my siblings, then standing next to my husband, and eventually holding the hands of my own children.

The parade never really ends. Next Fourth of July another will be headed down the same street. We will turn our heads in anticipation. The familiar sound of drums that keep the beat for the slow procession will be heard in the distance. Soon the musicians will appear, leading onward with bright, eager faces until their notes are muffled by the next band, just as spirited and fresh. And so it goes...year after year. The parade reminds us of what we were, and as we watch, we are young and hopeful again.

Poppy Is Reminder of Sacrifice

For most of us, the poem "In Flanders Fields" is a familiar reminder of Memorial Day. Written by John McCrae, it is a tribute to the fallen soldiers of World War I. The lines, which begin "In Flanders Fields the poppies blow / Between the crosses, row on row...," are often read aloud at Memorial Day services in tribute to those who perished in war.

Using the voice of the dead, McCrae addresses all of us who are left to remember them. This was a personal message as well, for the poet's inspiration was the death of his comrade at the Second Battle of Ypres in May, 1915. Lieutenant-colonel John McCrae was a military doctor and artillery commander who also presided at his friend's funeral. One can only imagine the emotions that prompted him to write the now legendary words.

Most of us were introduced to the poem in school and probably wondered at first where Flanders Fields was. But we learned it was a battlefield in France, and we understood that the soldiers who gave their lives asked to be remembered for their sacrifice where the poppies "mark our place."

Actually, the preponderance of poppies on soldiers' graves at Flanders was first noted during the Napoleonic wars. But it was in 1918 that American teacher Morina Belle Michael conceived the poppy as a symbolic reminder, and it has since been associated with Veterans Day, Remembrance Day, and especially Memorial Day. We grew up recognizing the fabric flower with its red petals and wire stem as a familiar adornment in buttonholes every year.

But it was merely an artificial flower to me as a child, protruding from the pages of my school books or wrapped around the strap of my bag. In time, the full meaning of the poppy was revealed to me, and I understood that this tiny flower meant so much more than that which blows "Between the crosses, row on row." It is a reminder of those brave young men whose voices reach out from the poem and touch us with so much humanity: "Short days ago / We lived, felt dawn, saw sunset glow / Loved and were loved." For they were just as we, but that their lives were disrupted and ultimately ended by a cause that they were called upon to defend.

Many years and many wars have passed since first these lines were written. And, with each generation, the meaning of a soldier's sacrifice must be taught to those for whom such debts are obscured by the pressing matters of mundane life. Memorial Day is a reminder to all of us.

For as the poem tells us, "If ye break faith with us who die / We shall not sleep, / Though poppies grow / In Flanders Fields." It is our faith—and gratitude—that preserves these everlasting blooms.

Disney Charms the Child in Each of Us

Why not Disney World?! It fulfilled both needs: a graduation present for my two nieces and an escape to Florida after another long U.P. winter. And although Katarina and Anna (graduating from college and high school, respectively) had been to the United Kingdom, they had never been to the *Magic* Kingdom. We, on the other hand, were familiar with its charms, and we couldn't wait to share the experience with the girls.

My love affair with Disney began as a small child when I watched the *Mickey Mouse Club* on television and was introduced to Walt Disney's many animated film characters. And to learn that these fantasies existed in a place called Disneyland was beyond my imagination. I was able to see it for myself when my parents included this magical place on a family trip to California in 1968.

I guess those memories inspired a visit to Disney World in Florida with my own children, who donned the Mickey ears and took in the spirit that fills everyone the moment they enter the park. And when Tinker Belle flew down from the castle, I felt my own heart flutter with fairy dust. We returned a few years later, and the characters of those classic films still came to life on the sweet streets of make-believe and walked among the crowd of adoring humans.

That's what I remembered, and that's what I wanted to relive and share with my nieces. We posed in front of the iconic castle, and I kept an eye out for Cinderella and her prince. But I soon learned that the girl with the glass slipper is not as popular as she used to be. Neither are Snow White and Sleeping Beauty. In fact, even the gift shops seem to have neglected these classic fairytale figures. In their place were several characters whose names were unfamiliar to me. There were still princesses, but their reigns were too recent for me to recognize.

Something else had changed, too, but it had less to do with this world of fantasy than it did with the larger world of reality. At the park's gates visitors were herded through metal detectors. Our bags were checked by security, a procedure that is now, sadly, a necessary routine.

It was Memorial Day, and the crowd, dominated by families, also had a representation of veterans who were honored guests. I was struck by the contrast of these brave Americans, many of whom had been wounded in foreign lands, and the little girls with them who were dressed as princesses from mythical places under the sea and atop frozen wonderlands.

What had not changed was the magic. We all merged into the crowd, wide-eyed Mouseketeers at heart, still believing in the creations of a man whose imagination continues to preserve the magic of childhood.

The Influence of a Decade

My mother admitted that when she and my father planned to get married, she assumed they would settle in his hometown in Michigan. However, my father, who was just leaving the Navy, wanted to start a career in Chicago. To make a long story short: my siblings and I were all born in the city. Our lives, naturally, were influenced by that decision.

It is not an influence that I regret for I was fortunate to have an upbringing rich in experience and opportunities. However, like most of us, I have wondered how different my life would have been if my parents had not made the choices that they did. I lived in the same house from age three to age twenty. Our neighborhood—with its assortment of characters—was where I learned about life. Would I have not learned the same things in some other environment?

Perhaps, but a particular time and place yields its own unique influence.

My parents grew up during the Great Depression, which had a great deal to do with their values and character. Had my father been born a year or two earlier, he would have been in World War II, a venture he regretted missing at the time. As fate would have it, he married and began his family in the opportune years of the fifties. I am a product of that era, as well as of the turbulent sixties, the decade in which I entered my teens. Although none of us choose these broader influences, they leave their indelible mark on our character.

In many respects I yearn for the more innocent and optimistic attitudes of the fifties, a time when things seemed to make sense. Yet I am often tugged by a desire to shake things up and expose what I believe to be unjust, a pursuit that has gotten me into more than a little hot water over the years. My sister, Carol, who is two years younger, had virtually the same experiences as I did growing up, and we share a similar perspective. My brother entered his pre-teen years when we moved to the suburbs, a homogenous setting that was conducive to his easy-going manner. By then it was the seventies, my youngest sister's most formative years. Her carefree, independent spirit may be a result of a less-restrictive upbringing in an era that was more encouraging of women's pursuits.

I suppose we cannot discount the inherent personality with which we are born. Still, it is interesting to consider how one's character evolves as a result of when and where we grow up. Perhaps those influences hold less significance in this technological world where it is virtually impossible to grow up in a sheltered environment—at least in America. But for those of us who truly are a product of our environment, our past is not only who we were, but who we *are*.

National Tragedy Remembered

When a national tragedy occurs, it becomes not only a part of history, but a personal memory from which an individual views his own life in a before-and-after perspective. This was true for Pearl Harbor and 9/11, and it is certainly true for the assassination of John

F. Kennedy. Although I was only a child, the President's assassination revealed a grim reality that ended my juvenile naivety.

Friday, November 22, 1963 began as any other school day for me. At lunchtime my sister and I walked home from our grade school across the street. We joined our little brother in front of the television to watch *Bozo Circus* while our mother prepared lunch. Suddenly, the children's show was interrupted with a news bulletin that the President had been shot. I told my mother what I had heard, but, unbelieving, she said that I must have been mistaken.

It didn't take long to find that this terrible news was, indeed, true. As I entered the classroom for the afternoon session, the teacher, clearly shaken, instructed us to bow our heads and pray. As this was a Chicago public school, we students—Protestants, Catholics, and Jews—had never done this together before. That minute of silence seemed the longest of my life.

What followed was the longest weekend of my young life. Like most American families, ours watched the coverage of events that began in Dallas and ended with the solemn funeral in Washington. Little was said in our living room. The grim black and white images captured moments that words alone could not and cast a pall that permeated every room of our home.

Yes, we watched the motor cavalcade and noticed Jackie's bloodstained suit. We saw the suspect—a bland-looking man who could have just as well lived in our own neighborhood—shot and killed on live television. We followed the hours of protocol that enveloped the funeral, and we witnessed, with a sense of personal invasion, the intimate moments that the Kennedys had to share with the world. I recall the dirge-like music that accompanied the long, long procession of the caisson down Pennsylvania Avenue. I felt most sad about the two children whom I judged did not fully understand the loss of their father. Their mother's eyes, clearly swollen beneath a black veil, conveyed a grief beyond my comprehension.

Until this event, I had viewed the President, as I did my own father, to be an invincible presence. In my protected world, protectors did not die. But that world—the safe, fairy-tale version—was shattered that day, as abruptly and irrevocably as the deadly shots from an assassin's gun.

College Dreams Clouded by Stormy Era

Most of my girlfriends in high school would have agreed that the most glamorous career a girl could hope for was that of an airline stewardess. However, we were more realistic about the options we had after graduation. There were basically three: secretary, nurse, or teacher.

I considered being a secretary, but that idea was dashed by my shorthand teacher, who assured me that, despite my typing abilities, my cryptic note-taking would never suffice in an office. Nursing was a noble profession, but my history of fainting at the sight of needles might prove inconvenient. Alas! I was good at reading and writing. Maybe I could be a teacher.

One of the best teaching institutions was Chicago State College. The tuition was very affordable, and I could commute on buses from my home (I didn't have a driver's license). My best friend also planned to attend, and I felt relieved to have my future in place by spring of my senior year. I had the lead in the school musical, a steady boyfriend, and a romantic image of college based—unrealistically—on the movie *The Graduate* and the fall issues of *Seventeen*.

But those images began to blur over the summer. Viet Nam, a place I had only learned about a few years earlier, was now a source of controversy that was expressed everywhere. Martin Luther King had been murdered in April. In June—the week I donned my prom dress and celebrated with friends—Robert Kennedy was shot and killed. Just miles from my neighborhood, demonstrations against the war rocked the Democratic convention with violent protests that erupted into bloody riots. The bubble in which I had existed was pierced by the arrows from the larger world, a place that presented challenges I had only begun to know.

I entered college that fall with strangers from all over the city. My best friend postponed school for another semester. My academic confidence had been that of a late-bloomer, and my scholarly ambition to major in English was an isolated choice among more intimidating subjects. Still, my heart thumped with anticipation for courses that included botany, European history, anthropology, and a physical education credit entitled "Latin American Rhythms."

So on that day in early September I walked across the campus with hundreds of others who also felt anxious and excited. We were handed green balloons in celebration of the school's centennial birthday. As thousands had before us, we were eager for the light that learning could provide. We were yet unaware that the horizon also glowed with the rising flames of war and protest. But we were soon to feel its heat.

A Year of Fire and Ice

Any college offers a feeling of independence for an incoming freshman, especially one with my background. My public high school had fairly conservative guidelines, including the dress code. I felt quite radical wearing jeans to my classes at Chicago State College. As exhilarating as freedom can be, change can feel awkward and uncomfortable at first. But change was burning down conventions at the speed of a wildfire in 1968.

Meanwhile I was trying to be a cool college freshman at a historic city school. Opened in 1868, it had been a teachers' college for girls. The front entrance opened to a beautiful park which had accommodated horse-drawn carriages. On warm days students still sat and read under the massive oaks. Reminders of those former days were also evident in the huge wooden lockers that once held long cloaks and broad bonnets.

The surrounding neighborhood's former elegance had eroded over the years, and the view from the college's windows revealed a jagged cityscape of dilapidated buildings. Fortunately, what went on inside the antiquated classrooms inspired me. The impressive faculty included my botany teacher, creator of the seedless watermelon; my speech teacher, a successful stage actor, and others whose accomplishments and publications fortified the college's standing.

I found my classes to be provocative, and I immersed myself in study with an ardor that bordered on passion. When my history teacher praised me for an analysis I had written, I became his devoted fan, foregoing social activities on Friday nights so that I could study for his Saturday morning class. And, although I was not exactly the image of the co-ed models in *Seventeen*, I pretended that Chicago

State's exterior gray walls were ivy-covered, and discovery of my writing talents would propel me to an exciting career.

But there were exterior forces that bled into this fortress of learning. Martin Luther King Jr.'s murder escalated racial tension. Our college closed for one day in November in response to disturbances at a nearby high school that left several students injured. But the worst would occur in January when protestors marched down the halls, demanding classes be closed in honor of King's birthday. When helmeted policemen entering the building, I ran in panic and nearly collided with an African American friend of mine. His mission of disruption was abruptly quelled by my appearance, and his expression softened. Then, with a sadness that bespoke our different plights, he uttered, "Gail, what are you doing here?"

That was the day I realized that the world I knew was over; there would be no return to innocent times. The future would be wrought with conflict, and there was no going back. The lines had already been drawn.

Turbulent Times Are Recalled

A rule that was strictly enforced in my grade school concerned walking in a straight, single-file formation through the hallways. This was achieved by following the lines which were engraved in the cement floor. "Square your corners," a teacher would call out, and we all marched on in obedience. I think back now on the following-the-lines rule as a metaphor for life before 1968. After that, all lines seemed to be crossed.

When I entered Chicago State College, I intended to "stay within the lines" as I always had. I was taught that following the rules led to a good education, which led to a good job, which led to a happy life. Before long, that equation seemed flawed.

The good education I expected was a mixture of inspirational challenges and esoteric agendas. While my anthropology class, for example, taught me to respect other cultures, and art history gave me an appreciation for all forms of creative expression, other classes disappointed me. Shakespeare remained dead with lifeless lectures, and an American literature course was sacrificed by a radical instructor whose sole focus was the writings of incarcerated minorities.

Teachers, as well as students, were affected by the wave of volatile politics. The day after students were shot by National Guard soldiers at Kent State, I attended my morning poetry class as usual. The teacher arrived several minutes late wearing a black armband. He reprimanded us for coming to school on what he said was a day of mourning. Conversely, one teacher boldly criticized sympathy for fallen soldiers, citing his defense that all soldiers enter war under a contract of killing. This was the time of the draft lottery, and most of us looked upon this system of being called to duty when your number came up as absurd. I knew boys who went to college just to avoid the draft. I knew boys who contemplated going to Canada. Of course there were those who joined the service voluntarily. But the number of boys who would never come home was growing. And we were all keenly aware of that.

It was a confusing time. While we marveled at the landing of men on the moon, our streets were filled with a crudeness unchanged since primitive man. I can remember riding my bicycle along Lake Shore Drive and having passengers in cars hold out their hands in a gesture of the peace symbol. Yet, I witnessed the chaos of running crowds, overturned police cars, and smoke in Grant Park as those in my generation resorted to violence as an expression of protest against the war, the government, the police…those over thirty. While many endorsed "flower power," they were also armed with rocks.

The Democratic National Convention that year brought some of the worst violence to Chicago when anti-war protestors taunted the police until the conflict became physical. While peaceful demonstrations failed to get much attention, violent ones like this made national news and deepened lines of opposition. The more I saw, the less I understood.

In truth, there were victims on both sides. My father, a policeman, described to us the abuse that they endured, the least of which was name-calling. They were the soldiers in the streets, doing the jobs they had always done, but were now labeled as "pigs" by those they had taken an oath to protect. In response to that particular insult, my father and other officers wore pins that mockingly read, "PIG: pride, integrity, and guts."

Not that all of the older generation supported the war. My father told me that if I were a boy and was drafted, he would have sent me to Canada. That was a strong sentiment for a man who regretted that, because of his age, he had missed serving in World War II.

Our generation had many poets, but the song lyrics, "Something's happening here. What it is ain't exactly clear," summarizes these disturbing times well. Since then I am reluctant to follow anyone's lines but my own.

Tragedies Touch World's Humanity

Although our lives, for the most part, are lived within small circles of family and friends, there are moments outside the perimeters of our personal havens that shake us to the very core of what defines us as human beings. The abominations perpetuated upon innocent victims often crystalize into a tragic memory that is shared, not just within our own nation, but by the entire world. The impact of the fallen towers of the World Trade Center is felt long after the dust has settled in the streets of New York, and other acts of terrorism here and abroad have left universal scars. Events that have inspired global grief are engraved on the eternal monument of historical tragedies: Boston, April 15, 2013, Paris, November 13, 2015...

It is in our nature to seek answers, to make sense of that which goes against all that we believe. But, of course, there is no rationale for such atrocities. Nothing within the realm of goodness can understand such hatred, and it is the cruelty against innocence that we find most appalling. So as horrors unfold in cities here and abroad, we ask ourselves how such terrible things could happen, how a world so dangerous and filled with violence can possibly be saved.

Perhaps it is because we ask these questions and because we react with emotions of shock and rage and grief in the face of unspeakable acts, that salvation *is* possible. And though it seems at times that goodness is merely a flickering candle in the dark, there is hope beyond the sparks of violence and carnage that continue to ignite the world. There is hope because we care, because we grieve for the slain and ache in sympathy for their families. It is our sense of humanity that saves us.

Of course we feel despair in the current tide of hate that threatens the globe, for evil exists. But so does goodness. We must have faith in the world powers that join us in the fight against terror, but we also have a powerful weapon within ourselves. It is the goodness which we are committed to preserving. And we must teach this to our children, lest they become lost in the mire that thrives on prejudice and hate, all too prevalent here as well as abroad. It is not our nationality but our *values* that separate us from our foes and bind us to the greater mankind.

As the poet John Donne said, "Every man's death diminishes me because I am involved in mankind...The bell tolls for thee." May the spirit of the fallen innocents unify us and give us strength. In this way the victims did not die in vain. That they have loved and were loved is the ultimate triumph of a life well-lived and a legacy that will go on in those who revere their memory. So long as we honor goodness, goodness will survive.

Small Trips Come with Big Packages

Even with a limited budget, a small vacation can have *big* results. Think of Chevy Chase's character in *National Lampoon's Vacation*: a highlight for his family's trip was seeing the world's biggest ball of string. When it comes to local attractions, size does matter. Tourists love big road objects.

I'm not sure when America's love affair with big objects began, but we have a *large* legacy across the country. Most of our ancestors were welcomed to America by the world's tallest woman. Thousands flock each year to see the country's largest heads at Mt. Rushmore. (It makes it all the more impressive that they are the visages of presidents, but I have a feeling that their sheer scope in stone would have a similar attraction if they depicted cartoon characters.)

Early in the last century businesses capitalized on the idea that big things can have big results. Is there any better way to advertise your service than to erect a giant ice cream cone or mammoth-sized chicken on your roof? The latter was a feature we loved to point out on the outskirts of Chicago. Another recognizable sight was the giant milk bottle in our grandparents' small town. It is sad to think that these are now gone. But there are still many large objects that capture our traveling spirit along the highways. One of our family's favorites was the giant astronaut at a diner west of Chicago. Each year after cutting our Christmas tree at a nearby farm, we could have lunch and pose under the 1950s icon. The tradition kicked off the holiday season, despite the fact that Christmas and space travel have nothing to do with each other.

In this area just drive north along U.S. 2 and see a menacing mosquito made out of metal, a colorful fish fashioned in fiberglass, and a leaping buck that defies any hunter's advance. Some attractions are even closer to home. Ever since I was a little girl, Big John has stood tall in front of the Iron Mountain Iron Mine. My sister and I would stare out the car window and quickly compare his dual face smiling from the other side of the sign. A more recent spectacle is the big bear across from the mine. Despite its gray cement color, which makes it appear more like a polar bear than a black bear, tourists are often observed posing for pictures in front of it.

We've all done that at some point somewhere, haven't we? It's hard to resist the pleas of delighted kiddies in the backseat who just have to stop and see the giant Indian chief, lumberjack, or miner. Next to these gigantic versions of local color, we look so small— except for our smiles. They are the grandest part of it all.

Veterans Deserve Dignity and Respect

Even with the present government shutdown, Arlington Cemetery in Washington, D.C. was open to the public. I was pleased that my visit would include this special landmark. All I knew was that this was a military burial ground. I was about to learn that it was much more than that.

The vast grounds, with their magnificent old trees and rolling hills, are astoundingly beautiful. The many paths throughout the park led to more memorial sites than we could take in on this hot September afternoon. America's long military history is represented with impressive war memorials such as the Battle of the Bulge and the Spanish-American War, but it also honors events such as the Space Shuttle Challenger and 9/11's Pan Am Flight 103.

Likewise, the graves themselves honored not only those who served in the armed forces but also high-ranking officials. Most were marked with the same white stones, the simplicity of which offers a uniform tribute within the Gardens of Stone. The most understated are two small stones that belong to Robert and Ted Kennedy. Their brother, John F. Kennedy, along with Jacqueline, lie nearby. On the hill above is the home that once belonged to Robert E. Lee.

But it is the average man and woman's life that takes on the most meaning here: those who grew up in a typical American home and answered a call that qualified him for the privilege of this resting place. On this particular day we could hear a gun salute in the distance. We also walked past a bench where a family gathered in solemn reflection around an elderly woman whose tears told of her recent loss. It was a story told here over 5,000 times a year.

But the most moving of all ceremonies was that of the changing of the guard at the Tomb of the Unknown. We joined a crowd of spectators for the hourly ritual that so beautifully expresses the military's appreciation for its brothers and sisters. As we stood in the heat, shielding our eyes from the scorching sun, the guard (one of the volunteers of the 3rd. U.S. Infantry Regiment since 1948) remained unflinching in his impeccable uniform and white gloves. The movements of the two approaching soldiers, like the mechanisms of a precise clock, awed those of us whose emotion continued long after our slow and silent departure.

I thought of the sign posted at the park's entry which read "Please conduct yourself at all times with dignity and respect." These words, meant to honor those who have served our country, are also appropriate for how we should live our lives every day. This code of behavior honors those who have sacrificed so that we might continue this privilege.

Country Dance Recalls Simpler Times

Every now and then, when I am scrambling to accommodate appointments, I wonder how people made social contacts a century ago. In a world before phones, cars, and electricity, everything was slower. Yet people in a community shared good times with each other.

I suppose that neighborly visits were more frequent, and people depended more on those who lived close to them. Rural life thrived on the good nature and resources shared by each family. Even local businesses had a more personal relationship with their customers. A country town and its surrounding area was a community that worked together out of necessity and socialized together out of a common bond.

I was reminded of that spirit at an event that was held as a special fundraiser in our town. My sister Carol was the creator and organizer of this event, and although the idea of a barn dance was initially met with some skepticism, the project proceeded with her faith that a small town could return to its country roots—and have fun.

Preparations for the barn dance reminded me of old movies in which naïve enthusiasts clean out an old barn so that they can put on a show. That's exactly what was done. The neglected second floor of the century-old exhibition building at the fairgrounds hadn't been used for years, and remnants of its past cluttered the floor and walls. It took days to clean, paint, and decorate the stark room, but the transformation was, indeed, something out of an MGM musical.

Guests entered a setting unfamiliar in recent years. Hay bales, baskets of wildflowers, and gingham tablecloths set a country mood, and the smells of a delicious farm dinner drew them to the tables. I noted that many had dressed for the occasion with denim shirts, calico skirts, red bandanas, and straw hats. It was as if everyone had long-anticipated this gathering, and when the musicians picked up their fiddles, there was a real feeling of celebration among the crowd.

As the caller instructed, we formed two lines. Soon we were skipping across the room with the music. Partners switched, and at some point everyone had grasped the hand of everyone else. Sheer joy accompanied the participants who wove through the moving circle. Business owners looped arms with their local patrons; teens and parents sashayed, and grandparents gently led children across the floor. The physical contact fortified the bond we felt, not simply as a community, but as friends and family.

At the end of the night, I watched as the departing cars formed a slow procession to the highway. Their headlights sent friendly beacons that finally merged with the glow of windows from the houses scattered about the town and surrounding hills. How warm and close they all seemed! Perhaps, we all felt closer tonight. It took an old-fashioned barn dance to remind us of how much we need each other.

Every Life Links the Past to the Future

The question of how old you are is usually answered in years, but the more accurate, if not elusive, response is one that cannot be expressed in numbers. We are not merely the sum of our own experiences but also those of others whose lives link us to the past.

I was born mid-century so I have a curiosity about events like the Great Depression and World War II that can't be entirely satisfied by simply reading about them. To really *know* what it was like to live in a previous time is to know someone who experienced it. Those individuals are the links that connect us to history, and the accessibility to those times is not as remote as it may seem.

My grandfather, who was born in 1893, lived an exciting life before he had a family. I would often sit on his lap as he watched boxing on television. His breathing was a comforting rise and fall, like the waves of the sea that carried him from Sweden at age sixteen. He jumped ship in Florida where he tromped through swamps and survived for days on bananas. Years later, his voice resonated with the sound of the rails and the horses he rode out West. His eyes reflected scenes from his Navy ship in World War I and from cities like Chicago, where he witnessed the tragic Eastland Disaster in which over 800 people died when their boat overturned in the Chicago River.

I couldn't know as a child that the beating of his heart reverberated across the decades from distant places, through tragedy and adventure, and echoed with the pulse that transcended centuries.

For my grandfather, too, was touched by people who had lived in times long before his birth, connecting him to a world in which the Crimean and American Civil Wars were fought, and the Industrial Age wrought machines that transformed labor. And his father, the great-grandfather that I never knew, was merely one more link away, no doubt having himself heard as a child the voices of elders who spoke of Napoleon and King George III. How could I know that these voices resonated in my grandfather's, linking him— and his son and eventually me—to the past?

But now as an adult I often think about how close the past really is. It is only as far as the oldest person you have known, the individual who has given you a personal glimpse into a world before you existed. These glimpses are gifts that one generation can share with the next. The children who hear them are truly blessed, as are those whose lives continue on through them.

Chapter 10

Inspired by Nature

Living in the Moment

I looked out my window today and discovered that the lake had finally thawed, a process that I have not seen occur so late in the season. Of course, we all knew that spring would get here eventually, but waiting seemed an endless vigil. It certainly wasn't like last year—or the year before. But, just the same, it is in our nature to compare them, isn't it?

Maybe one of the consequences of having lived a number of years is not being particularly surprised about anything that happens. That doesn't mean we won't grumble about it. Why is that? What is it about getting older that makes a person feel less enthusiastic and optimistic than someone much younger? You might say it is because we know better and have seen it all, but I have another philosophy that might explain why spring, for example, doesn't mean the same to a six-year-old as it does a sixty-year-old: We *remember*.

We remember and we anticipate. It is just as the poet Shelley noted, "...When winter comes, can spring be far behind?" We are so familiar with the cycle of seasons, that we can scarcely enjoy the current one before the next one is occupying our thoughts. We are already dreading the oncoming winter just as the August sun dips lower in the sky. As for those warm September days, the cynicism of experience merely sneers at those who think it will last. For if there is nothing else adults know, it is that nothing stays the same.

But try to remember when every experience seemed new and exciting. Try to remember when you had no knowledge of calendars or schedules, and you lived for the moment. It was a time when the first flakes of snow triggered a frenzy of anticipation for sledding, snowballs and snowmen. It was a time when Christmas seemed an endless distance away from Thanksgiving, but each day in between was marked by an enchantment that only increased its allure.

And spring? Spring was the awakening of a new world, one borne in a brilliant green never seen before and scented with fragrances never inhaled before. And summer? Summer was an endless string of carefree days played out one at a time on soft lawns, bicycle paths, and baseball fields. The start of school was weeks away—a distance too long to be of consequence. Life was only in the present. Time was paused and beheld like the vainglorious pose of a diver in mid-air above the water. Each moment was unique, each experience incomparable.

If we could see the world through the eyes of a child, we might appreciate the beauty and wonder of each day, a blessing in any season.

March Brings Sentimental Reflection

In March, the month I was born, I often reflect on how I have changed since those earlier birthdays. I no longer know the child, the teenager, the young woman who became the person that I am today. Yet, they are still there, and, especially at this time of year, they call to me.

How that birthday cake with pink flowers must have mesmerized the little girl who leaned over the single candle! There would be a sister next to her the following year and for many birthdays to come, wearing a matching party dress and equally excited to play Pin the Tail on the Donkey and drop-the-clothespin-in-the-bottle. Presents were toys played well through the spring, and life was a Disney fantasy acted out in their own backyard and imaginations.

What is that sixteen-year-old thinking as she walks to school, feeling the wrath of the city's worst month? Possibly, she is thinking about being with friends or the upcoming dance or even a babysitting job over the weekend. She might be planning to write in her diary or lamenting that chemistry class is impossible. She can date now and wonders if she is pretty and clever enough to be asked out. She hopes that this summer will be special, but it is only March now and so far away. Still, she dreams, and—Oh! Those dreams make the world brighter.

And how does March find her ten years later? The dreary winter melts outside the windows of her first house as a married woman. March seems especially long this year, for at the end of the month, her first baby is due. The nursery is stocked with a bassinette and tiny clothes for the little one, who finally makes her appearance on March 30. All the dreams her heart could hold are realized in this precious angel, a girl she names Emily Linnea. And—Oh! How that special love made the world brighter!

Marches arrive more quickly in the coming years, and there is scarcely time to notice another birthday. Days begin early. ("Do you have your lunch—your homework?") There are hurried trips to the store, scouts, music lessons...

But for those birthdays that light the beginning and end of the month, time stops. The earlier birthday is celebrated with a store-bought cake with pink flowers and handmade gifts and cards signed "Love, Emily" and "Love, Grant." The other birthday is celebrated with a homemade cake that has a Care Bear or Strawberry Shortcake or a unicorn—and presents wrapped in purple bows with pretty cards that read: "To Emily—with love..." It is love that blesses sweet, sweet March.

Since those years I have had many birthdays—some of them far from home, but I am never far from my memories, and—Oh! Those memories make the world brighter. Still.

Spring Cleaning Is a Game of Lost and Found

Spring cleaning is more aptly named for the *way* it arrives rather than *when*. One day you are shoveling snow, and the next day a burst of sunlight illuminates a cobweb in the corner of your kitchen. You look at your husband and exclaim, "That's it! I'm tearing my kitchen cabinets apart, and you're cleaning the garage!"

Husbands don't really mind cleaning the garage. It's a little like telling a child to organize his toy box. Hours later they are still playing with the first item they encountered. That's okay. Anything that keeps them occupied while you get something done is helpful.

Meanwhile, your journey requires stamina and bravery as you go where only spiders and mice have ventured in recent months—although you hope not! You start with one of the most inaccessible areas: under the refrigerator. Mere crumbs can't elude the vacuum attachment, but you spy something deep within the bowels of dusty coils that no tool can reach. You extend your reach with a fly swatter and slowly coax the fuzzy object toward you. "Aha!" you exclaim with excited recognition. "I knew that grape rolled under here!"

In fact, the rituals of spring cleaning often uncover lost and forgotten items. Changing the drawer liners requires that all kitchen utensils be removed first. As the items are lined up on the counter, you discover that you have three meat thermometers, and two of them were borrowed from your neighbor. You stick them in the back of the drawer and eventually forget that you have even one—a frustration when you are cooking that Thanksgiving turkey.

The hall closet is the last area of uncharted waters, and it calls for a sense of adventure as well as a flashlight. Unfortunately, you haven't seen the flashlight since last year's spring cleaning. A kitchen chair affords a view of the top shelf, which is strewn with missing gloves and mittens. None of them are pairs, but, ever hopeful, you add them to last year's box of matchless orphans.

Exhausted, it is time to check your husband's progress in the garage. You are pleased to see that he has ambitiously dismantled the pile of junk from the entire right wall.

"What do you think?" he asks with pride.

It is then that you notice the left wall, where nothing has been removed. However, that pile of junk from the opposite side of the garage is now stacked there, too! Before you can respond, he is happily playing with the switch on an object he recovered.

You can't help but smile. All is not lost. It is the flashlight.

Front Steps Provide the Best Views

Known as the cocktail cruise, a leisurely ride on the local lakes and rivers is a lovely way to enjoy the sunset and see your neighbors—if only from a distance. If I had a boat, I would partake in this lovely evening ritual of skirting the shoreline with one hand holding a cocktail and the other waving to the figures silhouetted against the brilliant setting sun. But I don't have a boat—at least, not one with a motor. (You can't hold a cocktail *and* paddle a kayak.)

As it is, I observe from the shore. Like the other day, I joined my family on my sister's dock after a late afternoon swim. When the children were finally waterlogged and headed to the house, we adults just lounged on the water's edge and stared out at the lake. The jet skis and zooming motorboats were finished for the day. But as the sun lowered, the pontoon boats left their piers and began their customary circuit around the lake. As they passed, we waved to each other, not really in personal recognition (for it is virtually impossible to identify faces) but in a shared appreciation of the beautiful summer evening.

Summer brings us all out-of-doors, even if it is just to sit on the front porch and watch the cars go by. This was a frequent pastime where I grew up in the city. Yards were tiny, but the front steps provided a view of the streets and, therefore, a parade of people and cars. Our house was in an excellent spot for this recreation as it was located on a major boulevard near a corner stoplight. As cars slowed for the light, we could clearly see the people enjoying the summer air through open windows and convertible tops. We would often recognize those we knew, and the red light sometimes provided enough time for a brief—albeit shouted—conversation.

But part of the attraction of "step-sitting" in the summer was what was going on across the street. To the right was the bus stop with its eclectic assortment of characters, day and night. But directly across from us was the school playground. And on summer evenings this was the setting for softball games. Chicago softball was an authentic and popular sport with a 16 (*not* 12) inch ball. These larger balls made a tremendous sound when hit with a heavy wooden bat swung by one of the strong young men who regularly assembled for these neighborhood games. A small gathering of fans gathered on the green park benches, but we had preferred seating on our own bleachers—the front steps of our house, where we always had the best view.

For it seemed that the whole world passed by our house in those days: kids on skates and bicycles, couples out for a stroll, cars cruising to the beach or hot dog stands, and the boys en route to their games. They were all there, the whole parade, viewed from our front steps on those warm and wonderful summer nights.

A Cold Swim Signals Summer's End

I have mixed feelings about going away in the summer. While it is a great time to travel, it is a short season here, and I am selfish about how I spend these days. My preference is to be outside with as little an agenda as possible. Just like the summers of my youth.

Yesterday, when the afternoon clouded over with strong winds, I acknowledged a familiar sense of regret. How many times this summer have I taken a leisurely ride in my kayak or enjoyed an afternoon dip in the water or even sat in the shade reading? Not enough. It is never nearly enough.

I called my sister who shared my interest in a swim. We set a time, but first there were phone calls to make and dinner to start and...well, it seems there are always distractions and delays. By the time I finally launched my kayak, the wind was fierce, and the waves made navigation difficult. When I entered Carol's bay, I surprised some fishermen who felt I made an ambitious journey. "Oh, it will be easier on the way back!" I countered.

I hurried the routine of pulling my boat up on Carol's shore and making a noisy ascent over the stone steps so as to scare away potential snakes. (I am told that pine snakes are not constrictors, but I am skeptical.) When I entered Carol's back door, she was just turning on the stove in preparation for dinner. Still, she grabbed a beach towel and scurried outside with me. A sense of fun filled our hearts. We were kids again.

Well, not quite. It took a few minutes of assuring the other that the water would feel fine once we were in. As children our bathing suits never had an opportunity to dry—nor did our hair, which the sun bleached into the crisscross pattern of our braids. Even as teenagers our suntanned skin was usually soothed by a late afternoon dip. Back then the day moved slowly, and summer seemed endless.

It was now *we* who moved slowly, maneuvering away from the seaweed and cold springs and floating just beneath the sun-warmed surface. The afternoon was waning and the increased wind suggested something more, perhaps a change in the weather. We continued swimming in a broad circle until a distinct chill could not be denied. It was time to get out, not for the last time, certainly, for there would be warm days ahead...certainly. Summer could not be over.

Water is a metaphor for our lives, containing and reflecting all that we are, have been, and dream of becoming. To swim on a summer's day is to recapture the moments of our youth and hold onto summer—just a little longer.

Summertime Is Comfortable

Although the summer weather has kept me in a state of ignorant bliss, I can't help but notice that some maple trees are changing color. But as long as the temperatures and sunshine are holding onto summer, I am not leaving my lawn chair. The season may have had a late start, but I am prolonging the bliss as far into September as I can. I am not turning on the heat in the evenings; I am not making soup; and I am certainly not putting on long pants and a sweater. I'm too comfortable with summer to get up and change this soon.

Easing *into* summer is a gradual process. You stop reaching for a jacket on your way out to get the mail. You stop putting your pajamas on at five in the afternoon. By July you've forgotten what an oven is for, and the only reruns you watch are the sunsets from your yard. Easing *out* of summer should be gradual, too.

Lately there has been a trickle of intruders in my eternal summer fantasy. Those organizations and activities that traditionally begin anew with the fall are sending reminders with dates cleverly inserted into phrases like "September kickoff," and "autumn brainstorm session." I am ignoring these notices. I don't want to go to a meeting. I don't want to wear shoes. Come to think of it, I don't really want to *go* anywhere.

I've become so comfortable with summer that my brain has gone on vacation, too. The only articles of clothing I wear are my nightgown and bathing suit—both outside. I am still catching up on reading my magazines that feature articles about the best vacation destinations and the dangers of not using sun protection. Of course it is idle reading. I am no more going to wash my hair in olive oil to protect it from the sun than I am going to bake a seven-layer cake for "a beach-themed party for forty of your closest friends." (Although the pitcher of sangria with berries "picked fresh by you" looks refreshing. Maybe I could make it with Kool-Aid instead of scavenging the woods for wild fruit.)

The truth is that I am not really in the mood for cooking during the summer (as opposed to my not-in-the-mood-to-cook-but-I'll-do-it-anyway attitude the rest of the year). Sometimes the only way I can recall what we had for dinner the night before is to examine the dried fragments left on the grill. "Well, I see bits of charred hamburger. I guess its hot dogs tonight."

We could go out, but then I'd have to put on shoes. I'm so comfortable with summer that I don't even want to wear something I have to button. I wish I could wear a bathing suit and t-shirt all year. But then I'd have to live somewhere else, and I'm too comfortable to move.

New Car Was a Neighborhood Sensation

When my husband suddenly stopped the car, I was sure that he saw a deer in the road. Instead, he backed up to our neighbor's drive and pulled in. There was excitement in his voice when he explained, "John's on his new riding mower." Of course, we just had to witness the maiden voyage across the lawn.

Our neighbor was perched on the seat of his new vehicle. His wife stood nearby, absorbed in the instruction booklet. John gave us a nod before tugging on a lever which dropped the blade that proceeded to munch at the long grass. We watched admiringly as John circled the yard on his shiny, four-wheeled, wonder toy.

This reminded me of the times years ago when getting a new automobile was a sensation in the neighborhood. The event was anticipated for days. The men stood in the alley and discussed the pros and cons of one brand versus another. But even the most ardent debater drew back in awed reverence when *any* new vehicle arrived on the block. A crowd gathered to greet the proud owner, who basked in the glow of his envied acquisition.

Getting a new car was a big deal back then. Families usually only owned one car, and it was expected to last for many years. Consequently, it was taken care of with pride. On any Saturday in the warmer months, at least one of the neighbors held a polishing rag in one hand and a can of Turtle Wax in the other. Preserving the paint's finish was as important as servicing the engine.

Of course, working under the hood was something most men also did routinely. But, as my husband explains, that's when the average man could get to his engine without tools that were as small and specialized as a surgeon's instruments. Like most mechanical things, cars were less complicated then. Elaborations on style were a matter of taste, but all were reliable and had heaters, radios, and trunks. What else did you need?

Still, when the cars for the upcoming year were premiered in September, hearts began to flutter. And when commercials for new models were revealed on black and white televisions, imaginations saw them in color. Even the glossy ads in magazines seemed inadequate to fully convey the long fins and whitewall tires of the most recent "dreams in steel." And seeing one up close, even in your neighbor's garage, was still something to talk about.

Simpler times, perhaps, but weren't those simple pleasures the best?

Past Is Seen with Selective Memory

Every summer people compare the weather and the presence of natural pests to the previous year. "I've never had as many ticks on me as this year!" "Where did all these bees come from?" "We never had mosquitoes here when I was a kid!"

I do not doubt that all elements of nature have their year. Temperature variations, drought, flooding, even the amount of snow can have an effect on summer's community of insects. However, memory is also subject to the rise and fall of seasons over many decades. Maybe—and I am only suggesting here—we just don't remember the *pests* as well as we remember the *best* of our childhoods. And that may be a good thing.

We certainly had mosquitoes in Chicago. And our neighborhood was about as different from a jungle as you could get: asphalt streets, cinder alleys, cement sidewalks, and an occasional dogwood with more bark than bite. The yards were scarcely wider than the narrow houses, and the grass barely reached the height of the mower's blades before an icy wind brought winter's killing frost. But we had humidity, and the mosquitoes loved it. So did we. We ran through sprinklers by day, unaware of the mosquitoes' presence beneath our feet. But at night the tiny vampires followed us as we leapt at lightning bugs. Although the itchy bites had us scratching away in bed at night, by morning our attention turned once again to the beckoning outdoors.

I never saw a tick in the city, but I remember them in the woods up here. On one excursion to my grandfather's camp, we romped through the tall grass and fished along the river bank. One tick remained a stubborn souvenir as it accompanied me home and took up residence in my ear. What I remember is the discussion of the adults as they debated how to remove it. My fear was not of the tick itself but of the burned match that was thrust into my ear to extract it. I much preferred the application of salt on a bloodsucker that had attached itself to my foot while I was swimming in the river. Despite those experiences I returned to the camp many times and played in the overgrown grass and swam in the river with no regard for repeat attacks.

My mother grew hollyhocks along our fence in the alley. Our neighbor had rose bushes and cherry trees. There must have been bumble bees, but I don't recall even one humming through the air en route to pollinating the flowers. I only remember the sweet smell of spring after a long, gray winter. I only remember the soft grass of early summer and the twinkling of lightning bugs on hot nights. Nothing can taint those memories.

The Yellow Days of September

If I had to pick a color to depict the mood for September, it would be yellow. It's the shade that best describes the elements I associate with summer's end: the pale leaves flickering in the golden beams of late afternoon, the dried crops in blond fields, and the final heat that lingers over the city in a yellow haze. It is the color of both brilliance and dullness, a burst of summer's departing sun on an exhausted landscape.

Yellow is the color of school days: Ticonderoga pencils, school busses and construction-papered bulletin boards. September, bathed in golden sunshine, brings memories of the beginning of school, just as it was on my very first day in kindergarten. There, upon a table of honey oak, I picked up a yellow crayon and drew a sun under which happy flowers grew. The girl next to me had blonde banana curls that bobbed up and down as she moved over her artwork. With a bravery inspired by my mother's direction to make friends, I ventured a question: "What are you drawing?" Dimples appeared as she smiled and responded, "A kitchen." I pretended to admire the black boxes she had scrawled and smiled back. And so little Alice with the Shirley Temple dimples and curls became my best friend.

In those yellow days of September we cut up bits of bread with safety scissors and put them on the classroom window sills for the birds. At snack time we put our fingers through the holes of Salerno butter cookies and plunged paper straws into the heavy cream that rose to the top of the milk bottles. We shared golden smiles and playtime giggles that only friends can know. Outside, the leaves were turning yellow-orange against skies as blue as Alice's eyes. Pumpkins turned to sunset tints while Alice's delicate hands traced jack-o-lanterns on construction paper. October, so bold in its grasp, ended the days of softly glowing warmth. Yet, we had created our own.

It was on one of these happy days that Alice announced that she was moving away. Then, suddenly, she was gone. I was too young and too hurt to understand. The classroom seemed darker with the oncoming clouds of winter.

September is a fragile month, heralding the coming autumn even as it mourns the loss of summer. The first day of school, year after year, filled me with sweet anticipation for new teachers, new friends, and new experiences. Now early fall reminds me of that to which I may not return: the simple days of childhood, the pleasures of playthings and playmates, and a time when dreams were outlined on manila-colored paper with fresh crayons. It was an innocent time borne out of green grass summers and mellowed over the gentle, yellow days of September.

Autumn Marks Beginnings and Endings

A former neighbor of ours was an avid gardener whose yard required excessive attention all summer. Despite the demands, she loved working outside. But come October, she would become depressed, hating to see everything she tended die and dreading the long winter ahead.

Of course, that is true: autumn signals the end of life. All we have planted and nurtured and enjoyed must disappear. But, perhaps, there is another way of looking at it: When one thing ends, another begins. The cycle of life continues, even as we mourn the loss of each stage.

This week we received the tragic news that our friends' son had died. The baby had struggled with an auto-immune deficiency that kept him hospitalized for six months, with the exception of one week in July when his parents were allowed to take him home to celebrate his first birthday. Those few days with his family were filled with love and optimism. We were all hopeful about his bone marrow transplant, but fate had other plans. The loss of a child is a grief most bitter.

Then, yesterday, news of another nature arrived in the mail. This time is was the birth announcement of a baby girl, curled like a pink cherub on the card's photo. How adorable! How happy her parents must be! All babies are a promise for the future. They are the embodiment of love and hope. The arrival of a child is a joy most precious.

I pondered on these two children whose lives are celebrated in two different ways this week. I considered the preparations each set of parents must make: one in accommodating the schedule of feeding and caring for a new life; the other in choosing the appropriate means of saying goodbye. In an ironic way the deceased child has accumulated a lifetime of love in his fourteen months on earth. Those he has touched have hearts so full that every beat that continues in them will resonate with his spirit. Love's continuing cycle does not end with the seasons, nor does it yield to the stages of growth or the very end of life itself.

The world often seems a harsh place, especially for those who mourn a loss. But nature can be a source of comfort as each season renews memories of those we loved. And as they return in our thoughts, their spirit will continue in our lives, as will ours in those who love us. Like nature, life is loss and rebirth. Even as we grieve, the cries of new life are heard. The cycle continues.

Fall Reminds Us That Nothing Gold Can Stay

Summer, as cool as it was, seemed to hang on a little longer this year. The grass stayed so soft and green that the verdant scene from my kitchen window looked more like June than September. But by late afternoon the sun had a golden tint that could only come with autumn. Our days, at least the longer ones, were numbered.

But when sunny days bring warm temperatures in October, our spirits are lifted as well. The white clouds that only recently outlined the summer sky drift slowly to the horizon, lingering on the edge of another lazy afternoon. How precious are those mellow hours of mid-day when the leaves in all their brilliance catch the sun, as if this bridge of trees might hold the light a little longer, but, alas, as the poet Robert Frost said, "Nothing gold can stay."

Autumn, though, gives a spectacular farewell performance. In a way it is a celebration, like the fireworks of July or the holiday lights in December. No sooner do we say goodbye to one season than the next one is wooing us with its special attractions. We need that. Not only in the seasonal gifts that nature brings, but in the ones we create to light the darker parts of the year.

Today is Halloween, and the very end of October glows with jack-o-lanterns and porch lights. Trees, like skeletons, rattle bony arms in the wind. Leaves, so recently fallen, are now dead and dry and swept into pyres. Only their scent escapes in wisps of gray smoke. Children, jubilant in their festive costumes, peer innocently from the dim yards. It is the adults who see beyond the night, knowing that tomorrow is November.

November is a dreary month, exposing barren fields once lined with regiments of green stalks and brown gardens where sweet vines had twisted toward the sun. The papery remnants of forgotten flowers flap in the wind. A line of squawking geese make a hurried escape toward an opening in the horizon. Against the lavender-gray sky the drooping sun is now a pale ghost that hovers over a silhouette of trees. For a few moments their jagged outline is tipped with white translucent light before it all disappears in shadows. Nothing gold can stay.

Still, we remember. It is human nature to recall the bliss of summer's carefree days. Perhaps it is the feeling of youth that we most associate with summer. That which buds in rosy splendor restores our faith that life is beginning again, that good things are yet to come. And the most tender of nature's gifts is the gold that turns to green, with all the promise of sweet youth.

We must cherish these gifts, for while they will return again, nothing gold can stay.

Shorter Days Can Enrich the Soul

As usual the first snowstorm appears during the height of holiday frenzy. Inconvenient perhaps, but snow and frigid temperatures are as much a part of the season as Santa Claus. While we may look forward to a white Christmas that is merry and bright, the winter season actually begins on the day that has the most darkness: the winter solstice.

The date is easily overlooked. December 21 is at the end of the Christmas countdown. It is overshadowed by a frantic agenda of shopping, baking, and entertaining. It is lost in a week that spins toward a crescendo of celebration. Yet, the winter solstice is a holiday itself.

Most of us think of the shortest day of the year as a hurdle that is eased by thoughts of approaching festivities. We know that, even in the bitter days of January, the earth will begin its ascent into longer days with gradual measurements of lingering sun. But the actual day when the sun is at its most southerly position is an occurrence that has always intrigued man.

There is an inherent part in each of us that feels the spirit of the shortest day of the year. We can sense it in the weakening light of late afternoons. Too quickly the sun dips below the trees, leaving us with a chill that haunts the evening. For just as the wonder of the awakening day offers promise, the setting of the sun, however beautiful, brings an ending, if only in that single day that can never return.

But night has its own beauty. The clearness of a cold winter night opens the sky to a spectacular view of stars. With some help from electric illumination, activities such as skiing and skating can also be enjoyed after dark. The night sparks imaginations, bringing fantasy to life. It is a time for reflection, bringing memories to light. Unlike the reality that daylight exposes, nighttime allows our perspective to be softened. The less we rely upon our eyes, the more we see with our hearts. The night is for romantics.

There is another way to look at the loss of daylight if you consider what is gained. An early darkness brings the family together. Children, as they did around ancient fires, huddle closer to those they look upon for protection. In the uncertainty that darkness arouses, comfort and hope are gained from loved ones. The winter solstice reminds us that earth has a cycle, and tomorrow will bring longer—and brighter—days.

"Miles to Go Before I Sleep" Is Winter's Theme

Despite the several inches of snow that already fell this fall, it was only today that I first put on my snowshoes for a walk in the woods. It was time, I thought, to stomp out a trail that Bella and I will follow all winter.

As I walked upon the new-fallen snow, lines of Robert Frost's poem, "Stopping by Woods on a Snowy Evening," echoed in my head. The same quiet beauty that gave the narrator pause held me still in my tracks for a few moments. The recent snow had covered all evidence of fall's dried brush, and the growth of summer was but a remembered dream.

Bella tilted her head in an inquisitive pose, reminding me of the narrator's horse who "…gives his harness bells a shake / To ask if there is some mistake." But after a moment, my little companion ran ahead, pursuing some elusive scent of nature beneath the snow. I remained longer to ponder the serenity that was so eloquently expressed by the poet: "The only other sound's the sweep / Of easy wind and downy flake." How lovely that sound is.

Frost was not a poet of great cheer: His verses often reflect a somber philosophy. This is especially applicable in winter, the season so closely associated with the end of life. Only weeks ago I was cutting down leafy branches that intruded on this path. How quickly winter steals the warmth of verdant green and rustic reds. How quickly the frost numbs and amputates its victims, leaving only a memory of what had been.

But we need the snow, too. It gives us opportunity to reflect on all that we have done and what yet is ahead. Only when winter clears the landscape of all distractions and puts before us a canvas of white can we see clearly where our tracks have led us.

Perhaps that unique feeling of solitude is the reason that I love the woods most in winter—except, I am not entirely alone out there. Interrupting my thoughts on this particular day were two crows circling above the trees, insistent in their private quarrel. They were ignorant of my human presence—ignorant of the activity that dominated my visits in other seasons: cutting down trees, erecting posts, nailing up signs to mark the trails. My tracks were unnoticed by those who inhabited these woods. But it is human nature to make plans, to make promises, if only to myself. And so I moved on.

The woods darkened around me, indifferent to my footsteps that would be covered many times in the coming snows of this long winter. But human vanity prevails. I have miles to go before I sleep.

Ghosts of Winter Haunt Memory

The festive lights of the holidays are extinguished, and dark winter holds us in its embrace again. There is sadness in this transition from jollity to somberness, yet it is not quite solitude. As I settle into a chair by the window, breathing in the warmth from a cup of tea and relishing the last rays of afternoon light, I am visited by memories.

Suddenly, the snowy panorama is a backdrop for scenes from my past. I stare through the frosted glass and see my own children as they were so many years ago, playing on the brilliant snow. Their voices are once again youthful and exuberant as they dance around a snowman they erected with their father. Mittens, stiff with ice, are abandoned as snow is shaped into balls in their bare hands and tossed across the yard. My son's cheeks burn with excitement. My daughter's long hair swirls about her laughing face. I memorize her beauty in this moment of ecstasy, knowing that I will carry the memory of that image for a lifetime.

But now pink streaks of daylight strain across the landscape, and I am somewhere else. A tall silhouette weaves down a slope and arrives laughing at my side. The skier is my father, who guides my awkward struggles along the trail. We sit together on the chairlift. He teasingly leans forward and shakes his skis. But I can never be afraid next to him. We look across the vista together, and I know that I will always cherish the world that he showed to me.

The shadows of evening are long now, and the darkness reveals a scene from my early childhood. From far away I can see the lights of a tiny house. The windows are steamed from my grandmother's cooking. The melody of her voice carries notes of her native Sweden. Outside, my grandfather scrapes the walk with a shovel. He stoops and rises above the piles of snow. His blue eyes, pale as the distant stars, see a child coming toward him. I am that little girl, clutching ice skates and smiling as I approach. The cold air is so still that I can hear my grandfather's breathing. The house lights beckon, and I can see through the window the faces of those I love inside. Oh, that I could preserve them there forever.

But the faces fade into the night that has enveloped the backdrop for my revelry. Instead, it is only my own face that I see reflected on the glass. Now that the darkness is complete, my visage, decades older, is illuminated by the lamp beside my chair. Gone are the images of those I have loved and lost. They are merely the ghosts of winter that haunt me still.

Chapter 11

'Tis the Season

Thanksgiving Connects Generations

My childhood recollections of Thanksgiving consist of the same traditions that continued throughout the years so that the holiday blends into one memory. Each home where family has gathered takes on the same ambience that has called us together for decades. Warm greetings ease into conversations, and a sweet anticipation stirs over appetizers and drinks. Then someone announces that all is ready and it is time to come to the table.

"Come to the table." What an invitation that phrase conveys! How familiar and comforting it is to sit at the Thanksgiving table once again: the *good* dishes and crystal stemware set with care; the unmatched pieces that serve the children at the card table; the centerpiece turkey, golden-skinned and ceremoniously sliced; the bowls and platters that are passed—and passed again; and the praise that glows like candle flames upon the happy scene.

But Thanksgiving is so much more than the meal we share together. It is even more than the celebration of that first Thanksgiving that symbolizes the shared bounty between the Pilgrims and Indians. Though non-religious, the holiday flows with a spirituality that unites all of mankind. It is a time to remember and appreciate all with which our lives have been blessed.

These blessings are universal, for the love of one another is at the core of humanity. When we share food, we share life's gifts. We remember that there are those for whom a daily meal is a struggle for survival, and "give us today our daily bread" is the humblest of humane acts we can offer to those less fortunate. Our holiday meal, wherever it may be served, is a reminder that our simplest blessing is that which sustains us.

As we come to the table on Thanksgiving, we should remember that there is a greater table that we share with others. Americans of different origins, beliefs, and circumstances also come together on this day. They gather with family, friends, or even strangers in homes, churches, restaurants, or shelters to share a meal that symbolizes that for which they are grateful. They follow in the footsteps of our ancestors and the many generations who have expressed their gratitude for all that America has given them.

For most of us Thanksgiving is touched by personal sentiment. The table at which we share our meal is also occupied by the spirits of those who are no longer with us. As we reach out for one another's hand and bow our heads, those we have loved and lost join us in heart and memory as we honor the past, give thanks for our present gifts, and pray that these blessings bring peace and prosperity to all who *come to the table.*

Be Thankful for Small Conveniences

Like most of you, I have a lot to be thankful for, especially when it comes to friends and family. I try to count my blessings throughout the year, but the traditional holiday for giving thanks is a reminder to be grateful for all that I have. That being said, there is also a lighter side to Thanksgiving Day that has to do with small blessings.

First, I am grateful that I was not a Pilgrim. I realize that there is much to admire in the simple life of a Colonial woman, but it required a patience that I do not possess. I could only cook dinner over a fire if someone else started, tended, and watched it for me. Meanwhile, I would be gnawing on raw ears of corn with the Indians, who seemed to have a lot more fun.

I am also grateful for my modern appliances. Having a refrigerator means I can purchase a turkey wrapped in plastic, instead of cutting the head off a warm fowl that has to be plucked and disemboweled prior to cooking. In contrast, I only have to give my frozen bird enough time to defrost. Keeping it in a paper bag in the refrigerator for several days is the most expedient thawing process, but I have often miscalculated the time needed for an especially large bird. This usually results in a lot of chipping away at the frozen innards of an ice-filled cavity. My grandmother used to make giblet gravy, but the thought of handling those slippery gizzards is too much like a lab experiment, although I have to admit that store-bought turkeys reduce the ick-factor by having their entrails packed in convenient baggies. They also have plastic belly buttons that pop up when they are cooked. Science is a beautiful thing.

Of course, the meal wouldn't be complete without our special dishes, which, for me, requires opening a lot of cans. That doesn't mean that I haven't deviated from the convenient recipes offered on the back of soup labels. I once attempted to make a traditional dish from scratch, but the process required so many ingredients and utensils that I kept losing track of what I was making. My family was just as confused and spent most of the meal guessing what the mystery casserole was. That was the last time I ventured down "Recipe Lane" without Campbell's soup.

I have accomplished homemade pies, but that requires reserving hours to allow for the delicate process and inevitable failure of pie crust. Eventually, I solved that problem by accepting anyone's offer to bring something. "Well, if you insist," I reply with genuine relief, "you can bring that wonderful pie that you make."

I feel a little guilty about condemning someone else to the kitchen for a day of struggles with lard and flour, but I dispel those feelings with the knowledge that I am contributing the table's main attraction: the turkey. With any luck it won't be as overcooked and gutless as I am.

Holiday Lights Are a Tangled Web We Weave

Outdoor holiday lighting has gotten out of control. Instead of the simple lighted wreaths or window candles, we feel compelled to install enough lights to land airplanes in the front yard.

My personal lighting nightmare always occurs on the windiest, coldest day of the year. I can hear the rattle of bulbs even before my husband emerges from the basement with a mass of twisted strings dangling from his arms. My job is to untangle them so that he can stretch the lines across the floor, plug them into an outlet, and check for any burned-out bulbs. During this process we invariably step on several and crunch them into the carpet.

My next job is to drive to the store for more light bulbs. Upon my return Richard is poised on a ladder that is balanced on one leg. I take my position at the bottom of the ladder, providing the appearance that I could thwart a fall. The only protection I can really offer is to repeatedly warn him *not* to fall. Sometimes it works; sometimes he falls.

This year I feigned eagerness for our yearly ritual in order to get the lights up while the weather was still nice. I even purchased extra bulbs and located the extension cords. The sun felt warm as I pretended to hold the ladder. I was even calm when Richard jammed the plastic clips under the impenetrable gutter guards. But as I ran for the trusty duct tape, the sky clouded over with an ominous winter gray. Sure enough, just as the last bulb was attached, Richard noticed that another twelve feet of roofline remained.

"Isn't there another string?" he asked in a tone that suggested I had thrown one away.

I accused him of putting the bulbs too close together. He accused me of hurrying him along and disrupting his craftsmanship. The inevitable trip I made to the store for more lights put a chill in more than our moods. A strong wind whipped at the lights as they bounced off the last stretch of gutter and shattered on the ground. Richard snapped orders like a doctor in surgery. "Another bulb! *Red!* Not *green!*"

It was dark when I picked the last of the broken glass out of the shrubbery. Richard descended the ladder and plugged in the lights, an action to which he added a weary "There!"
The lights gave a momentary glow of color before they were extinguished by a blown fuse.

In that silence that only married couples understand, we disconnected the strings and rearranged a network of extension cords into different outlets. Finally, now cold and exhausted, we duct-taped the loose ends to the siding and tucked dangling lines behind the shutters.

"Good enough," he growled. I couldn't agree more.

Shopping Is Not a Dickens of a Good Time

In Charles Dickens' *A Christmas Carol* holiday shopping is heartwarming and quaint. Smiling people pause to chat on charming cobblestone streets illuminated with the soft glow of lantern light. Carolers provide seasonal background music, and shop doors open to the tinkling of welcoming bells. Merry shoppers find the perfect gifts and cheerfully carry them through the snow-dusted streets on their way to picturesque skating ponds and cozy cottages.

According to Dickens, Victorian Christmas shopping was sheer bliss. Easy for him to say: He never had to find a parking space. There is no time to purchase roasted chestnuts while you circle the mall parking lot. Shopping requires a stiff upper lip—and comfortable shoes.

Today it seems that no matter what items are on your list, everyone else has the same ideas—except they got to the store before you did and purchased the last ones. Ever resourceful, you scour the aisles for creative alternatives. You find a stack of adorable sweaters for your little niece, all in sizes that she may grow into in ten years. You spot what you think is the perfect nightgown for Aunt Sarah—until you notice the words "Hot Mama" on the back.

What about pretty stationery? A salesgirl scoffs at this inquiry. "No one *writes* anymore." She directs you to the electronics department. The displays are written in hieroglyphics. The clerk suggests a gadget that can store a library of information in the space of a pinhead. Before you can ask why, he has assembled an array of cords across the counter for connections—to *what*, you have no idea. The thought of getting a nice book enters your head, but the "pinhead" reference suddenly makes reading actual words on a page seem ridiculous.

By now the mall is heaving with people who all share the same trance-like expression. The temperature has risen to ninety-five degrees. Music from overhead speakers drowns out their voices—and their thoughts. Someone stumbles, and the ripple effect knocks you into a specialty store called Soap Box.

Despite the heat, your sore feet, and the distraction of hearing "Have a Holly, Jolly Christmas" for the nineteenth time, the smells inside the Soap Box are encouraging. You spew out a list of gift suggestions: Perfume? Hand Cream? Body lotion? Bubble bath? Looking all of thirteen, the salesgirl blinks without expression and tells you, "We only have soap."

The voice of Burl Ives echoes across the parking lot as you search for your car. You are resigned to the fact that this holly, jolly Christmas will be a *clean* one for everyone on your list.

Greatest Gifts Come from the Heart

When we returned to school after the holidays, it was typical for our teacher to have us write about what we did over the break or what we received as a special gift for Christmas or Hanukah. It was an assignment that was generally met with enthusiasm as all of us had stories to share about our holiday experiences.

When I look back at those innocent times, I am reminded about how much things have changed, as well as what has not. I'm sure that I wrote about my newest doll or visiting my grandparents. For most children these are still holiday highlights. The toys may have become more complicated and expensive, but the excitement of receiving just the gift you wanted still brings joy, and being surrounded by family at this time of year is still a cherished tradition. The difference is that it is increasingly more difficult for families to be together on the holidays.

This was made dramatically clear to me several years ago when I gave an essay assignment to my own students. I asked my juniors to write about their most desired holiday wish. They were assured that their personal expressions would not be shared with anyone except me, and I took them home to grade them over the Christmas break. What I expected to read about were gifts of video games and fashionable clothes and the anticipation of seasonal feasts with extended family. I couldn't have been more wrong.

My sixteen-year-olds poured their hearts into these essays. Perhaps it was because the opportunity to express themselves in this format allowed them a safe outlet for their deepest of emotions. As their teacher I knew little about their personal lives or family situations and was, therefore, a neutral sounding board. However, what I learned made neutrality impossible. My heart was touched by the soulful requests of these teenagers.

Not one of them yearned for an extravagant present. Those who desired any material gift at all did so for someone else. Some expressed a wish for a new appliance, a reliable car, or money to make a parent's life easier. Some asked for a job for a parent or to have "my mother stop crying." But the majority had a single request that family members could be together for the holiday. Some described a heartbreaking separation from a mother or father. Others recalled happier times when grandparents were still alive and how much they loved and missed them.

These revealing accounts say a lot about the true meaning of Christmas. When we think of what to give someone, it should be remembered that our *presence* is the best present, and the greatest gift of all is love.

Cutting Tree Continues Legacy

We started a new tradition after we moved here to the Northwoods. Over the Thanksgiving holiday our son selects an evergreen tree from our woods and cuts it down for our Christmas tree. I accompany him as he carries it back to the house, and Bella prances alongside with a discarded branch in her mouth. It is a happy excursion.

The Christmas tree is the centerpiece of holiday decorating, and it carries emotional attachments. I remember as a child how some of Chicago's vacant lots transformed into fragrant forests overnight. In choosing a tree my father tended to overestimate the size of our small living room, a problem that my mother later addressed with a saw. Once decorated, I never tired of watching the glowing bulbs reflecting off the metallic ornaments and quivering lead tinsel. The Christmas tree transformed our living room into a holiday fantasy.

In the sixties several of our neighbors purchased the popular artificial trees. Silver, blue, and even pink versions were a little too modern for our family. Still, they didn't leave a trail of needles to haunt the carpet for months. When Richard and I were first married, we bought a green "bottle brush" variety for our first apartment. The assembly presented the same challenges every year, and the plastic tree eventually found a new home in my classroom.

Our own children insisted upon a real tree, as well as a role in picking it out. No matter where we shopped for a tree, Emily and Grant always took off in separate directions with periodic shouts of "I found a good one!" Settling on the right one was always a well-debated compromise.

There were also excursions to tree farms west of the suburbs that offered the opportunity of cutting down a tree yourself. Sometimes just getting to the location on rural roads was a challenge. One year we cut a tree down on property that turned out *not* to be a tree farm at all. Another time Richard's bare hands got so cold while we searched for the perfect tree that when he finally cut one down, he sliced his numb fingers, too! Our next search was for a bandage to stop the bleeding. Thereafter, we bought our tree from the neighborhood Boy Scouts.

The first Christmas after we lost our daughter, the holiday decorations remained boxed in the basement. I didn't want Christmas, but my son protested. "We have to at least have a tree." When he brought one home, I compromised by placing a few ribbons on its branches. Somehow, the unadorned evergreen offered a little comfort at that difficult time.

When Grant comes home for Christmas, he gets to see his latest selection transformed with a lifetime of mementoes. After all, what would Christmas be without a tree?

Christmas Magic Is No Surprise

Remember when you were a child at Christmastime and wished and hoped for that one special gift? You may have written to Santa or even dropped hints at home, but you could never be sure that you would get what you really wanted. And if you did find it under the tree on Christmas morning, the element of surprise was part of the gift itself.

That may still be true, but as we get older, it gets harder to be surprised, especially if you have family members who are about as subtle as, well, reindeer on a roof. It begins with those obvious hints around Thanksgiving. "So," your spouse will say, "if I were going to buy you a sweater, what size would you wear?" I guess that eliminates the surprise of finding out that your husband thinks that you are several sizes larger or smaller than you actually are.

It's not as if loved ones don't want to surprise you: They just want to be sure that you will like what they give you. My husband, who has managed to surprise me with wonderful gifts over the years, had an imagination meltdown last year and asked several times for some ideas. I needed a new bathrobe and had lost a favorite pair of earrings so I suggested those items. I could still be surprised by what he might pick out, right? Well, something told me that wasn't happening when he posed these questions while we were shopping: "Where can I find the women's robes?" Later—while awkwardly holding a robe-sized box—he asked cryptically: "If I got you earrings, would you prefer the hoops to be the size of nickels or quarters?"

But I guess my father's flair for nuance takes the cake. Always a practical gift-giver, he found a deluxe electric can-opener/knife sharpener on sale in the newspaper that he thought would be perfect for my mother. No, he didn't say anything. He didn't have to. For several days the newspaper ad with the item was posted on the refrigerator. Mom's only element of surprise was whether he would remember to purchase it before the sale price expired.

The last Christmas gift my father gave my mother was a watch. I went with him to purchase it, and he knew exactly what he wanted, pointing with confidence to his selection at the jewelry counter. Mom still loves that watch, mostly because he picked it out himself for her.

I know how she feels. Although wind-up watches have long been out of fashion, I still cherish the pretty wristwatch my husband gave me the first Christmas we were married. And I still take it out and wear it on special occasions. But the most treasured gift was the one he gave me the Christmas before we were married. After forty years, *that* surprise still sparkles.

Decorations Preserve Memories

Last year my sister and I visited a friend whose holiday decorations included numerous vintage items. She proudly showed us ornaments that once were on her mother's and grandmother's trees. Her favorites, like the Snow White and Seven Dwarfs ornaments, were from her childhood. We encouraged her to display these unique treasures, as well as an Art Deco box containing a set of Christmas tree lights from the thirties. These were not just vintage decorations, they were memories.

Along with those personal memories were indications of the times they were from. The old aluminum icicles twirled under the lights with hypnotic charm. But the ornaments purchased in the 1940s had paper tops, which conserved metal during World War II. Rosemary smiled as she identified each piece, and I realized that memories, like the delicate glass of the oldest items, were both precious and fragile. Keeping these items helps to preserve those memories.

Rosemary's collection brought back memories from the holiday trees I remember…heavy lead tinsel, hand-painted ornaments, and swags of thick garland. Our family's tree also had strings of blue and yellow Swedish flags draped across boughs from which hung ornaments in colors that ranged from traditional red and green to the metallic pinks and turquoise so popular in the fifties and sixties. Upon our front door was a large, plastic Santa face, cheerfully greeting those who entered, and the front windows glowed with electric candles encircled in red felt wreaths.

Few of these items have survived the years, but I treasure the ones I still possess. Each year I begin attaching the tree lights by plugging in the old set that belonged to my Grandma Signe. I love the twisted wires of red and green and the bulbs of sculpted glass, which have faded a bit but still glow with holiday magic after all these decades. And although the old ornaments seem too fragile to survive another season, they are carefully placed on the tree where they belong. These sentiments from family and friends tell the story of Christmases past.

Rosemary gave us ornaments that she and her mother had made, and these will become traditions on our trees as well. She felt happy that we would appreciate them and take care of them. Holiday traditions are delicate memories that we often entrust to others so that they will continue to bring meaning and joy. In the case of these beautiful handmade ornaments, the efforts to create them will be appreciated, even by those who did not personally know the creator. Maybe that's because we share a common bond that continues generation after generation: preserving our Christmas memories.

A Charlie Brown Christmas Turns Fifty

Yeah, how did *that* happen? Watching *A Charlie Brown Christmas* on television each December is one of my favorite ways to herald in the holiday season. The charming special with its hip animation and jazzy score is as fresh today as it was when it premiered in 1965. Charlie Brown and his friends are just kids. I was just a kid. How can any of us be fifty years older?

1965. That was the year our family drove to Florida to visit my grandparents. There was nothing *jazzy* about traveling twelve-hundred miles in a station wagon, and there was nothing *hip* about my grandparents' damp cinder-block house. In fact, when you are accustomed to Chicago's white Christmases, the idea of a brown one is a little depressing.

And, apparently, it wasn't even safe to go outside. My grandmother, who for months had told my parents that they just *had* to visit this wonderful, sunny region of the country, now had some warnings for her grandchildren that made Florida seem more like a strange planet. She guided us to the carport, the safest vantage point to observe these alien dangers.

"See those beautiful flowers there?" she said while pointing to brilliant pink blooms on a bush outside the house. "They are poisonous so don't eat them!" And there were deadly snakes. "One little boy thought it was a candy wrapper, picked it up, got bit and died." And in addition to there being spiders the size of headlights, scorpions lurked about as well. "Just check inside your shoes!" Good Grief! Spending Christmas in Florida was like spending Christmas on Mars!

Like Charlie Brown, I had a hard time finding the Christmas spirit although there was no lack of spirit in the decorations. Just like Snoopy and his electrified dog house, the commercial aspects of Christmas flashed like neon signs, but from snowless roofs and palm trees.

Following Christmas traditions that year was a little like Charlie Brown's futile attempt to direct the school pageant: Everyone was expressing the holiday spirit in his own way. We weren't dancing, but we were running on the beach, diving into the salty waves, and collecting sea shells—unusual activities for us, but also a lot of fun. My younger siblings turned into Peanuts characters as their play echoed noisily throughout the house. But no one really minded. My grandmother served her wonderful coffee cake and cookies; my grandfather played his mandolin; and we stayed up late to hear stories and share laughter—just the way we always had.

And my grandparents had a traditional, real tree—decorated with their familiar ornaments and lights. It took up a lot of space in the little living room, but I think Charlie Brown would agree that all it needed was a little love. In fact, that's all that Christmas really needs, wherever you spend it.

A Time for Reminiscing

One of my favorite holiday memories was watching my children bound down the stairs on Christmas morning and kneel beneath the tree in anticipation. I held the camera as they squealed out, "Just what I always wanted!" Vivid still are the images of their smiling faces as they asked, "Do you like what I gave you, Mom?" Though the gifts themselves fade from recollection, those sentimental moments remain.

When my siblings and I had our own families, we were fortunate to live close to our parents with whom we all celebrated on Christmas Eve. Their home was filled with the familiar scents and sounds of that night's festivities, embellished over the years with the addition of excited grandchildren. But on Christmas Day we were all in our own homes with our individual families so my parents came to us to deliver gifts and share Christmas greetings.

This tradition, that my mother called "making the rounds," began in the afternoon and concluded at our house. By then the holiday lights glowed softly in the pale light of dusk. The children would spot their car and excitedly proclaim that "Grandma and Grandpa are here!" Moments later the front door burst open with a flurry of packages and greetings. "What did you get from Santa, Grant?" "Is that a new doll, Emily?" "That turkey smells wonderful!"

After dinner we settled into the living room. Once again the camera was brought out to capture the faces beaming over a new toy, a pretty sweater or a flannel shirt. Hugs were exchanged, wrapping paper was gathered, and cookies and tea were served on the coffee table. The children sprawled across the floor, occupied with their new gifts. Richard and I sat opposite my parents while a glowing fire lent its warmth to the tranquil scene of Christmas night.

Thus began one of my favorite traditions, listening to my parents reminisce. We shared recollections of holidays in the city, like the decorated windows of downtown's department stores. Mom reached back to her childhood when Chicago was accessible by streetcar and extended family gathered in their South Side apartments. We laughed at her stories about favorite or peculiar aunts and uncles. Dad recalled his youth in Michigan and the Swedish relatives who inhabited his small town. Names and faces drifted through the conversation as we remembered those now silenced by the passing years.

Perhaps, long from now, my voice will be heard in someone's memory—bits of recollected stories told before a fire on a Christmas night. These warm memories will connect a family, even beyond our own lives.

Christmas Morning Is for Children

Christmas Eve may be calm and bright, but Christmas morning is usually a contrast to the more silent night. Maybe it's the anticipation that builds through the long holiday season, but Christmas morning holds a special magic. Even in sleep the eyelids of children flicker with excitement until they bolt up in bed with the realization that it is finally—finally!—Christmas morning!

Parents have their own pace as they stumble downstairs in drowsy celebration. Wasn't it only a couple hours ago that they finished assembling that toy and wrapping the last present? Mom is looking for the camera, and Dad is wondering if he could get a cup of coffee before the frenzy of unwrapping gifts takes over. Eventually, Mom and Dad settle into their chairs to share in the wonder. After all, Christmas morning belongs to children.

I remember well this magical time in my childhood and, especially, sharing it with my sister. We always opened our gifts with the utmost care and delicacy, relishing every moment of suspense as if that were part of the gift as well. But when our brother came along, something happened to decorum on Christmas morning. Tissue paper was a thin barrier between his eager hands and the coveted toy. Within seconds he was driving his metal Tonka truck over our dolls in bulldozer ecstasy. His mission of destruction continued all day.

There were also Christmas mornings disrupted by the coughs and sniffling of colds. That didn't damper our enthusiasm for opening our presents. But one year the stomach flu invaded our house for the holidays, and playing with our new toys was temporarily on hold. They remained under the tree while we recuperated in bed.

A couple days later we awoke very early, eager to get to those toys. We also had our appetites back, and the tiny tea set was perfect for a makeshift breakfast that morning. We assembled celery and crackers on the doll-sized plates but wanted something special for the cups. Boiling water for tea was out of the question, but we found an interesting alternative in the refrigerator. A bottle of red wine, leftover from Christmas dinner, was the perfect complement to our menu. In fact, it tasted enough like grape juice to justify a second pouring.

Then our parents woke up. My mother took one look at the opened bottle of wine on the kitchen counter and quickly disrupted our tea party. After that episode we only served water or ginger ale in our china cups. It really made no difference to us—or our dolls.

The Most Sentimental Time of the Year

At this sentimental time of the year, we often recall the holidays of our youth. I am blessed to have had wonderful Christmases with my families in both Chicago and Michigan. Sharing Christmas with everyone was often hectic, but it created treasured memories.

On Christmas Eve we celebrated with my mother's family who lived only a few miles from our own Chicago home. The house was filled with relatives and friends, most of who exhibited the same boisterous, Irish temperament and filled the tiny rooms with gaiety and laughter. My grandfather fixed cocktails with olives and cherries and served them in fancy glasses. My grandmother played the organ while my sister and I gave shy renditions of Christmas carols. We sat in layers of red organdy with velvet ribbons around our waists and long hair. Our mother had put a thin coat of Vaseline on our patent leather shoes, which we impatiently tapped in anticipation of the early arrival of presents.

As the only children in the family, we were alternately teased and doted upon by my mother's younger brothers. They convinced us that Santa was on his way, and we listened all the way home for his sleigh bells in the snow-lined city streets.

Christmas morning was wrapped in tissue paper, but not for long. Such wonders emerged from under the tree! Some gifts came in duplicates for my sister and me: cowgirl outfits, matching dolls, and robes in pink and blue. Others we shared: miniature cookware, a phonograph with records, and board games that would occupy us for hours. How splendid to go to bed that night in a new flannel nightgown while clutching a special Christmas doll!

But there were other years when we abandoned our newly-opened gifts and loaded the station wagon for the long trip to Michigan to have Christmas with my other grandparents. We'd arrive long after the pines along the highway had disappeared in darkness. Packages, suitcases, and sleepy children filled the little living room already crowded by the tree Grandpa had cut from the woods of his beloved camp. Grandma emerged from the kitchen and scooped us into her arms. The table glowed, and the Swedish feast was comforting and familiar. Gifts were exchanged. Grandpa played his mandolin. Christmas began again.

Christmas Remembered

As I trim the tree with tinsel,
It reflects a distant scene
That my parents spread before us
As a promised Christmas dream.

Colored lights recall the city,
That old house where windows glowed,
Voices singing at the organ,
Uncles, candy, toys and bows.

Now when cold still tingles fingers
Handmade mittens used to warm,
I recall our Northern Christmas,
Grandma's kitchen, Grandpa's arms.

When my table's set with candles,
Someone else's hand I see
Places bread still warm from baking,
And the magic smells I breathe.

It is Christmas I remember
When I dream of them at night,
Tunes from mandolins that haunt me,
And the sound of sleigh bells, light.

Holidays Linger with Leftovers

This is certainly the season for expressing good will. It is also the season for expressing good cooking, good baking, and good snacking. Good gracious! I don't know about you, but I am *goodied* out! I am also *cookied, candied*, and *eggnoged* out! It's not my fault. It's not anybody's fault. Although the holidays bring the best *out* in us, they also put the best *into* us.

Our will power was exhausted at Thanksgiving. Since then, culinary temptations have been appearing around every corner, usually in adorable containers. Cookies in decorative tins, Chex mix in a Santa bowl, and candy canes in a "one horse open sleigh" are pure sabotage.

Even the simple act of sitting requires a festive reward. Suddenly the coffee table is covered with appetizers shaped like snowmen. The lure of spicy cheese dips that are intended to be scooped up by anything crunchy and salty is beyond any normal human's resistance. Sentimental holiday movies just seem better with cookies and hot cocoa. How can you even concentrate on the football game on New Year's Day without a plate of sloppy appetizers on your lap?

I guess we can put a little of the bingeing blame on our relatives. They make all your favorites over the holidays, in enough quantity to send you home with buckets of leftovers. One compliment about a bean casserole will result in an annual deluge of it for years. Compound that with all the other special dishes brought through your door and it's a perpetual feast. You can't just ignore your loving aunt when she pinches your cheek and says, "I know how much you love my potato salad so I made five extra pounds just for you."

The potato salad lasts almost as long as the holiday ham. Slices the size of boot soles are carved away at dinner. The exposed bone is carried away for soup—and yet the meat continues on in sandwiches for days. Bits of ham appear in a creamy, mystery mixture that is spread over toast for a creative imitation of chipped beef. You assume that this impromptu recipe *had* to be the last of the holiday ham, but you were wrong. For just when you thought that you saw the end of the Christmas pig's reign, a casserole emerges from the oven with generous pieces of the miracle meat cavorting with chunks of potatoes. By the third day the casserole has shrunk to a saucer-sized leftover in the refrigerator. On the fourth day it is served with an unidentifiable Jell-O salad and headless gingerbread men. That night you burp and an unmistakable "oink" comes out of your mouth.

Just when you decide to call a halt to the holiday fare, the button pops off of your pants. Of course, that only means one thing: room for dessert!

'Tis the Season to Eat, Drink, and Be Wary

Despite the slow start to winter, the season is always a long and lingering one up here, especially when it begins with such frivolity and then comes to a crashing...lull. You can just get a little sense of that when you walk into the kitchen the morning after Christmas and all you see are cookie crumbs on the floor and bits of tissue paper under the cabinets. You may have been like a transformed Scrooge the day before, but it's back to humbug the next day.

Of course, the holiday spirit is still running through the week—rather like the blinking lights that you put up in November that are now getting on your nerves. Sure those red and green bulbs are festive, but it would be nice to have the plain bulbs back in the outside lanterns so you can actually find the front door in that dim light without tripping over the bushes.

Meanwhile, your Christmas tree is having a meltdown of its own. A couple of the heavier ornaments—someone's idea of a clever gift ("Look! It's an ornament *and* a coffee mug!")—have slid off the branches and rolled under the couch. The tree is so dry, you're afraid to light it one more night, but then most of the needles have already fallen off. They stick to your clothes, along with the tinsel that inevitably floats off the tree and clings to your hair. By December 26 you look more like a Christmas tree than that balsam you decorated a month ago.

Oh, there are still parties and holiday get-togethers after Christmas, which are welcomed treats. What are not so welcome by now are the treats themselves. It's been so long since your body ate an actual meal, your stomach is starting to resemble a cheese ball—a *giant* cheeseball. You don't even use utensils anymore: Everything you eat comes on a toothpick. Let's face it: If you cut yourself, you would bleed eggnog—which is about all you have in your refrigerator right now, besides the chip dip and cocktail wienies you were saving for breakfast.

Part of you yearns to return to normalcy. You might even wake up on December 26 and declare, "I am going to have a big breakfast, hearty enough to eat with a fork, and a cup of coffee that is not flavored with gingerbread or peppermint or served in a cardboard cup."

Your wife, who is clearly not ready to abandon her holiday traditions, hands you a plastic platter of leftover appetizers, all conveniently stabbed with toothpicks. She points to the coffee pot, hidden behind an array of paper goods adorned with snowmen and reindeer. "There's a coffee mug under the couch," she says. "Hang it back on the tree when you're finished."

She disappears in a flash of light. Or so it appears until you brush something from your eyes. It's a strand of tinsel. That's it! You really need to take those decorations down—if they don't take you down first.

Family Talents Are Lost in Translation

When cousins from Sweden arrived for an extended visit, my family planned an experience that paid homage to our roots while creating an American display of hospitality. Nancy hosted a Swedish Christmas and served homemade glogg, while my brother provided a sightseeing tour of Chicago. They came to visit our homes in Michigan a few days later, and Carol and I provided activities that we hoped would continue a warm welcome for our distant relatives. However, as the week wore on, language and culture differences had us siblings wondering just how *distant* these relatives were.

By the end of the week it was apparent that our efforts to provide an American-style good time was often lost in translation, and the ideas for entertaining our Scandinavian kin had become as dry as my American Christmas tree, the needles of which could be heard dropping as we sat in the silence of my living room on New Year's Eve. Suddenly, Nancy, emboldened with glogg, proposed an impromptu talent show in which each of us would demonstrate a trick or skill. There's nothing like a quirky challenge to unleash the court jester in the typical American.

And my family, bless them, are not only typical, they are about as *average* as you can get in terms of talent. A few of us actually play musical instruments, but—to give you some idea of our sense of appreciation for the mediocre—my mother's occasional performance of her one-woman-kitchen-band always brings down the house. So when my brother-in-law displayed his double-jointed dexterity by twisting himself into a pretzel on the carpet, it was met with applause from us—and looks of confusion from the overseas crowd. My nephew's impressions of well-known people were, apparently, only well-known in this country. Even my son's illusion of pushing a whole pencil up his nose—a real crowd-pleaser in our family—failed to tickle any funny bones in the stoical Scandinavians.

If I was going to tickle anything at all, I was going to need a master in comedy—or, in this case, the *mistress* of comedy. I scurried upstairs for a quick change into my Lucille Ball costume, returning minutes later with my best impersonation of the wacky redhead from *I Love Lucy*. As if our winters aren't cold enough up here, the frosty looks on our relatives' faces lowered the temperature another twenty degrees.

Apparently, the classic American comedy was not as widely-popular as I thought, and my performance required some *'splainin'*.

As for the rest of our acts, well, suffice it to say, our cousins from the North eventually showed signs of slight amusement, if only reacting to the oddity of our performances. Since their talent was in *reserving* emotion, we'll take that as rave reviews.

Holiday Storage Is a Tight Fit

I'm not sure exactly how this happened, but I am blaming the Christmas pig. The straw swine was a gift from visiting relatives. Apparently a traditional, seasonal figure in Sweden, the little porker put everything off balance in my holiday storage plans. I could just barely get him into a box filled with other decorations by pressing his ears down under the lid.

Still, he refused to go back into that same box the following year. In fact, his defiance was duplicated by a reindeer whose antlers defied any of the containers reserved for home décor. In desperation I placed both of them in a cardboard box, where they remained until the following year when they rejoined the Christmas zoo in my living room. But their odd-shaped heads presented the same problem this January 2, my official day for putting the holiday decorations into storage.

And they weren't alone. Two new ornaments were too large for the compartments reserved for tree decorations. And a candleholder that looked so delicate on my table was now as awkward as a tree branch. Even Frosty, the glittery snowman, threatened to wait until spring before he went into hibernation. Last year all of these items had been successfully stored in their appropriately-labeled boxes. So—unless the mice are juggling their contents—*what happened?*

I have a theory about the accumulation of Christmas décor that is akin to the theory of survival of the fittest. Only the most durable of ornaments can survive the process of trimming and un-trimming the tree, which usually results in the breakage of one ornament each year. If my husband helps me in either of these tasks, at least two are smashed. This justifies the addition of a couple new items each year, thus allowing for a rotation that maintains a balanced ratio between the number of decorations and the amount of storage space. At least it did until the pig entered the picture.

I tried making more room by eliminating some of the packaging on other décor. But even tissue paper between the more fragile items proved too bulky for the confines of their storage bins. My head spun with possible solutions, and I briefly considered stuffing the fluffy tree garland in with the Christmas village houses. But that real estate was already crammed with the overdevelopment of Main Street's shops, as well as countryside expansion with plate-sized skating rinks and fleece-covered ski hills. Even one more miniature tree would prevent the entire winter-wonderland from being contained together under one plastic lid.

The straw pig was staring at me. How could that oinker derail a train of twelve perfectly organized boxcars? Well, I guess I have no choice but to purchase another home for my holiday decorations—though I'm sure there will be no vacancies in it next near.

Reindeer Caper Backfires on Amateur Sleuths

The white deer looked stately on our frozen lawn. Handcrafted from interlocking pieces of plywood, the decorative reindeer were secured to the ground with metal stakes and adorned with bright red bows. The problem was that these frisky fakes just wouldn't stay put.

Although the stationary deer were appropriately posed in peaceful snow-grazing, we awoke one morning to discover that their positions were dramatically altered to represent quite a different scenario, one in which one animal was "mounted" upon the other. Although we quickly rectified the situation, the vandalism reoccurred the next night and proved to be a source of annoyance, as well as embarrassment.

We assumed that some teenagers were having a little fun with our yard art. Even some members of our family found the playful staging humorous. My sister's husband was particularly amused. In fact, Jim enjoyed the deer maneuver and its effect on us so much that when the vandalism ceased, he decided to continue the antics himself. That's right, my brother-in-law—a lawyer, no less—sneaked over to our house one night and re-created the scene of the crime. Not that he confessed, but a family informant spilled her guts. That's when my husband and I plotted revenge.

The plan was simple: We would set the deer up on Jim's lawn and pose them in the same inappropriate manner that he did on ours. (We'd see who was laughing then!) We waited until eleven o'clock at night to disassemble the deer and place them in the trunk of our car. (We didn't want any of our neighbors to think that we were staging our own deer at night!) By the time we pulled up to my sister's house, it was predictably quiet and dark. With a flashlight in one hand, and the video camera in the other—I wanted this caper on film!—I assisted my husband in removing the plywood pieces from the trunk. It was hard to distinguish antlers from legs in the dark, but we finally managed to assemble them in the front yard in that memorable tableau that was now captured on tape. We giggled all the way home.

We knew that Jim would see the deer when he left for work, and we expected a phone call that morning. But when that day and the following day passed without a word, we began to wonder. Of course, he would assume that we did it. Was he angry? How could he be? He started it! Maybe he was plotting a counter attack. Well, we certainly weren't going to call him and admit our guilt. So we just waited.

A couple evenings later the entire family gathered at my brother's house for his birthday. Richard and I were certain that Jim would seize this opportunity to confront us in front of the family. What we weren't prepared for was no reaction at all. Jim behaved normally, as if nothing at all had happened. Hadn't he seen the deer in the yard?

I pulled my little niece aside and asked if her father had seen the deer on their lawn. "Oh, yes. The lady across the street called and told him. He said some kids must have done it."

I hadn't considered that a neighbor might complain, but I figured Jim was still getting his just desserts. Nonetheless, the fact that he hadn't accused us was making us suspicious of him—or what he was planning to do next. We decided that the charade had gone on long enough. I made a general announcement for everyone to gather around as I had something to show them. Then I slipped the video tape into the television and waited while the crude camera work revealed our midnight caper. Even with all the fumbling and whispering in the dark, you could figure out that Richard and I were the culprits who executed this escapade of revenge.

Suddenly my sister shouted to her husband, "I told you they did it!"

Richard and I wanted to know why he would have any doubt, but Jim just shrugged with disbelief. "I didn't think you would drive all the way over here in the middle of the night to do all this." Well, he was wrong!

Once the laughter died down, we inquired about our deer. After all, the holidays were over, and we wanted to put them away. That's when Jim surprised us. "Oh, the police have them." Police! I imagined my pretty white deer with the red bows being hauled off in a patrol car like…like common criminals! My daughter was especially upset about the missing deer and called the local station the next morning to arrange for someone to pick them up.

That would be me. The next afternoon, there I was, following a female police officer across a lot to the station's storage building where they held stolen goods. The garage door opened to reveal, among the bicycles and electronics, my two deer, each marked with large evidence tags dangling next to their red bows. As I tucked them into my car, the officer asked how the deer managed to get twenty miles from home.

I couldn't tell her everything, but I quickly explained that my brother-in-law had posed our fake deer inappropriately, and we were returning the joke in his yard. "You see," I said struggling for a better explanation, "he has a weird sense of humor." Then, pointlessly, I added, "He's a lawyer."

The expression on the policewoman's face told me that she didn't get what she wanted for Christmas—and she never has. I mumbled a cheerless greeting and drove away.

My husband and I put the deer back in the rafters of our garage. We just hoped they stayed put—at least until next year.

Another Year Goes up in Flames

What is it with men and fireworks? I don't mean watching them; I mean creating them. Although these pyrotechnic displays are usually associated with the Fourth of July, the males in my family believe that New Year's Eve also calls for bombs bursting in air. It seems that anything worth celebrating is best expressed with explosives.

I'm not sure how this tradition got started. A few summers ago bags of fireworks arrived with those who dismissed them as merely "sparklers." We all attended the local fireworks display, but that only ignited the pyromaniacs' enthusiasm. Later that night the children were holding their ears as their fathers propelled gyrating rockets into the black sky.

Apparently, the winter holiday season is also a festival of lights—and flames. On this New Year's Eve the men watched the clock as if it were attached to a bomb (little did I know!). My suspicion arose when the men all decided to take a walk in the snow.

My sisters and I followed the moving line of lit matches to the deck above our boathouse.

With an excitement more characteristic of little boys, they had lined up their "toys" on the railing. My protests were overwhelmed by assurances that the harmless objects would "just go up, sparkle, and go out." I stood back and watched as they lit the first one. It sparked...then wobbled and fell off the railing.

Undaunted, they tried another. This time the firework did what it was supposed to do: A grand display of shooting sparks erupted as it spun about in a frenzy of smoke. Unfortunately, it did all this while it was lodged between the railings of our deck.

It wasn't long before the air was glowing with floating embers. Gloves and hats were abandoned as repeated efforts to light another "really cool one" continued. Occasionally, a female voice would suggest that it was really cold, getting late, and time to go in. My brother-in-law, Jim, just batted at the sparks that landed on the new jacket he had borrowed from my husband. Well, someone had to break it in, I guess.

When all the fireworks were finally extinguished, we turned on the yard lights and gathered the shredded remains that were scattered over the ash-covered snow. The scene resembled the Hindenburg Disaster. The sulfur haze dissipated as we walked back to the house. But suddenly, as I gazed up at the real stars, I realized with dread that it would only be six months before they'd be at it again.

Chapter 12

Boathouse Philosophy

Our Bella

It is spring again, and I have returned to my perch above the boathouse, a sun-warmed room in which both writing and viewing the lake satisfy my soul. For our Bella these early days of May heralded the fishing season, a period that didn't end until the waves of autumn left icy scallops along the shore. Even in winter she would lie in restless slumber, re-living her tireless pursuits beneath the rippled surface of her beloved lake.

I remember the day those long legs first found freedom in the water. We had moved here in the sweltering heat of mid-summer and sought relief from our labors in a short swim. Bella, at age one, had never swum before, and she now paced along the shore in a panic as we urged her in. She proceeded cautiously into the water until her steps gave way to paddling. One look of surprise, a sudden gasp, and she was off on the endless journey that filled her life with joy.

Nothing could distract her from that endeavor. As soon as she scarfed down her breakfast she was pleading with us to open the door so she could go down to the lake. Her daily ritual began with scouring the shore for fish and then swimming out in a broad circle past the pier and through the reeds. Her dark body was a familiar sight to those who passed by in boats, especially those who shared her love of fishing. Sometimes they would shout out a greeting to her, but Bella's eyes never wavered from her purpose. Eventually, it became necessary to call her in to rest each afternoon. After the whistle sounded, she would obediently, albeit grudgingly, come out of the lake. But invariably she would pause, and we could see her staring up at us through the pines while considering that perhaps we weren't watching, and she could slip unnoticed back into the water. She held that hopeful pose until the second blow, which she answered with a full gallop up the hill and onto the patio, where she reluctantly acquiesced to my command to "shake, shake, shake" before coming inside. "Good girl, good girl!"

Of course, there was a reward for that. It was lunchtime for Dad, and that meant a piece of his sandwich for her. Mom didn't allow begging or table scraps, but, Oh! Those savory offerings from Dad's armchair! There was a code between them, and Bella waited in her patient, regal position for those treats, always receiving them in gentle appreciation. Her sweetness shone in her eyes, expressive orbs that communicated unconditional love to her beloved family, especially the man to whom she had become a constant companion.

Born on the very same day that Richard retired from teaching, June 4, 2004, she was my gift to him. It was love at first sight when I first held the only female puppy in a litter of Labradoodles. Her black body curled up in my lap as I drove home. I looked at her enormous feet, the drooping ears that flipped up on a head that was too big for her body, and as I said aloud, "You are beautiful," her name came to me. Richard and Grant were washing their cars when I pulled into the driveway and surprised them. "This," I introduced, "is Bella."

While intelligence is genetic, and obedience merely discipline, sweetness is an inherent trait that blesses only the most special of dogs. Bella's love for everyone she encountered was returned in heartfelt expressions from the members of her family and her many dedicated fans. From nearly knocking you over with an enthusiastic greeting to putting her sleepy head in your lap, no one could resist Bella. Nor could she them.

True, she liked to lick small children and pull off their hats as she chased their sleds down the hill. True, she followed people to their vehicles and asked to go home with them—what would have been a regrettable ride as she always paced like a caged tiger in the back seat. True, she became anxious whenever we left her at home and would eat an entire loaf of bread to show just how much she missed us. True, she just couldn't get through an entire night without getting in bed with us—and always on my side. And true, she was spoiled and could always command a "Bella rub" with one wave of her upheld paw.

But most true is that we will miss every quirky, adorable, ridiculous thing about her. On Christmas morning we will miss Bella's strategic tearing of the tissue paper on her wrapped toys. We will miss her wild anticipation when her brother calls to say he is just minutes from home. We will miss her tail-wagging greeting when I pull into the garage and her excited leaps as she bounds ahead of us for the boathouse. My trails will be lonely paths without her inquisitive movements beside me, and the lake will be a vacant mirror without her reflection upon it. The places that she warmed at her perch by the window and next to us on the couch are now merely haunting reminders of the place she had in our home and our hearts.

So great was Bella's love for us that it masked her pain as she nobly continued in her old steps. But it was in her eyes. She couldn't understand and, in the end, neither could we. Her final car ride was strangely quiet as we brought her home for the last time. We put her to rest beneath a pine tree near the water so that she would be close to her beloved lake. Our dear, sweet fisher-girl. Sweet dreams.

Every House Tells a Story

I was only three years old when we moved into our house in Chicago, but I have a recollection of the day we arrived. I was intrigued by the area under the front steps, a kind of hiding place that I stooped to explore. There in the dirt was a red metal telephone, which I immediately recognized as a child's toy. Inside the house another set of stairs that led down to the basement left its impression. Above my head, nailed to a beam, was a wooden plaque etched with a house and the words that I would eventually learn to read: "Home Sweet Home."

Both objects were sources of curiosity for me because I couldn't understand why anyone would leave them behind. Certainly the child who owned such a delightful toy would be missing it. And what of the parents who left behind the sentimental plaque? In my childish brain was a sense that a home, and everything in it, belongs to a family. Such personal possessions must have had meaning for these other people. Now, they were merely part of the house's past.

But I believe that, apart from its physical construction, a house has a soul. It is created from the people who have inhabited it over the years. The hopes of a young couple who start a family together are contained in the fiber of the building. The floors echo with the steps of babies and running children and aging grandparents. The kitchen absorbs the aromas of thousands of meals: breakfasts prepared before the sun rises on winter mornings; dinners simmering on the stove; and baked specialties lovingly prepared for holiday feasts. The walls, too, retain the spirit of those who lived within them. The years accumulate like the layers of varnish on hardwood floors. Generations of family members make their marks, dropping a favorite dish that scratches the floor or scribbling with crayon on the painted woodwork. And on the wall the pencil lines that measure growing children are faded but not forgotten. All the years of soap and polish cannot erase the human beings that made their marks.

A house has bones that take the weight of change. It flexes over the years with additions and renovations while retaining the memory of what had been before. Signs of the times are woven into the house's frame, tracing the advent of plumbing, electricity, telephones, and cable lines.

If a house could speak, it would repeat the sounds that filled it over the years. Among them would be the noise of everyday living: the clatter of dishes, the splash of bath water, the conversation at dinner time, the giggling of children, and the whisperings in sleep.

If you listen to the creaks and moans of an old house, you might hear its voice and imagine its history. The story it tells is the story of our own lives.

Beauty Is in the Eye of the Beholder

The restaurant afforded us the perfect view, as well as a platform for people-watching. We ladies were impressed by the consistency of Charleston's reputation for style. The women prefer to wear dresses in public. It may be a continuation of their Southern Belle heritage, but it certainly makes an appealing statement about femininity.

Of course, the men also take great pride in their appearance, and this did not go unnoticed. Because we were sisters vacationing without our husbands, our dinner conversation generated discussions that would probably not have occurred if they were with us. One was about the physical attributes that make a man most attractive. One related question, frivolous as it may seem, actually sparked an interesting debate. Nancy leaned over with the intriguing query, "What actor, from any time, do you find the most attractive?"

While we are three sisters and a sister-in-law, the variations in our ages showed in our preferences. It seemed apparent that an actor's attractiveness is dictated, in part, by the current trend. Depending upon when your preferences were established, you may prefer or reject certain styles and types when it comes to the opposite sex. Society may dictate what beauty is, but the definitions from our youth tend to stay with us.

That even applies to the attractiveness of a movie star. Chances are that if you thought an actor was handsome when you were in your teens, his former image will still hold that appeal for you now. Cary Grant, William Holden, and Gregory Peck were still popular screen idols in Carol and my childhood. With their sleek suits, clean-shaven faces and neatly combed hair, they emanated sex appeal. This standard shaped the image we had of the ideal man. But what we considered classic good looks is apparently not timeless.

My younger sister shrugged with indifference at our handsome heroes and offered her own candidates. However, I was unfamiliar with most of them, having never seen their work. The ones I did recognize seemed boyish and sloppy. We exchanged more names—and reactions: "Really—him?" We even analyzed our choices. It seems that modern preferences are for rumpled hair, chin stubble and a goatee. We older women prefer a clean-cut look— even, apparently, on an old goat.

The debate was clearly split along generational lines so I called in a neutral vote. I asked our thirty-something waitress about an actor that most of us agreed was attractive. She smiled politely and said, "I never heard of him."

I guess the adage "Beauty is in the eye of the beholder" relies mostly on how much you *be older*!

Mothers Treasure Keepsakes

Recently I was given some family memorabilia that included a Valentine's Day card. On the back was scrawled in pencil, "To Billy, from Wallace." The message was written by my father to his cousin when they were children. It seemed peculiar for me, my father's little girl, to see his handwriting as a little boy. Yet, I couldn't help responding to it as a grown woman who has also been the recipient of such childlike sentiments. No doubt my great-aunt had kept this card as a memento of her son's correspondence, and now, nearly eighty years after it was written, this Valentine's Day message found its way into the hands of yet another mother, the daughter of the sender.

Most mothers have a place for such things. Children's drawings, cards, and handiwork are precious documents. Awkward hearts drawn in crayon with the words "I love you" are difficult to discard. So they are placed in a drawer or special box and kept for years. They are the reminders of a child's simple feelings and fleeting youth.

When I taught a class on memoir writing at the local library, many of the attendees shared stories and items they had brought for inspiration. One woman talked about a collection of letters she had discovered that were from her father to her mother. What surprised and touched her was that her mother had moved them to her nightstand drawer toward the end of her life. The daughter teared up as she related the loving contents that represented the feelings of her parents toward one another. Now these letters were a special gift bestowed upon her, continuing the legacy of love that was a part of her family.

It seems that the most precious gifts are those that are the most simple, even ordinary. Don't you remember the art projects you made for your mother: construction paper baskets, the figures made of modeling clay, the jars of colored bath salts, and the macaroni necklaces? Though the objects may be lost or broken over the years, the notes that accompanied them may have survived—for mothers tuck those words away.

Mothers are sentimental. Among my souvenirs are the corrective shoes my daughter wore as an infant, a baby blanket that was made for my son, and an assortment of their first drawings. One Mother's Day card that I treasure is illustrated with colored pencil. My daughter drew a smiling sun over a beach with palm trees. Two figures are walking hand in hand. It is the two of us. Over our heads is written, "My mother's special day." Although it is stored in a box with other memorabilia, it is always close to my heart.

Acting Your Age Can Be Subjective

Years ago, while discussing age and attitudes with my grandmother, she looked at me and said quite seriously, "I feel exactly the same way that I did when I was eighteen." She was seventy-five at the time, and I have often pondered those words over the years. Is youth *really* a state of mind? Or is it simply a state of *being*, subject to time restraints and physical changes?

Well, that depends on who you ask, of course, or more precisely, *when* you ask. Being young at heart is easy when your heart is young. Tears, temper-tantrums, and euphoria are par for the course at sixteen. So are bungee-jumping, snowboarding, and back flips off a diving board. But give that youngster six more decades, and his wild ways will be reduced to understated irritations and mild amusement. Anything that involves jumping up and down will likely stay down, and any activity that refers to the word *back* will likely hurt later.

While a teenager is permitted to be irrational, most of his thoughts are subject to hormonal urges. On the other hand, Grandpa's harmless flirtations will most likely be viewed as those of a dirty old man. We excuse the youth because they haven't had enough experience to know better, but we expect the maturity of adults to govern their minds as well as their bodies. And it does—most of the time. But the real question is whether or not a mature adult would think or behave differently if he were not confined and limited by the restrictions of his age.

That interesting query was the subject of a short story by Nathaniel Hawthorne called "Dr. Heidegger's Experiment." The title character presented a magical potion to his aging and ailing friends who were led to believe that the drink was from the Fountain of Youth. But before the doctor would administer this drink, his guests were asked if they might repeat the mistakes of their youth if their bodies were suddenly restored. They unanimously rejected such an absurd idea. After all, their age and experience taught them to know better. However, no sooner did the elixir start its physical transformation, and another transition ensued. Soon they were all resorting to the very behavior and vices that had corrupted them in their youth. Once the restraints of old age were removed, so were their inhibitions. Youth, it seems, is its own excuse.

I want to clarify that my grandmother always behaved as a lady. She knew better than to repeat mistakes, burn bridges, or make a spectacle of herself. But she was also a girl who never forgot the value of having fun. While that may not produce the same physical effects that the mythical Fountain of Youth was claimed to alter, simply having a good time seems to be a remedy for *feeling* old.

After all, if age is a state of mind, then *thinking* young is a state of bliss.

Hugs Embrace What We Need Most

I judged the little boy to be about four years old. His mother was preoccupied with placing items on the counter for checkout at the grocery store. For some reason the child suddenly lowered his head and began sobbing. It was not a temper tantrum, but something was creating this emotional reaction. The mother leaned over, put her arms around the boy, and took a long moment to comfort him until the tears stopped. The hug, like magic, did the trick.

I'm sure that hug was accompanied by words—the gentle, healing words that a mother uses to quiet a child—but the hug itself was the central expression in this situation. The power of that simple gesture is perhaps the most healing of all human contacts—or inhuman, for that matter. (Just ask any loving pet owner.)

Soon after that incident in the store, I witnessed a similar encounter at a gas station where I observed a dog in the pick-up truck ahead of me. The animal paced frantically back and forth, clearly anxious for the return of his owner. Just as obvious was the approach of his master, whose appearance prompted the dog's enthusiastic leap into the front seat. The man leaned over and gave a reassuring hug to the dog, who, satisfied with the contact, settled himself next to the driver for the ride home. Even dogs need to be reassured that they are loved, but I suspect that the man benefited just as much from this loving gesture.

These examples fortify a story that I heard years ago from an educator at my daughter's teen retreat. It was apparent in the smiles and tears of the participants that the week had been an emotional, if not life-altering, one for these kids. The speaker alluded to this in a reference to a boy from a previous summer whose experience had a highly singular impact. We were told that the teen had always been big for his age, and his size discouraged physical affection from the time he was a young boy. When the members of the retreat's close-knit group expressed farewell hugs on the last day, he broke down in sobs. It had been years since anyone had hugged him.

In my last years of teaching many things had changed. Spurred by the threat of lawsuits, our district adopted a strict policy in which any form of physical contact with a student was forbidden. Although this seemed innocuous enough, it also included the occasion of patting a student on the back, lest this gesture be misconstrued as a confrontation. But it also meant that we couldn't put an arm around a child who was hurting or hug a student good-bye at the end of the semester. Although I understood the necessity of a policy concerning physical contact, it was sad that we even had to censure hugs. Sometimes that's the very thing we all need.

Conquering Fears Enriches Life

As long as we keep moving forward through life, every birthday is a milestone. Staying put because it's easier or staying the same because it's comfortable is one of my greatest fears. That's why I finally faced another phobia of mine and agreed to ski in Vale, Colorado.

It wasn't the actual skiing in the mountains that delayed this decision; it was the terror of riding the sky-high lifts that paralyzed me with fear. But declining an exciting opportunity in life was even more disconcerting. So instead of succumbing to my weakness, I rose to the challenge.

Not that it was easy. Although I had faced mountain heights via car on several summer vacations, the Rockies in winter on *skis* are no less intimidating. My sweet niece leaned over in sympathy, "They look steeper than they really are." But I knew I had to get up in order to get down. And it began with a gondola, a Cinderella coach destined for an ice palace in the sky via a magic cable that I hoped was not made of pumpkin vines. I sat facing uphill and tried not to look out or think—thus averting an urge to express my emotions in uncontrollable screaming.

But once I was on my skis, I took a moment to scan the panorama of white peaks against a brilliant blue sky. It took my breath away—literally. That's what happens at over 11,000 feet, especially when nervous anticipation is added into the equation. But this venture was about moving forward, and I did just that, following my sister's family of seven down trails that I navigated, not with ease, but with great determination. "I can do this," I repeated to myself, especially on the chairlifts, which featured safety bars that offered psychological comfort. I took on the challenging trails with as much confidence as I could muster. Till I fell.

Nothing serious, but I felt foolish as I caught my breath and struggled to rise so I could catch up with those waiting below. A man stopped and said kindly, "It's not a race." His remark reminded me that if I fall, I fall, but I don't have to keep up with those who are younger or faster. I can make my own trail and be quite happy at my own pace.

It was a belief that I clung to the next day when I became separated from my family, who had skied onto a different course and disappeared from sight. My heart raced as I continued on alone in the blinding snow, having to navigate several trails and lifts on my own. I finally met up with them at lunch. I decided to make my sister feel a little guilty so I stomped across the lodge and asked half-jokingly, "Remember me?!" But the truth was that I was feeling pretty proud of myself for overcoming my fears and mastering the challenges.

On the last day we all posed for pictures next to the elevation sign at the highest plateau before taking on one of Vale's challenging "back bowls." As Nancy swerved onto an ungroomed slope, she shouted, "I love this!" Another skier sped by while concurring: "So do I!" Our laughter erupted like the spray of snow behind our skis as we took our singular paths down the mountain, united in this exhilarating moment in the journey of life.

Items Are Objects of Affection

My nephew was preparing for his first year away at college. We discussed some of the items he would need to take with him. I smiled when he told me that he always loved my Kool-Aid and wanted to make his own at school. Touched by this sentiment, I offered to give him a pitcher for this comfort drink. Suddenly my young niece protested, "Not the brown one!"

Of course, not the brown one! The old Tupperware pitcher is a longtime staple in my kitchen and has served Kool-Aid to all the children in my family for years. From the time each of them could open the refrigerator door by themselves, the sight of that chocolate-colored container meant Auntie Gail had one of their favorite drinks prepared. As with many products that are "new and improved," nothing beats the one to which you are most accustomed. I've tried new pitchers that are slimmer, larger, heavier, and lighter, but they were all disappointments. As far as I am concerned, nothing beats the brown Tupperware pitcher from the 1980s. Besides, how can I part with anything that's been lovingly used by our family for so long?

Some household items just become too dear to abandon. Functionality is one thing, sentimentality is another. While any decent hammer does a decent job, the old tool that belonged to Grandpa is a precious keepsake that keeps a job precious. You're not just pounding a nail; you're doing a job that continues a tradition that was begun long ago.

The things that we value the most usually don't have any intrinsic value. Plastic, wood, even paper items are invaluable when they accumulate a past. I have a dull pair of scissors that remain in a bathroom drawer. They have a loving history. I used then to cut my children's hair when they were young and could only sit still for a few seconds. I also used them to snip the tags off purchases, especially exciting for my children when they were clipped from their new school clothes. Those scissors also cut wrapping paper for birthday presents, string for homemade kites, and cardboard for science projects. No wonder they are rusted and bent. No wonder they are irreplaceable.

When I read about people losing possessions in a fire or weather-related tragedy, I am reminded that those are only things, and things can be replaced. However, I wonder about those items that have been part of their family traditions for many years, and I also realize that not all possessions can be replaced. Like my simple brown pitcher, some items serve a place in our hearts as well as in our homes.

Friendships Need Nurturing

Remember when friendship was as easy as knocking on a neighborhood kid's back door and asking if he could "come out and play"? Once you had mastered the *play nicely* aspect of a relationship, having friends was as simple as a game of tag where you take turns being "it."

Adult friendships are more complicated. They take root in the shallow soil of common circumstances. They have to be nurtured, and even then they require a delicate form of gardening that is not immune to the elements of the ever-changing environment in which we live. People alter their habits and interests, move away, divorce, suffer illness or tragedy, or merely lose touch. Many friendships simply wither and disappear over time.

I was reminded of that one January when a Christmas card was returned to me with a stamped message of "no forwarding address." The card had been sent to a friend whom I hadn't seen in seven years. We used to live just houses away from each other and had boys the same age. We both cried when she moved out of state. I visited her a few times. I also sent her Christmas cards, even a letter of support when a second marriage failed. But our communications dwindled and our relationship vanished. Perhaps it was easier for her not to remain my friend.

Friendship can be a source of strength, but it can also be a challenge.

I have thought about the different friendships I have had over the years, and many of them grew out of mutual circumstances. These were people I worked with every day, or served with on a committee, or sat next to at our children's band concerts and ball games. I saw them in church or the store or at school. Common interests made us acquaintances, but sometimes our personalities just clicked. We called each other just to talk. We had coffee in each other's kitchen. We even got our husbands together to join us for dinner or a movie.

But when situations change, friendships can easily fall by the wayside. If your children are no longer in the same activities, or you withdraw from a commitment, the bond is severed. After losing touch you may wonder how much of that friendship was only a convenience?

At this stage of my life I realize that friendships are gifts worth preserving. This month I sent a few notes to remember some old friends. One of them was a practical joker to whom I mailed a photo of myself sitting on my snow-filled patio and holding two glasses of wine. I wrote underneath: "I'll just sit here holding these until you come to visit."

If she lived closer, I would simply knock on her door and ask, "Can you come out and play?" That's a request that any good friend would understand.

To Stay Happy, Keep on Dancing

One of the sweetest memories I have of my grandmother is of her dancing. Every evening my grandfather played a few tunes on his mandolin. Grandma would often sing the words in Swedish, then, suddenly, her feet would skip across the floor in quick dance steps. Her movements were as light as a young girl's, and her face glowed with the joy of the moment.

Even if my father did not inherit his mother's agility as a terpsichorean, he had a dance move of his own that consisted of alternating heel-toe hops on each foot, performed with or without music as an expression of spontaneous frivolity. For my mother, all it took was the right song on the kitchen radio to have her break into an impromptu jitterbug—something that she can still do with an impressive flair.

Dancing is a natural instinct, I think. Babies who haven't even begun to walk will bounce to the beat of a lively tune. And even those for whom the years have stiffened their joints, a rhythmic sway to the music can seem a rejuvenating panacea.

It is not our instinct but our inhibitions that hold us back from dancing to the music. Why is that? Maybe we are too self-conscious when it comes to such a physical and personal expression. It takes courage to let the music move you—and then actually go out there and *move*. One of my daughter's friends told me that Emily "always danced as if no one were watching." That phrase makes me smile because it described not only her enthusiasm for dancing but the joy she found in expressing herself in so many ways. She never shrank from an opportunity to have fun.

I try to follow that example, but it isn't as easy to do when you are older. At a recent local concert where over 400 people sat politely and stiffly in their seats, I was determined to get up and dance. But it was my mother who initiated the act, leaning over and saying, "C'mon, girls!" Of course, Carol and I joined her in the aisle. So did several others. Fun is contagious.

It is October again, and that always brings memories of my wedding, especially the fun we had with relatives who stayed at my parents' house all that week. One evening in particular was filled with merriment as family stories were told and Dad put on some music for dancing. Carol and I did a choppy foxtrot to Scott Joplin's "The Entertainer," bouncing and laughing across the floor.

Yet, with all its richness, October also reminds me of that which is lost. There is a melancholy in the departure of leaves. But—Ah!—the celebration they have on their way down—turning, spinning, twirling, and floating—dancing for the sheer joy of the moment.

All That a Heart Can Hold

Most of us have been the authors of those childish sentiments printed on handmade cards and presented so proudly to our mothers on Mother's Day. And some of us have been the recipients of those precious tokens of our children's love. The cards usually express a child's appreciation for all the things his mother does for him. But the list rarely touches upon the greatest sacrifices a mother makes.

Because in addition to taking her children to baseball practice or ballet lessons, hosting sleepovers, and making the "greatest pancakes in the world," a mother gives much more of herself than her children usually know. They know their mothers as sources of love, which they often symbolize in the childish scrawl of a crayon heart. But at the true center of a mother's being is her capacity to love with such depth that her own happiness is contingent upon that of her children's happiness.

Getting up at night to soothe the fever of an infant is only the beginning of the worries a mother carries. If only a kiss and Band-aide were enough to heal the wounds that children incur: the hurt feelings from thoughtless people, the disappointments over not making the team; the broken hearts over unrequited love. If only an ice cream cone could quiet the frustration, anger, and fear that an adolescent experiences. If only wise advice could keep a rebellious teen away from temptation and harm. If only a mother's love were enough to conquer all.

But because it isn't, a mother worries. And that doesn't change as her children grow up. I am reminded of that many times within my circle of friends. Although most of their offspring are grown and married, there are still concerns for their well-being. There are still worries for a child who loses his job, separates from a spouse or struggles with a serious illness or addiction. A woman may proudly shows photos of her grandchildren, but her smile fades when she thinks of their parents' recent separation. She considers the financial and mental toll ahead and bears this in her own way, silently and bravely holding together, because mothers must be strong.

Yet, they still worry. They worry even while doling out cookies and smiles and hugs. They worry about you driving at night, getting enough rest, and being lonely. They worry that you will not find all the happiness that you deserve, and they bear your heartache as their own.

For all the things a mother gives and does, her greatest sacrifice is in the feelings she keeps in her heart. The depth of that love is something only a mother can know.

Year Passes in Familiar Cycle

The start of the year occurs at a peculiar time, coming as it does on the heels of holiday celebrations that are brought to a crashing halt on January 2. The year begins at the entrance of a long winter's lull that, despite its monotony, moves with a pace that blurs the months. Perhaps that is because we have passed this way so many times before.

You are not alone in lamenting, "Where does the time go?" It is a legitimate question, albeit rhetorical. Everyone knows that the passing of time is continuous, unstoppable, and inevitable. But the interpretation of its speed is relative to one's age. For children, time can seem to move with excruciating slowness: a week before Christmas may as well be a lifetime away.

Adults like to manage time as if it were a tangible commodity. It is human nature to divide the day into parcels, prioritizing the hours for business and pleasure. We have all been there—rising before the sun, burning the midnight oil, and finding time to do whatever it is we do. Ironically, the faster we move, the faster time seems to go.

Henry David Thoreau said that "Time is but the stream I go a-fishing in." Easy for him to say: He wasn't married, had no job, and had nothing else to do except look at nature and listen to the birds. Besides, he was a young man. The stream from which he lived still appeared an unlimited source. It is with age that we contemplate the shallows and heed the current. Time is but the stream that trickles toward an unknown bend.

When I was a child and learning how to head my papers in school, I was perplexed about the date. As each day passed, a new number followed the changing month, but the numbers in the year seemed permanently fixed as they never seemed to alter. My naivety lacked a broader perception. Like everyone else, I came to know the turning of cogs and wheels that progress the days into months and the months into years. Now the revolution of the seasons is as familiar and steady as the beating of my heart.

Ever since man established measurements of time, we have recorded our lives with the precision of those timepieces. The afterlife may be for eternity, but, while we live, we are subject to the earth's timetable—as well as the one we create for ourselves.

A successful man watches the clock because "time," as they say, "is money." But a wise man watches the sunsets, too, for as we know, time is precious. We enter and leave this world alone, but the time we spend here and those with whom we choose to share that time makes all the difference.

A New Daisy Blooms in June

There were plenty of butterflies on this June day, but they were all in my stomach. The long car ride only accelerated my nervousness. What would she look like? What would she *be* like? All I knew was that this little stranger was waiting for us, and we couldn't wait to meet her.

Any doubts vanished the moment I laid eyes on the ball of black fur that toddled over on four spindly legs and proceeded to tug on my purse strap. She was the smallest of the litter but certainly not the meekest, a fact she proved by struggling to get out of my arms and venture into Richard's lap as we drove to our son's house. "This," I told Grant with the pride of a new mommy, "is Daisy." As she melted into his arms, he noted the fragility of this baby Goldendoodle.

We had all been accustomed to our gentle, sixty-pound Bella, including her habits and favorite spots. She had grown content and comfortable in her routine, and so had we. This new pup showed a stubborn curiosity that can best be described as sassiness. I don't recall that Bella, even at her most rambunctious stage, was anything but polite and apologetic about her behavior. But then it has been twelve years since I had a puppy. You tend to forget.

It all came back to me on that first night. The crate I had readied with a blanket and soft toy proved to be a curiosity that lasted for about five seconds, the same amount of time it took for me to close the gate. We were astonished that such a piercing whelp could erupt from a body that fit inside my husband's shoe! I couldn't subject my son or his neighbors to such mournful howls so I put Daisy in bed between Richard and me. That lasted about ten seconds, which is how long it took before she fell between the mattress and footboard. Oopsy-Daisy!

My last resort was to sleep on the floor, a decision that resulted in a restless compromise while she explored the confines of the bedroom and amused herself with the doorstopper spring that repeatedly twanged with reverberations.

Finally, she nestled beside me and tired herself out by gnawing on the buttons of my nightgown. I awoke early with the same instinct every new mother has when her baby is about to wake up or cry or, in this case, pee on the rug.

Twelve years dulls the memory. I had forgotten what it was like to be out in the yard at 5:30 in the morning urging "go potty" while pulling grass and stones from my puppy's mouth. I must appear quite a sight dodging the timed sprinklers while Daisy clings to the hem of my robe by her teeth. I have also forgotten what it is like to safeguard the house from a hurricane that registers a force of 6.5 (pounds) on the "wrecktor" scale. We've partitioned off parts of the house, but the storm we call Daisy is beating down the barricades with the determination of rising flood waters. She's got us just where she wants us, and we can't go far because she has hidden our shoes.

In fairness to our little force of nature, she is affectionate, entertaining and adorable. It's just that we are older and more set in our ways than we were when we had our other puppies. We've become accustomed to our relaxed schedule since retirement, and that included having a dog that flopped down on the floor with a satisfied sigh when we settled down for the evening.

Even simple outings like going out to dinner or a movie require planning that we haven't had since we hired babysitters for our children. Suddenly, our lives revolve around Daisy's schedule. I can go out with my hair a mess, but I'll be darned if we're leaving the house before she has pooped! (The success of that mission is directly disproportionate to the immediacy of our departure time.) But when we gently put her in her crate and quietly walk down the stairs, her panicked yelping is as unnerving as a smoke alarm for which there is no replacement battery.

And, yes, we will take her to an obedience class, and we have already taught her a few commands. But she is still at an age when even a training treat is trumped by the irresistible charm of a twig on the ground. The fact is we are training *ourselves* again. Richard is doing well with *sit* and *stay*. His reward is a sandwich. I put it down right next to his water bowl.

I admit that this acquisition was inconvenient with a busy schedule over the summer, but when is a puppy ever convenient? What we know is that it was very lonesome around here without Bella. She will always have a special place in our hearts, but as I cradle this new puppy in my arms and smile down on that tiny, silly face, I know that there is more room in our hearts to love again.

Touch from Past Is Unexpected

Most of us have awakened from a dream and wondered, "Now, where did *that* come from?" People and events we scarcely remember will pop up in an unrelated scenario of a dream sequence. The reference may seem trivial and remote. Often the dream is forgotten along with all the bits of our past that we brush aside in order to get on with our daily lives. But sometimes the dream haunts our thoughts with an insistence that it *did* come from somewhere—or someone.

No matter what your age, you probably spare little time for nostalgic daydreams. A busy schedule may even minimize the melancholy that often comes with dwelling on what used to be. An active daily routine helps us focus on the reality of now. But sometimes, out of the blue, a subtle disturbance invades our present world. A familiar sound, scent, or sudden image catches us unaware, and we are abruptly taken to another time and place. It is in these unexpected moments that the past taps us on the shoulder and takes us by surprise.

Some years ago during the Christmas season I paused to listen to a pianist who was hired to entertain customers as they shopped in a large department store. The grand piano was placed in the center of the main floor, and I sat in one of the nearby chairs for several minutes enjoying the music, which included requests, while patrons scurried aimlessly through the aisles.

Suddenly, a woman paused next to me, seemingly transfixed by the particular tune. Finally, she spoke, though her remark was only half-intended for me. "Every once in a while my husband stops me," she said wistfully. Just as I struggled to understand the import of those words, she added meaningfully, "This was his favorite song." With that she gave me a tender smile and moved on into the crowd.

Such moments are unexpected. You may be bent over some project of wood and nails when you pause to study the hammer you are holding. In an instant, an image of your father appears to you in a haunting replication of the same gesture. You can see his hand grasped about the tool, and you are suddenly watching him from a child's perspective once again.

Hasn't someone hurried by you, leaving a familiar scent that reminds you of that special aunt's perfume or a favorite uncle's aftershave? The memory brings them back to you for a sweet, albeit brief, reunion.

If there are angels, I believe that they carry messages from those who can no longer speak for themselves in this world. They come, regardless of the distance of time, and touch us with an unexpected visit from the past. Even as we hurry toward tomorrow, the past will stop us with a sign that is as gentle as the flutter of wings.

Views from My Boathouse

It was a warm afternoon, and although the wind was discouraging, I just couldn't stay inside. I wanted to write, but I also wanted the sunshine, the water, and the trees. A solution awaited in the room above our storage garage by the lake. I packed up my computer and carried it down to the boathouse. There from my windowed perch were my beloved views of the water through the pines.

There is a myth that writers have to wait for inspiration. If that were the case, very little creative writing would be accomplished. However, it is true that certain locations have atmospheres that are more conducive to creativity. For me, the lake has always been my muse. It began when I made up stories at my grandparents' cottage. The water was the perfect element to set my imagination in motion. I was convinced that mythical creatures inhabited the unseen depths of the lake, and they surfaced in tales told over campfires. Secrets were whispered to me through the pines overhead, and I translated them into my stories. Writing them down became my passion.

Recently, I looked at some of those early writings—slanted lines in pencil on dime store tablets. I had even illustrated the cardboard cover of my first "book." Beyond the immature language and simple plots, I could recognize an element of myself that remains: a love of storytelling. I don't claim to be the best at this, but it is a process that I enjoy more than anything else that I do.

My writing process has changed a little since then. I no longer sprawl across the plank floor of the tiny cottage in an effort to write by the light of the fireplace. Nor do I bend over a pad of paper while I dangle my feet from the dock. It would have been beyond even my vivid imagination back then to think that I would eventually be living here and clicking out my thoughts on the keys of a computer.

Yet, sitting here by the lake, taking occasional glimpses out the boathouse windows as I search for just the right words, I recall the little girl that was first inspired by this scene. I inhale the familiar scents that generate a whirr of cogs and wheels in my brain. Thoughts flash like glints of sunlight on the moving water. And then the story rolls across my vision, growing and changing like the clouds that float above the three lakes. Perhaps it is the panorama's tranquility that permits my creative transport. I only know that of all the places I have been in my life, the boathouse has my favorite views.

About the Author

Gail Galotta was born and raised in Chicago. After a career in teaching she moved to the Upper Peninsula of Michigan, where she became a columnist for a local newspaper.

In addition to *Views from My Boathouse* Galotta's writing includes plays, poetry, short stories, and a children's book, *On the Tips of Angels' Wings: The Story of the World War II CG-4A Glider.* Her plays include *Crossroads*, *The Christmas Letters*, and a dramatization of Charlotte Armstrong's novel, *The Trouble in Thor.* Her short stories have earned honors, including a first place fiction award through Michigan's General Federation of Women's Club for her short story, "The Weight of Seasons" in 2007. The Upper Peninsula of Michigan Writers Association named her "Best Emerging Writer, 2008," after earning numerous honors for her non-fiction and poetry.

Galotta lives in Vulcan, Michigan with her husband, Richard, and their dog, Daisy. She is active in community theater as a director, actor and playwright. An avid fan of *I Love Lucy*, she has given lectures on the iconic television show, as well as presentations on memoir writing and local history. When she is not writing or directing—or involved in some "Lucy and Ethel" predicament—Galotta enjoys the outdoors, especially her *boathouse views.*

Made in the USA
Lexington, KY
15 May 2018